CW00641727

HOW MODEST ARE THE BRAVEST!

Courage from the beaches of Normandy and beyond

Ken Tout

Helion & Company

Helion & Company Limited
Unit 8 Amherst Business Centre
Budbrooke Road
Warwick
CV34 5WE
England
Tel. 01926 499 619
Fax 0121 711 4075
Email: info@helion.co.uk
Website: www.helion.co.uk
Twitter: @helionbooks
Visit our blog http://blog.helion.co.uk/

Published by Helion & Company 2018
Designed and typeset by Mach 3 Solutions Ltd (www.mach3solutions.co.uk)
Cover designed by Paul Hewitt, Battlefield Design (www.battlefield-design.
co.uk)
Printed by Hobbs the Printers, Totton, Hampshire

Text © Ken Tout 2018
Photographs © as individually credited
Maps drawn by George Anderson © Helion & Company 2018

Every reasonable effort has been made to trace copyright holders and to obtain
their permission for the use of copyright material. The author and publisher
apologize for any errors or omissions in this work, and would be grateful if
notified of any corrections that should be incorporated in future reprints or
editions of this book.

ISBN 978-1-912390-72-4

British Library Cataloguing-in-Publication Data.
A catalogue record for this book is available from the British Library.

All rights reserved. No part of this publication may be reproduced, stored in
a retrieval system, or transmitted, in any form, or by any means, electronic,
mechanical, photocopying, recording or otherwise, without the express written
consent of Helion & Company Limited.

For details of other military history titles published by Helion & Company
Limited contact the above address, or visit our website: http://www.helion.
co.uk.

We always welcome receiving book proposals from prospective authors.

Contents

List of Photographs

List of Maps

Acknowledgments

Sincere thanks are due to the following whose help, added to basic information from unit and formation records, made this project possible.

Chapter 1, Hollis: Brian and Veronica Hollis, Steve Erskine, Major (Rtd) Tony Warriner MBE, Charles Hill, Brian Bage, The Green Howards Association.

Chapter 2, Bazalgette: Dave Burrell, Bomber Command Museum, Canada, Nanton Lancaster Society, W.R. Morris.

Chapter 3, Blackburn: Daughter Andrea, Kim Taylor-Galway, David Stover, subject's communications with author. It is hoped George Blackburn's trilogy, *The Guns of Normandy, The Guns of Victory* and *Where the Hell are the Guns?*, will be reissued by the Canadian publisher Rock's Mills Press in the near future (original editions published by McClelland and Stewart).

Chapter 4, Bridge: Sue Gordon-Williams, Arthur Lockyear MBE, Anghie Cooley, Derwent Hill Centre, Firth Park School, Sarah Stoner.

Chapter 5, Cain: Francie Clarkson, Rosemary Diplock, Bob Hilton and Andrew Burden (Para archive), Pauline Johns (IoM).

Chapter 6, Cardy: Linda and Ken Fallen, Christine Carter, REME Museum, subject with author.

Chapter 7, Chapman: Dick Chapman, Janet Morris, Nanette Williams, John Riley, Welsh Pony and Cob Society.

Chapter 8, Close: Joanna Jones, Richard Close, Major (Retd) Colin Hepburn, Jock Watt, Brigadier Christopher Dunphie, subject with author.

Chapter 9, Eardley: Roy Eardley, Jeremy Condliffe and the *Chronicle Series,* Congleton, Cliff Charlesworth, Simon Cooper.

Chapter 10, Göstl: Manfred and Hazel Toon-Thorn, Gerhard Stiller, Rick D. Joshua, Peter Mooney, Claire Hué, Gerhard Nogratnig (Min. of Justice), Martin G. Enne (Univ. of Vienna).

Chapter 11, Hammerton: Mike Hammerton, 'Remember Le Havre' Association, subject's *Achtung! Minen!,* subject with author.

Chapter 12, Harper: Gordon Harper, Kevin Sayles, Geoffrey Cooper, John Brown (former mayor, Hatfield Woodhouse).

Chapter 13, Jarzembowski: Janus Jarzembowski, Zbigniew Mieczkowski, Polish Institute and Sikorski Museum, Agnieszka Skolimowska.

Chapter 14, Murphy: Jay Root, Dave Phillips, 'Remember Murphy', Matthew Rector, USAG Fort Knox, David Stover.

Chapter 15, Rose: The Denver Post, Steve Ossad, Marshall Fogel, Belton Cooper, Donald Duckworth, Association of 3d Armored Division veterans.

Chapter 16, Rossey: Cedric Condon, Dominibue Keiffer, Bill Laing, Pete Rogers, *Les Fusiliers Marins* (Association), Commando Veterans Association.

Chapter 17, Tilston: Colonel (Retd) Rae Marting CD, AdeC, Essex and Kent Scottish Regiment Association.

Chapter 18: Wittmann: George Isecke, Hubert Meyer, Rick D. Joshua, Joe Ekins, Peter Smith, 'Rad' Walters, Brian Reid, Pat Byass.

Chapter 19, Lotton: Myriam Lotton, Mairie de Saint Aignan-de-Cramesnil, subject with author.

Merle: Daniel Borzeix, 'Buzz' Keating, subject with author.

'Harry': Shelagh and Denis Whitaker, Brigadier Pascal Mathieu, *Stadsarchief* Antwerp per Martine Reussen.

van den Hoek: Floris van den Hoek, Louis Kleijne, Filip Bloom, *Verzetsmuseum* Werkendam.

Chapter 20, Regimental Duties: Northamptonshire Yeomanry Association.

It is perhaps of interest to reflect that, in two of the actions referred to, the unit war diary was destroyed during the battle and the responsible officer was killed. Each diary had to be reconstituted from notes and memories of the survivors. Much appreciated has been the expert help of my neighbour, Mike Woolley, who happens to have spent a lifetime working on tank gun sights. He was therefore delighted to read and comment on drafts, as well as advising on my technical disputes with my computer, a genus which did not appear in schools in my day, and which were not available for *Tank!*.

As always my wife, Jai, supported in making work at home comfortable and efficient. She herself had been Chairman during the development of a pioneering NHS Foundation Trust (Mental Health). She therefore shared with me the interviewing and counselling of veterans in their 60s and 70s who still showed evidence of continuing Post-Battle Traumatic Distress Disorder, leading to some of the comments in the book.

The initial idea for the book was encouraged by Gill Jackson before a period of frustration ensued. Duncan Rogers at Helion then came to the rescue, being ably supported by Tony Walton, George Anderson, Vicky Powell and staff.

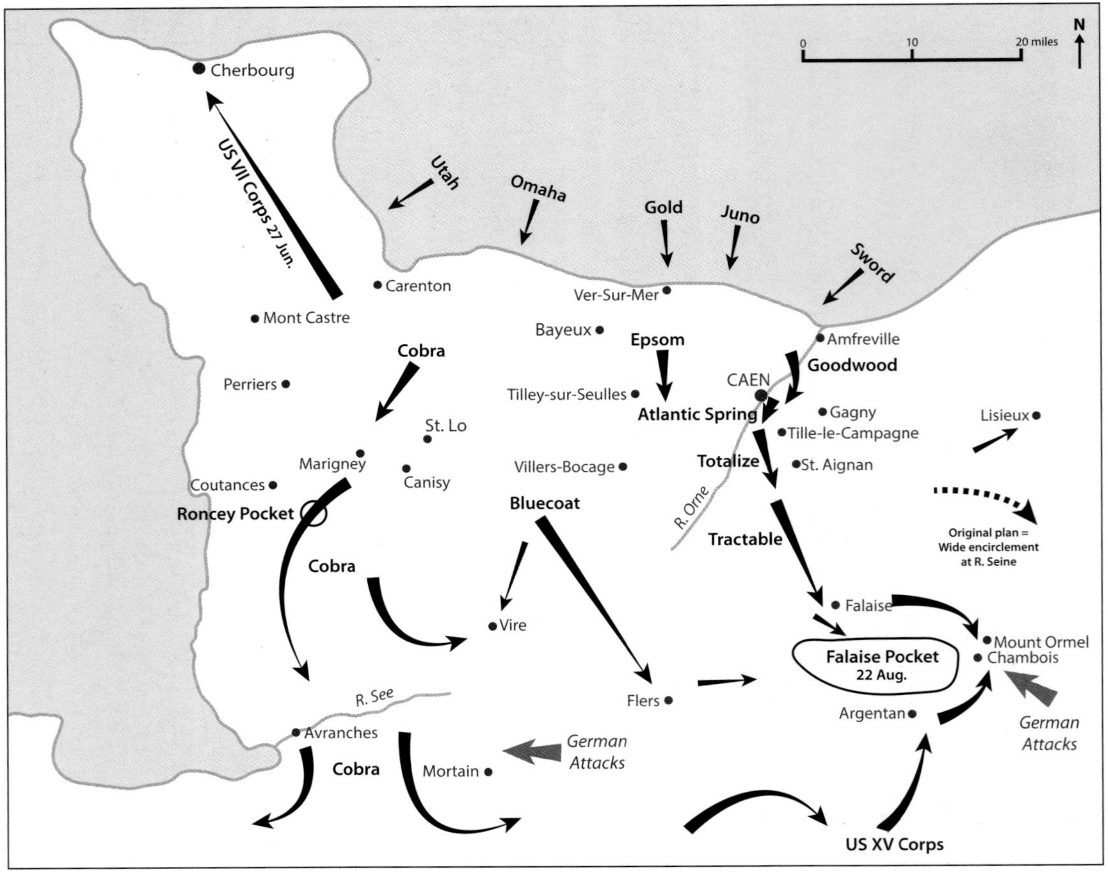

Map 1 Normandy.

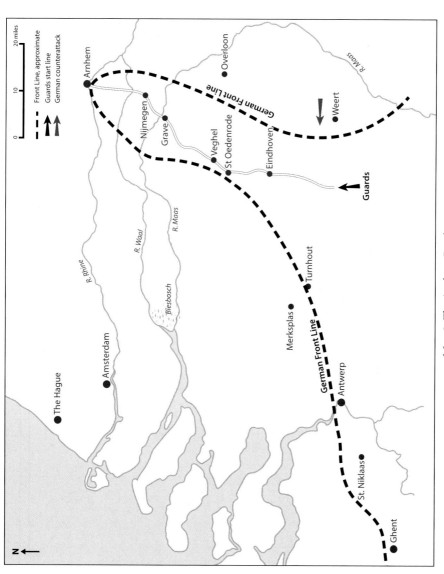

Map 2 The Arnhem Road.

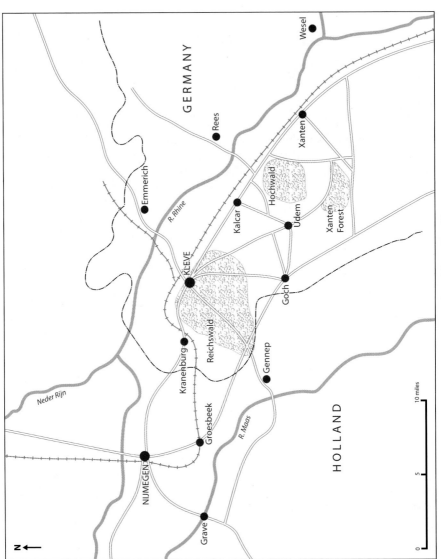

Map 3 Reichswald Hochwald.

Introduction
Why 'the Bravest'?

The idea for this book was fired by watching the film 'The Dirty Dozen', (MGM, 1967) widely acclaimed by critics. That plot supposed that the American Army had to coerce into service a gang of undisciplined, convicted criminals, in order to undertake a mission of such extreme peril that the average soldier would be incapable of tolerating it.

This view suggests that, in the trenchant words of critic James Berardinelli, "soldiers are often society's outcasts, the sociopaths and misanthropes who kill and rape. The heroes are a group of thugs."

For me this 'Dirty Dozen' portrayal was inaccurate, even abhorrent. I was privileged to be accepted as a comrade by truly brave men in battles of some significance in 1944, such as Operation *Totalize*. In my experience, at the moment of ultimate crisis, it was always the quiet man, the modest man who stood up to be counted.

The first bravery medal awarded to my tank squadron, in an action in June 1944 supporting the company of none other than CSM Stan Hollis, VC, the Military Medal went to Trooper Martyn, G. When it was announced, the reaction was almost universal: "Which is Martyn, G?" He was a typical unobtrusive, dutiful crew member who remained anonymous until that day when he decided to stay in his knocked-out Sherman, liable to 'brew up' at any moment. Alone, he calmly fired his machine gun into the huge surrounding *bocage* hedges, alive with enemy infantry, to cover the rest of the crew as they carried the wounded commander to safety.

The idea was born: to study a number of warriors who displayed outstanding valour and about whom I might have some modicum of understanding, such as having served in the same or similar actions, and so on. It would not be simply a list of heroes who had won the Victoria Cross. It would extend to warriors achieving what might be called an 'aggregate of continuing valour', worthy to share these pages with winners of the VC, the *Militaire-Willems* or similar awards. The list would include representatives of various nations and different arms between D Day and VE Day.

It would be necessary also to probe beyond the man of action in uniform in order to enquire about his pre- or post-battle persona, thus offering a contrast to the convicted criminals of the cited film. I knew Blackburn, Cardy, Close, Hammerton and Lotton, but, as to the other subjects, I had no idea of their out-of-battle characters. Some of them might have been braggarts, bullies or reprieved criminals. It was a surprise to learn about Baz's affinity with his banjo and his Bible; or Hollis's and Chapman's long, idle stints of fishing; or Cain's merry sense of humour.

In no way can this book be classed as an objective or academic study. However, it may have some value springing from the front-line soldier's peculiar sense of comradeship across arms or regimental prejudices, and often his empathy with the enemy. Seeing the smoke of the burning of Wittmann's Troop, then rolling across Gostl's machine-gun ditch, or climbing over the ruins left by Baz's master bombing, as well as watching Jarzembowski's comrades accelerating into their first vengeance action, and following the red rear light of one of Hammerton's clumsy contraptions, finding a way across unknown slopes in the darkness; these were all unique privileges. For me such memories highlight and colour the hard facts as formulated subsequently by the longer-term research and criticism of others more qualified.

Whilst selecting the individuals who are featured in these pages, I also checked on at least an equal number of other similar heroes without finding one who might havebeen of the '*Dirty Dozen*' genus. They must have existed. But I was fortunate enough not to serve with one.

1

Stan Hollis

Company Sergeant Major Stanley Elton Hollis, VC, British, 6th Green Howards (infantry)

The quiet man sat patiently on the harbour wall at Whitby, his fishing gear extended, waiting for the mackerel to bite. His small son, sitting alongside him, imitated his father's actions, learning both skills and patience. With a calm sea the mackerel were slow to bite. Time passed. Holidaymakers and day trippers bustled or loitered past, taking little notice of the two fishers, poised as still as sculptures. But perhaps an occasional local passer-by paused and remarked to a companion, "See that man fishing over there? He's the Landlord of the Green Howard pub in North Ormesby. Did you know that on D Day he … "

D Day – 6 June 1944: the greatest invasion armada ever assembled surges over the horizon and homes in on the Normandy beaches. They come by their thousands of ships and tens of thousands of warriors. The British and Canadians are tasked to capture the vast sweep of beaches from Arromanches to Ouistreham. But first there is the wild boiling broth of storm-tortured sea to challenge heavily-laden men clawing their way down scramble nets. Then the further stretch of holiday sands now blemished and obstructed by Rommel's devilish defensive contraptions. Beyond, rises the gentle promenade with its laid-back private houses, hotels and cafes. And, in among it all, the low grey concrete slabs of heavy gun emplacements and machine gun pill boxes with a clear view of the entire open battlefield and anyone who should stand forth upon it.

While the massed guns and rockets of the Allied fleet poured fire at the shoreline and beyond, and while small landing craft, myriad and busy as scurrying ants, ferried the first troops through the surf, the enemy tightened fingers on triggers of guns loaded and traversed ready. In spite of the intensity of Allied fire, a German machine gunner of the 716th Infantry Division might well have had some grounds for confidence although, as always at battle's outbreak, filled with apprehension.

Portrait of a warrior, the intrepid Stan Hollis. (Courtesy of the Trustees of the Green Howards Association)

He and his comrade crew were almost totally encased in a thick, reinforced concrete shell, virtually impervious to bullets, hand grenades or even some larger shot. He looked out through a tiny slit high enough only to accommodate the slender barrel of his machine gun, and wide enough only to allow it some traverse. No human being, he believed, could approach directly over those wide, open spaces outside. If the pillbox did become surrounded, a quick exit through the back door would take the crew along a trench to the next line of defence.

Above all, he knew that his machine gun, the MG 42 *Spandau*, was the terror of the infantry battlefield. On the Allied side the reliable American Browning thudded away patiently, the brilliant British Bren chattered a little more urgently, yet both fired at a speed which the human ear could encompass, able to count the individual shots. But the *Spandau* fired furiously with a single rasped sound as of ripping calico, so fast that the human ear could not distinguish nor the brain calculate its rapidity. The gunner knew that his light pressure on the trigger for a mere second would expel 20 bullets in an almost solid echelon of flaming death. Twenty per second, 1,200 per minute, aiming to destroy flesh and bone within an arc of certainty of 200 yards and more.

The gunner might well ask, "Who could possibly expect to evade such a fiery web of wide-sprayed explosive force? What lunatic enemy soldier would dare to charge directly at such a weapon?"

There was one who would dare. And he was now disembarking.

The Germans had constructed a battery of heavy guns on the gentle slopes of Mount Fleury at Ver-sur-Mer (Gold Beach, King Sector). These guns were capable of causing tremendous havoc, both along the exposed shore and among warships and landing craft out at sea. It was imperative that they be destroyed and the site occupied by ground attack at the earliest possible moment. The task had been allocated to the

6th Green Howards. This battalion, with its partner 7th and the 5th East Yorkshires, formed 69th Infantry Brigade within the 50th (Northumberland) Division with its distinctive 'TT' (Tyne/Tees) shoulder flash. The 50th had fought through the Western Desert, landed in Sicily and now was being asked to take a pivotal role in the D Day disembarkation.

Within the division one man had already established a reputation for his readiness to lay his life on the line when his comrades were in extreme peril. Stan Hollis had joined up in peacetime as a private. During the 1940 Dunkirk disaster he had served with distinction, achieved promotion to sergeant and suffered the first of his five serious wounds. He had recovered to fight in the desert, gaining further promotion. In Sicily he was again seriously wounded. But by D Day 1944 he was fit to continue in his rank of Sergeant Major of D Company, 6th Green Howards.

Rather than an instant act of heroism, his first contribution to the invasion was almost a comedy of errors. Aerial photographs and reconnaissance had indentified a cuboid object as an enemy pillbox on the promenade at La Riviere, the chosen landing site. As his launch rode in to the beach, Hollis grabbed a Lewis machine gun and fired a full magazine of bullets at the pillbox. There was no answering fire. The first Green Howards ashore discovered that the menacing pillbox was merely an innocent passenger shelter at a tram halt. The comedy did not last long. In handling the overheated gun, normally used with tripod, Hollis had burned his hands severely, later stating that it was the most painful wound he had ever suffered, because with far more serious wounds shock often cancelled out immediate pain. There was no time to hesitate. Into the water and run! A violent crash! The Green Howard splashing along at Stan's elbow had been blown up, virtually disappearing. Battered but furious, Stan charged on.

The Green Howards opened out and advanced cautiously through a minefield and along the streets. Their hearing, so essential to identify direction and weight of firing, became paralysed by the pandemonium of noise. Their sight became impaired by the rapidity and violence of brilliantly flaming explosions and the all-enveloping smoke and dust. But they felt a way forward, trying to maintain formation over uncertain ground in the murk, probing past houses, hedges and street crossings. Company Commander, Major Ronnie Lofthouse, accompanied by CSM Hollis, kept close to the point men, verifying the route, checking the flanks.

Suddenly Lofthouse halts and points along a hedgerow. "A pillbox! There! A pillbox!" Only 20 or so yards away, partly hidden amid bushes, is a camouflaged hump moulded into the landscape. Only the tell-tale slits betray its purpose. No further word of command is needed.

There is 20 yards to run towards the flaming muzzle of a *Spandau*, one or maybe more guns, and this is the gun that fires 20 rounds a second. Discretion surely cries "Get down! Take cover!" But no! In a brief glance Stan Hollis sees movement inside that slit in the concrete. A gun muzzle! Instantly, the trained fighting man is galvanised into suicidal action. Heavily laden maybe, but sprinting madly, he fires his Sten gun into the slit, right up to the very slit. Miraculously surviving, he vaults on to the top of the pillbox. Reloading the Sten, he pulls the pin from a grenade, leaning over to throw the grenade into the pillbox. Another burst of Sten follows, and frightened enemy soldiers stumble out and surrender, shouting, "*Kamerad!*" The remainder are lying still.

Onward and down into the trench beyond and another pillbox: a headquarters control post. Again running hard, leaping, firing furiously. More enemy hands are raised: "*Kamerad! Kamerad!*" The *Spandaus*, which could have enfiladed and annihilated the plodding lines of infantry as they pushed forward unsighted, are now silent. Twenty-five shocked prisoners can now be waved away to the beach, adding yet another statistic to this one man's contributions to victory.

CSM Stan Hollis's act was later considered worthy of the supreme award of the Victoria Cross, a mission fulfilled beyond the normal call of duty. Surely now was a moment to pause, to take a deep breath? A vain hope: Stan's D Day was by no means ended yet.

Pressing on, the lines of Green Howards had stormed the battery. But there was no time to celebrate. Orders were "Press on! Press on!" Inevitably, as the advance continued, casualties mounted, officers fell and reorganisation was needed. The major now gave Stan responsibility for commanding 'A' platoon, out on the flank, while the main Green Howards line moved forward into Crepon, achieving the longest advance by any unit on D Day.

Just beyond Crepon lay a farmhouse, le Pavillon, backing on to a large open rhubarb patch. An enemy field gun, supported by *Spandaus*, had been harassing the advancing infantry. It was located in hedges about 50 yards beyond the farmhouse. A group of infantry had tried to charge the gun but had been cut down by machine-gun fire. Major Lofthouse now agreed with Hollis's novel plan: try to destroy the enemy gun by using a PIAT mortar, aiming from the shelter of the house. The PIAT was not the most accurate or reliable of weapons, but it was the only larger piece to hand. Hollis took his platoon forward, occupied the house and fired the PIAT. But fate was unkind; the PIAT shot narrowly missed its target. The enemy gun crew, duly alerted, traversed the big gun, aimed and fired. The shell smashed into the upper storey of le Pavillon. Sections of roof came crashing down. A few shots more and the gun would demolish the house. Deluged by showers of masonry and tiles, Hollis ordered his men to withdraw. Duck and run, duck and run, firing to their rear.

As he was reporting back to the company commander, there was a frenzied burst of firing between the enemy in the field and a machine gun in the house. Hollis was informed that two of his men had stayed behind in the ruined building, and were now cut off by the enemy. His response was "I took them in. I will get them out." This was problematic because the men would have to cross 50 yards or so of open space under intense fire. Grabbing the Bren gun, Hollis marched forward, crunching rhubarb underfoot, into open space. He fired low, spraying the enemy's lair, looking fearsome: a big, muscular man, huge fists dwarfing the Bren, jaw-line like a ridge of granite, piercing eyes, his face bloody from minor injuries, one caused by a sniper's bullet. Raking the hedge behind which the enemy lurked, he dominated them, forcing them to keep their heads down. The two Green Howards isolated in the house took the opportunity to escape. Hollis, still totally exposed, maintained his fusillade before himself retiring in good order. It was a remarkable feat of arms considering his gun was loaded with ammunition only enough for a mere 30 seconds of unbroken fire!

After the battle, high-level discussion took place as to whether this action at le Pavillon merited a second award of the Victoria Cross. This would have been unique: a VC and bar on the same day. Eventually the authorities balked at the idea and it was decided to award one Victoria Cross to cover the two actions. Green Howard Captain 'Bolo' Young, later badly wounded and evacuated across the beaches by Hollis himself, said: "In full view of the enemy, who were continually firing at him, he went forward alone using a Bren gun. When the fighting was heaviest Hollis always appeared … and by his own bravery he saved the lives of many of his men." That assessment is confirmed by the official citation, which added: "It was largely through his heroism and resource that the company's objectives were gained and casualties were not heavier, and by his own bravery he saved the lives of many of his men."

Within a very few days Hollis had carried out another act with similar disregard for his own safety. At Cristot the lead tank troop had been knocked out by the enemy. The *bocage* hedges along the main road were virtually impenetrable to infantry. The only way forward was thus down a steep stony cart track hemmed in by hedges, across a country road and back up the continuing cart track. At the top of the track, the enemy had dug in a *Spandau* pointing down the narrow funnel of advance. Once again Hollis took the situation literally into his own hands, rather than ordering in men of lesser experience. He flung a hand grenade high towards the machine gun pit, and the German gunners instinctively ducked down, awaiting the explosion. The hiatus gave Hollis time to sprint down the track and get near enough to subdue the gunners, using his sometimes unreliable Sten gun when they rose up again to fire.

The Cristot attack complements the two D Day actions, illustrating some interesting variants of Hollis's bravery. At the La Riviere pillbox, Hollis's action might be seen as purely instinctive, a choice between becoming a running target or a recumbent target, equally vulnerable. On the other hand at Cristot, no sergeant-major would have incurred disrepute if he had ordered in a section of infantry, waited for another tank or asked for an artillery 'stonk', rather than launching himself down the track. There were ample options and time to choose.

One of the strongest considerations in battle is always self-preservation. Its messengers are pain and fear, and it reacts at the merest scent of danger. Stan Hollis would have had time to choose between personal safety and self-sacrifice in the pause before throwing the Cristot grenade. Even in the split second reaction at the La Riviere pillbox, there could have been the same process, condensed into a blinding moment of truth: to dive for cover or charge? However, when it came to the rhubarb patch at Crepon, Hollis, as a racing enthusiast, must have been well aware that he was risking the highest of odds on his own death or some terrible mangling. That awareness could echo and echo as he walked on. However, his deepest thoughts at such moments remain forever his special secret.

Recent newspaper coverage on the inauguration of a home town memorial to the VC awardee described Stan as a hulking figure with "a volcanic temper and huge fists". Could the aggressive attacks which he carried out on D Day have been no more than the natural actions of an unpredictable individual let loose with a gun? It is clear that Stan was brought up in an industrial area where a man needed to be able to 'look after himself'. More than once the young Stan had eloped to the Merchant Navy, again a situation where the need to be able to use one's fists might be expected. Even in later years, as a pub landlord, Stan encountered drunken men who wanted to 'take on' a VC recipient. But the general verdict of wartime comrades, family and pub customers seems to point to a more reserved and gentle person when not facing considerable provocation.

Nobody knew him better in 1944 than close comrade Green Howard Private Charlie Hill, who states: "I never once heard him raise his voice to a fellow soldier except when shouting commands on parade." Charlie fondly remembers an incident just before D Day. Like all those waiting to embark the next day, the battalion spent that night under canvas within a barbed-wire concentration area, the exits guarded not by their own sentries but by Military Police. The youngest soldiers like Charlie were at an extreme of trepidation with thoughts of tomorrow and imminent death or ghastly wounding. CSM Stan, so many grades higher than these youngsters, gathered a group of them together in a tent, Charlie included. The CSM then formed a pontoon school, playing by the flickering light of a paraffin lamp, late into the night. The fears of the young lads were submerged in the fun of those moments.

Further memories of Charlie's included the sight of Hollis jumping up on to the turret of a tank and using his Bren gun to flush out a sniper from a tree. On another occasion, as they hurried past a wounded German who lay screaming, one of the Green Howards suggested putting the German out of his mystery. Charlie remembered Stan's response: "No! Give him a chance to live."

Perhaps the fondest moments for Charlie were in the darkest reaches of the night. There were no continuous trenches, 1914-18 style, offering a semblance of linked comradeship and support. In 1944 two infantrymen shared a rough temporary slit in the ground, cut off from everyone else. Facing the infamous Hitler Youth, who were supremely trained in field craft, there was always the possibility of a swift, brief but bloody raid. At moments like that, Charlie and companion would be thrilled to hear the soft swish of boots in grass and look up to see the CSM standing upright against the sky above them, then crouching down in comradeship and asking in a low voice, "Alright for cigs?" Stan could always find some extra cigarettes for the lads.

One episode at this time had a permanent effect on Stan which again marked him out as a sensitive man. The company had taken prisoner a 16-year-old boy from the Hitler Youth (12th *SS Panzer* Division *Hitlerjügend*), a rare event as those youngsters were taught to fight fanatically to the death. Perhaps the Green Howards were too kind to prisoners, for generally members of the ordinary *Wehrmacht* units were treated according to the conventions of war, often with good humour. In this case the young lad saw an opportunity, seized a gun, and no doubt shouting *"Heil Hitler!"*, shot two men. Stan again was quickest to react, shooting the lad dead before he could do more harm. The killing of such a young boy haunted Stan forever. Daughter Pauline once heard him mutter "I've got blood on my hands", referring specifically to the lad killed in cold blood. But at such a moment, knowing the background of *Hitlerjügend*, there was no alternative but to shoot immediately and not just 'shoot to wound'. Where *SS* prisoners were involved, this was not a unique incident.

On 26 June the author's tank squadron was sent forward to support Stan's company in a typical 'straightening of the line' attack which was launched on 27 June near Lingevres. They were now deep in the jungle fastnesses of the *bocage*, with vast hedgerows, high banks, narrow lanes and tiny sequestered fields, a topography dating back hundreds of years and intended to safeguard against wild animals and human marauders. Amazingly, Allied planners had done nothing to provide some resource for ploughing up or cutting through the hedges. A tank gunner's view was therefore often as little as 50 yards; 200 yards along a lane was a distant vista in the *bocage*. No infantryman could see through the roots of a hedge, let alone penetrate it. A rifle-man's view was negligible. Tactically the *bocage* area around Cristot and Lingevres may have been the most difficult and dangerous terrain in Stan's vast experience.

Stan's battalion later joined in the great battles to close the Falaise Gap and cut off the entire German army. Untypically the end came not with Stan advancing, regardless of danger, but patiently sitting at Company HQ in counter-attack posi-tions, waiting for Major Lofthouse to return from conference.

Out of the silence a six-rocket volley of the familiar but hated 'Moaning Minnies' (*Nebelwerfer* multi-barrel artillery) soared, screamed and fell. The signaller next to Stan was killed instantly. Stan himself was riddled with shrapnel, including head injuries which would require a steel plate insertion. It was his fifth serious wound. This time there was no way back. It meant the end of his active army career at the point of battle. The date was D+48.

Brigadier Powell, of the latter day Green Howards, summed up this outstanding career:

> Stan Hollis was a remarkable resolute fighter. He was one of those people who, through the force of his own personality, could change the course of a battle. Remember he fought all through the war from Dunkirk to the Western Desert to Sicily, and Normandy.

It was even more remarkable if one harks back to Stan at age 17, apprenticed into the Navy. There he was critically stricken by blackwater fever and discharged back to civilian life suffering from resultant lung problems and deemed unfit for naval service. Surely he could have served out the war in some useful but much safer capacity?

Thus departed from the battlefield a unique warrior whose experience included being wounded and virtually stripped of all his clothes by a bomb on Dunkirk beach; being captured, battered and then escaping in the North African desert; and elimi-nating an enemy machine gun in Sicily, with a consequent Mention in Despatches. Along the way he acquired special knowledge which would be programmed into his mind, as, for example, in respect of the fearsome *Spandau*. He knew the multi-purpose machine gun was not without its faults. Its high rate of fire and muzzle velocity could cause muzzle lift, distorting the aim, especially if the gunner was distracted; overheating restricted the *Spandau*'s ability to fire longer bursts; pauses were required to change the belt or drum as well as to replace a burned-out barrel. But none of his immense knowledge would deprive the brain of its automatic reaction when warning of the probability of intense pain or imminent personal obliteration.

One ace that Stan had up his sleeve, after long battle experience, is that he would have considered his own skills to be far higher than those of the average German coastal defence division machine gunner, even when the gunner wielded a *Spandau*. From what he saw of his own raw reinforcements, Stan could assume that many ordinary *Wehrmacht* conscripts would be far more afraid of death and wounding than he himself would ever be, having survived so much. This confidence, added to the determined use of surprise, carried him through the worst of his battles.

Son Brian identified a probable motive and also a vital personal attribute of Stan's:

> He'd escaped Dunkirk and had his cheekbones shattered and skull cracked as a prisoner of war [in the desert]. Perhaps that made him go for it. I think it was the sheer determination on his face that would have scared the Germans. They just knew he'd kill them if he got to them.

The award of the Victoria Cross brought CSM Stan Hollis immediate fame, but it was not to last for long as, with peace declared, people generally wanted release from war issues, and he himself did nothing to encourage continuing renown. Granddaughter Amanda throws some light on his reluctance to court fame, with a story about a custom later in his life. As a publican, he collected bottle tops for a charity working with the blind. He accumulated piles of the bottle tops in a drawer, and Amanda discovered that underneath the bottle tops he kept his Victoria Cross. Lesser mortals would have framed it, displaying it prominently over the bar of the pub.

After the first burst of public acclamation there was little continuing interest and few prospects of favoured work, even for the holder of a VC. He had no job to go back to. He had been apprenticed to the Merchant Navy before the war, but was invalided out suffering from blackwater fever. He had driven lorries and was used to hard work in tough times. Now, at first, Stan was restricted to post-war jobs at a labouring level. However, both he and his wife Alicia applied themselves to the grinding additional task of training to become pub landlords. Successfully qualified, they took over the Albion in North Ormesby, near Middlesbrough, which was then renamed The Green Howard. It quickly became a shrine to the regiment.

Son Brian sums up Stan as follows: "A lovely father to my sister [Pauline] and I, and a thoughtful partner to my mother, and a good father to my future wife." Granddaughter Amanda remembers simply "his huge smile". The clientele of the pub were regarded as family friends rather than mere customers. Stan himself was not, like some publicans, a natural raconteur or comedian, but joined cheerfully in any jokes or lively banter. Sing-songs often started up in the evening, and plainly heard would be Stan's voice, trained as a lad in the choir at St Cuthbert's Church, Ormesby.

Inevitably, from time to time, some 'well-tanked up' stranger revealed an ambition to test the valour of the giant VC. On such occasions Hollis was inclined quietly to take the usurper outside where, no doubt, the man who had looked Death itself straight in the eye at close quarters, could settle the matter with a CSM's *coup d'oeil*. But both Brian and Pauline remember that, once or twice when a woman had been insulted, it was the big fists which dealt out retribution.

More to Stan's taste was sitting fishing with Brian on sea walls at Whitby or Saltburn, indulging in his favourite pigeon racing or taking time off for the 'gee-gees' at Redcar. Stan had been a pre-war pigeon fancier. Sadly, even in the Second World War, casualties among pigeons, used as battle messengers, had decimated the population of trained homing pigeons. Learning about Stan's love of and success at pigeon racing, the Queen sent him some pedigree birds from her own lofts. Either on the pigeons or the horses he enjoyed a bet, but never exceeded the limit which he set himself. Such was the constraint on family finances that he stopped smoking in order to afford school fees for Brian and Pauline.

Occasionally an echo of fame would disturb the placid routine. When the film 'The Longest Day' was released it was suggested that Stan should meet up with a German officer to publicise the screening. He refused, saying that he could never forget enemy atrocities which he had witnessed. Nevertheless, on another occasion the Green Howards Association proposed to return to a *Wehrmacht* officer an Iron Cross which had come into the association's possession. It was considered politic to seek senior veteran Stan's agreement. The reply came back: no objection to returning the medal to its proper owner, but no enthusiasm for meeting the officer.

This is not surprising when one considers the demons with which the erstwhile warrior was still wrestling. His family is to be commended for publicly discussing these intimate details. At times Stan would lock himself in a room to deal alone with all his ghosts when the torment became unbearable. Only in the most special privacy of war veterans' reunions is it clearly confessed that many veterans have suffered similar, if lesser mental tortures for many years. At the end of the war there was no provision for honest debate, appropriate treatment or decent recompense. Like many, CSM Hollis's mental wounds were quite as honourable as the steel fragments in his foot which still caused it to bleed if he stood for too long a period behind the bar. Who knows what part the various wounds, physical and mental, would have had in producing the stroke which led to his death at the early age of 59?

As at D Day, the culture of the British Army was of the 'stiff upper lip' variety. Talk among rankers about mental fatigue or breakdown was frowned upon and neatly disposed of under the label 'cowardice'. But some men suffered total mental collapse. Those who were clearly incapable of continuing in battle were swiftly shepherded down medical channels to psychiatric treatment and eventual rehabilitation. For the rest of us it would have been impossible, considering the limited contemporary skills and high costs, to provide psychiatric assessment and treatment for countless Post-Traumatic Stress Disorder cases resulting from experiences like the D to VE Day battles. We walked away, happy at the time, with a demob suit and an unexploded bomb of terrors in the mind.

Here CSM Stan Hollis, VC, provides a measure and touchstone for study of the ultimate in battle fatigue. In 1945 it was not realised, and perhaps is not yet fully taken into account, that 'Post-Battle' Traumatic Stress Disorder is distinct in two ways from what might be termed civilian PTSD.

The first aspect relates to the way in which a 1939 civilian who, like choirboy Stan, was probably raised to obey injunctions like 'Thou shalt not kill' and 'Love thine enemy', had to be drilled and perverted into an insensitive killer. He became an instinctive killing machine, often using the most ruthless and horrific methods of assassination. Then at war's end he was left to find his own way back through the darkest tunnels of the mind towards the normal behaviour of civilised society. Stan Hollis would, on reflection, have considered that the shooting of the Hitler Youth boy in cold blood fell within this 'killing machine' category. How often the spectre of the Hitler Youth lad reappeared in that locked room in the pub can only be imagined.

The second battle stress factor is related to the syndrome of losing a comrade to 'the bullet with my name on it': the 'why him and not me?' obsession. The demise of a dear comrade could prompt a massive conviction of guilt for having failed to turn the bullet upon oneself, even though logic argued that one was powerless so to do. Again the vision of a comrade dead at one's side could come back long afterward and haunt one's own continued existence. Stan would recognise in this category the soldier blown to non-existence when shoulder-to-shoulder with his CSM on the D Day beach, or the several soldiers squandered in a pointless charge across the rhubarb patch at le Pavillon.

It has been suggested that the death of that soldier on the beach stimulated all Stan's aggressive tendencies and caused him to charge blindly at the pillbox minutes later. It is likely that Stan's incentive, his driving force, was always more complex than that. It was not 'just another soldier' who died. Stan often insisted that the men under his command were not subordinates but friends. They were friends who pre-war had survived the tough times of an industrial area in the North-East, they were friends who had joined up together, they were friends who had fought the enemy together. And as some of the original friends were buried along the way, at Dunkirk, Alamein or Sicily, they were followed by younger recruits who were absorbed into this special bond of friends. Added to this was Stan's sense of responsibility, as evident in civil life as in battle. Being the elder and wiser among so many friends, with life or death responsibility, Stan Hollis went confidently into battle sustained by that friendship. And at the worst moment of peril he would be turbo-charged by the vision of friends dying around him.

Such an assessment implies a man of considerable perception and sensitivity. His daughter-in-law Veronica can vouch for him in that respect. She was at the long, impatient wait point of expecting a first baby and was feeling disorientated, depressed and with little present stimulus in life. Stan discerned this problem and said to her in effect, "Why not come and work in the pub for a couple of days a week? Stay as long as you want. No need to do anything. Just sit behind the bar and talk to people. And I will be there for you." This suggests considerable sensitivity in a man brought up in an era, and in an area, where some men might not have been too aware of, or concerned about, the personal feelings of a heavily pregnant woman.

When the praise and adulation became too much for the modest publican, he tended to respond with a standard disclaimer: "There wasn't only me doing these things. There were other people doing things as well. And the things that I did, if I hadn't done them, somebody else would have."

If one might dare to argue with the redoubtable warrior, there might not have been a "somebody else". On the other hand, because he "did those things", it inspired many others to master their own personal fears, rise above their previously perceived potential and serve far beyond the demands of mere duty.

2

Ian Bazalgette

Squadron Leader Ian Willoughby Bazalgette, VC, DFC, Anglo-Canadian, 635 Squadron (Pathfinder) RAF, killed in action 4 August 1944

Lying on his open air bed in the Tuberculosis Sanatorium at Harpenden, with his mother visiting, the 13-year-old consoles himself by strumming on his banjo and reading his Bible. Is this lad the kind of raw material needed for one of the most intractable and exhausting tasks at war?

Wrestling with the rudder of his wrecked Lancaster bomber, the pilot gives the order, "Fix my crash belt around me. Tight! Then jump! Quick! Jump!" Throughout a long life, Flight Engineer George Turner would never forget this calm order from a leader who has perhaps only minutes left to live. Jump while there is still altitude enough, if only a meagre 1,000ft. With three engines dead, the plane is burning, losing height and threatening to fall like a devastating bomb on the village just ahead.

This day they should all have been on leave but had forgone the opportunity. So now the fit members of the crew – Cameron, Goddard, Godfrey – must jump. Sadly the mid upper gunner and the bomb aimer, Leeder and Hibbert, have both been gravely wounded and cannot exit, cannot be aided. Any moment now the Lancaster must explode here in mid air. Their only hope is a planned crash landing.

The pilot continues to fight the jinxed aircraft, not their usual plane and not the most reliable craft in the squadron. The normally tough, resilient four-engine Lancaster bomber staggers along, fatally wounded, with its starboard wing a tornado of flame. That same inferno is now shooting blazing shards into the body of the aircraft, where leaking petrol swills about the floor. A moment ago its nose was aimed dangerously at the village centre, but the crippled plane is veering at last, avoiding the church steeple, away from the village, the pilot's eyes straining towards a flat expanse of enticing green meadow. But it is still so far ahead!

Cameron, Goddard, Godfrey and Turner all jump. Secured in his seat, miraculously still in control of this blazing time bomb, Ian Bazalgette flies on, wrestling towards touch-down on that beckoning green expanse, enticingly nearer, already

Baz's 'Goodbye' to mother at the end of his last leave. (Courtesy of Bomber Command Museum of Canada)

seeming to rise up to embrace the exhausted wreck of an aeroplane. A moment or two more?

Godfrey saw it all as he parachuted down: "He did get it down in a field about two fields away from where I landed. But it was well ablaze and with all that petrol on board it just exploded, a huge fire ball."

Overhead, Paddy Cronin, in another Lancaster, also watched: "I saw the whole event, even to the landing of the crippled plane by Ian, which then blew up. I thought at the time he had made it as he had landed. But unfortunately there was a ditch in the way which the plane struck and this caused the explosion which killed them all."

The Lancaster and its surviving crew were now down in enemy-occupied territory, just outside the village of Senantes in northern France, and German troops might be expected to investigate without delay. Doug Cameron, landing farthest away, did encounter Germans and came under fire but managed to avoid them. He made contact with the official Resistance, who co-opted him into their *reseau*, in which he served for the remainder of his war. The other three crew members were hustled into hiding by French civilians until the tide of Allied liberation swept past the village. There now ensued a period of illicit obsequies and homage by stealth.

Villagers reverently carried the bodies of Hibbert and Leeder into the church. Coffins were made and the bodies laid in state before the altar. A funeral service was organised for the afternoon of the coming Sunday, 6 August 1944. However, during that Sunday morning German troops arrived and announced that the bodies must be buried in an official war graves cemetery. The bodies were taken away, but the Germans cast only a perfunctory look over the wide-flung wreckage of the Lancaster, now barely recognisable as an aeroplane.

The villagers then processed to the crash site, laying down rich banks of flowers as a tribute to the man who gave his life to avoid crashing into the village itself. It was only during this act of arranging flowers that the remains of Ian Bazalgette were discovered still underneath the shambles left by the disaster. A casket was prepared to await burial but, remembering the fate of the bodies of Hibbert and Leeder, the villagers dispensed with fanfares or a church requiem. They hid Ian's casket in a cellar and waited for liberation. Paris now being free, the mayor of Senantes communicated with Free French authorities in the capital and obtained permission to hold a funeral for Ian on Sunday, 8 October.

Meanwhile, through confused channels of information as the war moved across the continent, the news reached Ethel, Ian's beloved sister. She had been working with the 9th United States Army Air Force (USAAF) in Normandy and was now stationed at Ceil, only 30 miles away from Senantes. Learning of the proposed burial of Ian, she was conveyed by her superior, a USAAF colonel, to the village on 3 October. Thus it was that, in that remote village as the war continued, a member of Ian's family was able to attend as chief mourner on 8 October. He was buried in the local graveyard with full military honours, French, British and American. In spite of later plans to move the body to an official War Graves Commission site, Ian Bazalgette lies forever in that rural churchyard, his anniversaries dutifully celebrated by the local people who will never forget.

If the circumstances of Ian's burial were unique, and his progress from a tuberculosis cot to a master bomber's seat unpredictable, his earlier life course also deviated from the norm for a boy of that time. And there was a famous name to be maintained.

The name of Ian's great grandfather, Sir Joseph Bazalgette, was one to be remembered and respected, especially by Londoners. He was directly involved in saving the lives of thousands of residents of the growing, wealthy but insanitary city where, in the mid-1850s, untreatable cholera was rife. After the 'Great Stink' of 1858 – when hot weather exacerbated the smell of untreated human waste in the Thames – Sir Joseph was allowed to expedite his long-proposed design and construction of 1,300 miles of new sewers. These proved to be of dimensions and stability which would not only be a world wonder of that century but would prove adequate into modern times. Along the way he constructed the Victoria, Albert and Chelsea embankments. He demonstrated two characteristics clearly inherited by his great grandson: he was untiringly persistent in pursuing the cause he believed in, and was recorded as "risking his own life in the cholera-ridden cesspools to save the lives of others".

One grandson, Charles Ian, was of a more wanderlust nature and decided to attempt farming in Alberta, Canada. There he met and married Marion Bunn, daughter of a nearby English immigrant. When Ian Willoughby Bazalgette was born, on 19 October 1918, the family found itself in some confusion because Charles Ian preferred to be called Ian and here was another Ian. So from early days the younger Ian was called Will, though himself preferring Ian. Conforming to the rest of the family, Ian pronounced his unusual surname 'Baz-el-jet'. To add to the confusion in historical records, the larger family of RAF Bomber Command chose to address Ian Willoughby by the familiar term 'Baz'.

Before long Charles Ian tired of farming and took the family back to England, where Ian/Will went to school in New Malden in south-west London. Aged 13 he contracted tuberculosis, which in those days before streptomycin was a killer disease; 50 percent of those contracting it died and many survivors continued to suffer serious effects. The only possible cure, apart from surgical collapsing of the lung, was up to a year of open-air recuperation, which cure Ian endured in the Harpenden Sanatorium and at the Royal Sea Bathing Hospital in Margate. Even the pleasant-sounding sea bathing element could not detract from the prolonged torture of recovery. So on one day (6 January 1932) Ian recorded in his diary:

> Rather a ghastly day ... no appetite for breakfast ... I didn't feel like doing anything, I just lay still ... After tea I played my uke. After that my troubles began thoroughly. I felt bad. I worried both mother and myself. After supper I worried again. I started reading my Bible. I felt better.

However, by July 1939 Ian was well enough to volunteer and be accepted into the Royal Artillery. He then found himself on searchlight training near Shrivenham, which was then in Berkshire. A comrade remembered him as "combining a tremendous application to his duties with being bubblingly irreverent and full of fun". On commissioning as a 2nd lieutenant he was posted to the 51st Highland Searchlight Regiment in Scotland, but he soon found the swivelling of searchlights, and even experimenting with the new radar, not active enough for him. He applied for a transfer to flying and in June 1941 was accepted into the Royal Air Force Volunteer Reserve.

Throughout his training, although consistently marked as 'above average', Ian Bazalgette displayed idiosyncracies which marked him out from the crowd. He was still something of a home bird; he did not smoke but he sent his cigarette ration home to his father, wrapped up in his dirty laundry, which his mother Marion continued to undertake. He also had a quirky sense of humour. A letter home related: "With some Canadian trainee observers we borrowed bikes and we found the most outstanding collection of WAAF [Women's Auxilliary Air Force] personnel with very little interference from the RAF. We were afraid of being chased up dark lanes and raped."

At last, on 19 September 1941, Baz was flying a Wellington bomber on a raid to Saarbrucken in western Germany, being attacked by two *Focke-Wulf* 109s, one of which was shot down. This was the start of a period of warfare with 115 Squadron, later flying Lancasters. Losses of Bomber Command planes were increasing and German anti-aircraft defences were impressive. On one occasion Baz's Wellington was caught in the apex of several searchlights and became the target for a number of anti-aircraft batteries. In order to escape, Baz had to go into a steep dive for thousands of feet and then back up in a steep climb. As a result of fuel starvation, both engines cut out, then at a critical moment they started up again. Time and again he brought his plane back with damage, a bent propeller or a collapsed undercarriage.

The worst experiences were often the minor but very personal tragedies. Thus Baz recorded:

> Very sad thing happened recently. An old friend of mine landed as second pilot of a Lancaster. I went and had words with him. Immediately afterwards the plane took off again, crashed and he was killed. It is not known precisely why the crash occurred. A tragic waste.

Baz completed his first tour of 30 sorties, and on 1 July 1943 was awarded the Distinguished Flying Cross with the commendation "his gallantry and devotion to duty have at all times been exceptional". Now acting Squadron Leader Bazalgette, he was not amused when success in battle led inevitably, as the system dictated, to a posting to train new pilots at an OTU.

The Operational Training Unit was itself a dangerous place. A Canadian Bomber Command survey found that out of 10,645 names on a memorial (of RCAF crews killed), 1,064 were killed at OTUs. This was due to the use of worn-out planes and the speed of training required to supply more crew as Bomber Command casualties mounted alarmingly. Even so, this was not challenge enough to satisfy Baz. He began a process like that of his great-grandfather, to pester the authorities until they heeded his pleas. His senior officer, Group Captain Hamish Mahaddie, DSO, DFC, AFC, who had most power to help Baz's cause, found himself almost bemused between irritation and admiration.

In one letter Baz wrote: "It is my dearest wish to have another personal affair with Germany. A few keen types around the Group are anxious to get back with me." Mahaddie responded: "Please take no action officially until my own horse-dealing methods have been completed." The pestering paid off. In April 1944 Baz, with his crew of "keen types from around the Group", all hand-picked and all of instructor status, flew their first 'mock up' as Pathfinders, prior to active service with the elite 635 (Pathfinder) Squadron.

Meanwhile, the life of a typical RAF pilot continued at base, and Baz would write to his mother Marion: "Everyone in the mess was in a very good mood, bags of laughter and dirty songs (with me as lead singer). A new WAAF Officer is quite attractive. The wolves are after her already." He had been spending time with a WAAF who was "taking my course of six easy lessons in love-making but we both kept roaring with laughter"; no action ensued. Back in his private room his Bible was by the bed, as in the Sea Bathing hospital, a constant antidote to worries.

If Baz might have appeared to be something of a tearaway when off duty, his demeanour in the air was impeccable. George Turner paid him this tribute:

> Baz was a wonderful skipper. When we were flying he was a discipline master. No one was allowed to speak on the aircraft's inter-com unless it was really necessary or an emergency. But when we were not on duty, we were one happy crew together. If anything we were real devils.

The mission of the Pathfinders was to go into the target area ahead of the massed formations, markibng the objectives using smoke or fire indicators. One or more Pathfinders would then remain over the target area to order any necessary corrections during the main bombing, as well as to report back. Since the war, Bomber Command has been subject to much criticism because of the fire storms caused in civilian areas of cities like Dresden and Hamburg. There seems to be a tendency to believe that this was Bomber Command's only contribution to the war. For the D Day landings, however, a substantial force of the Allied air fleets was deployed in direct support of the liberation of Europe. The air armadas had two main objectives: in Normandy it was essential to destroy the launching pads of the V1 flying bombs which were devastating areas of London; heavy bombers would also be used as additional artillery, supporting ground troops in major battles. On D Day itself, setting out from the base at Downham Market in Norfolk, Baz acted as a Master Bomber in an attack on the German batteries at Longues in Normandy.

The first major raid supporting Normandy land battles was on the city of Caen in July 1944. The aim was to take out the German defences around the west and north of the city. For the troops on the ground it was a massive boost to their morale to watch, and have ears deafened by the apparently endless formations of heavy bombers homing in on Caen, especially after a month of futile, costly ground attacks. It also gave the spectator a clear impression of what the air crews had to endure.

As the first Master Bombers headed for Caen, it was as though a massive solid curtain of fire rose up from the ground and spread into the sky, leaving no possible way through for what, by contrast, was a relatively frail flying machine, a Master Bomber alone. Yet the individual planes, and then the following masses, ploughed straight through the blazing screen until the bombing eventually eliminated the German anti-aircraft batteries. Baz was later informed that, down below, "the troops broke through without trouble".

In fact the tank troop which was sent in immediately to test for ways through the ruins found otherwise. The area was not merely destroyed as to houses and streets, but was ploughed over again and again by blockbuster bombs which piled up hills and dug massive gulfs so that for three weeks Caen became impassable to Allied armour. The saturation process was proving to be the wrong tactic for land battles, and the air chiefs had to think again.

In Operations *Goodwood* and *Totalize*, the method was refined. In the latter battle, On 7 August 1944, the Master Bombers aimed at bombing a route parallel to the tank columns and only half a mile away. Air Chief Marshal Sir Arthur Harris himself thought it impossible. Undeterred, the Master Bombers ran a test raid, proved their point and subsequently bombed as proposed with unprecedented skill. But Baz was not there that day.

He and his crew were scheduled to go on leave on 4 August. Another pilot, who was on the Battle Order for 4 August, had been sent to York. Now, because of thick fog in the York area, he was unable to return to Downham Market. Replacement crew were not available, such were the casualties suffered by Bomber Command as a price for bombing well-defended German locations. Indeed, Baz had been asked if he could extend his tour, possibly by opting out of the occasional operation, because it was so difficult to find flight commanders of sufficient skill and experience. So he and his crew agreed to undertake this extra operation, which would at least see them one 'op' further along the count towards the end of their tour of duty.

They also felt that they had 'drawn the short straw' because their own familiar Lancaster, M for Mother, was unavailable. They were forced to take T for Tommy, which was notorious for a number of incidents and for having had a pilot who 'burned out' his planes. It was also known that this was the third day for attacking the same relatively small target, and that the German anti-aircraft forces around the target were intact and efficient.

The mission for the day was to bomb a V1 Flying Bomb storage centre at Trossy St. Maximin, not far from Paris, employing a force of 10 Pathfinders and 61 main formation bombers. Baz certainly felt a personal interest in destroying the V1s, because he had shared the underground shelter at home with his parents, had spent part of his last leave reinforcing that shelter and also taken refuge with his sister Ethel under a metal table with a mattress spread on top. His mother had written desperately: "We had another hellish noisy night last night. I hope that we shall soon be coping satisfactorily with the thing, counter-steering it back to Germany, for instance."

Any premonitions arising from drawing the short straw were reinforced by the immediate events as the target at Trossy came into view. Rear gunner Doug Cameron observed: "A solid sea of flak filled the width of the bomb run." Into it flew the first Master Bomber in line; it was hit before being able to mark, exploded and the crew of eight were all killed. The second plane was also hit before marking and was unable to continue. Baz was now lining up T for Tommy for the inevitable straight, steady approach which was necessary for accurate marking and bombing. Then T for Tommy was hit, the bomb aimer grievously wounded, the starboard engines knocked out and their petrol tanks set on fire. Baz held the plane firm, and, with the bomb aimer out of action, carried out the marking and bombing by the more complicated method from the pilot's seat, with a lesser view than that enjoyed by the bomb aimer.

As the bombs fell the bomb doors jammed and T for Tommy went into a spin. Two of the crew wrestled to close the bomb doors. The mid upper gunner was asphyxiated by fumes from petrol which flowed from leaks and was threatening to burst into flames at any moment. Recognising that the English Channel was too far away, Baz turned and headed for the front lines of the advancing Allies, or any flat, open space.

Reporting on the chaos within the plane, the Flight Engineer George Turner insisted: "You'll have to put her down, Baz. We're badly on fire. You'll have to put her down." And, miraculously enough, Baz did in fact put her down.

And could it not have been, in that one climactic moment, however brief, that the master pilot exulted, "I've done it. And with God be the rest"?

Squadron Leader I.W. Bazalgette had completed his log book sheet for July 1944 and signed off. There would be no sheet for August. In a space at the bottom of the July sheet, the responsible officer at Downham Market had simply written and signed: "August 4 – Ops – Trossy-St.-Maximin – MISSING."

It is likely that much of Baz's character was moulded by his brush with tuberculosis. It was certainly an awesome situation for a 13-year-old to be faced with, the prospect of losing a lung or even dying, the only escape being via many months incapacitated in an open-air sanatorium. Indeed as he waited to be transported to the sanatorium he wrote: "I read the Bible until mother came in and put the light out. Then I said my prayers. One more of my precious days at home gone. It won't be long before I go."

If that kind of sentiment should appear a little immature, he was, when well, a highly intelligent and well-read youth. He had an avid interest in classical music and corresponded with music publications. On one occasion he noted another reader's confusion concerning the string quartet which Beethoven wrote as a tribute to Bach and which varies around the notes B-A-C-H. The reader had complained that there is no such note as H on the piano. Ian/Will wrote in to say that the Germans called our B flat 'B', but they used the letter 'H' for what we call B natural.

Similarly he was able to explain, when someone accorded Bach a minor rating as a composer, the meaning of Beethoven's pun that Bach's music was *"nicht Bach sonder Meer"* – not just a tiny stream (*Bach*) but an ocean (*Meer*) of music.

But once awarded his pilot's wings and let loose in a motor car or a plane, he could be as wild as anyone. His sister Ethel had volunteered to do secretarial work with the USAAF. One day a Lancaster dived low and 'buzzed' the USAAF headquarters camp, causing the staff to rush out in dismay. Only Ethel realised, and later gained confirmation, that it was her brother who was showing off.

Indeed, in spite of the Bible by his bedside, Baz displayed a constant irreverent streak, writing:

> Delightful atmosphere in the Mess here tonight. Central heating is on. But a fire is roasting the Group Captain's bum. A little knot of pleasant people is gathered around the piano making a silly din. I shall now join them and sing all the dirty songs I know.

One Pathfinder comrade, Flight Sergeant Larry Melling, DFC, was impressed by Baz:

> He had a tremendous sparkle in his eye is the best way to describe it. He stood out among the people who were there. He was an inviting sort of person. He was always the first person to volunteer for a job, no matter what sort of job it might be. Even though he was a Squadron Leader he wasn't above pushing a car to get it started or pumping up somebody else's bicycle tyre.

At least in his earlier RAF days Baz himself did not feel so eminent, and indeed betrayed a sense almost of inferiority:

> The Mess here really gets me down. I have an inferiority complex through being in a place where every other person has a DFC and two former squadron members were awarded the VC. The difficulty is that they don't talk to you and everyone stares when you enter the Mess. Oh well, bugger them!

But from the extremely close proximity of the same confined airplane, Doug Cameron saw a very different and confident leader: "Baz had the diplomacy to consult individual crew members on any issue concerning their responsibility; and the decision taken always appeared to be that of the particular crew member, thus promoting the collective confidence of the crew."

Away from the responsibilities of warfare, Baz retained his interest in the more subtle and wonderful aspects of life. His growing collection of gramophone records was no hasty selection; when he wished to purchase a recording of a particular piece of music he would take the trouble to listen to all the available recordings by different orchestras and conductors before deciding which of them to obtain.

He had a deep appreciation of nature. Looking out from the near prison confines of barrack rooms, he watched and recorded the changing seasons: "The moorhens have hatched now. They keep their brood in shallow water amongst the reeds, but the pike snaffle the odd one, I fear. The nightingale has begun to sing."

He was a connoisseur of flowers and spent much of one leave planting a complete garden of selected roses for his mother's delight. Ethel, his beloved sister, was well aware of his love of flowers and was therefore deeply moved, beyond the normal sentiments of bereavement, when she was first taken to the site where the plane had crashed and where her brother's body had lain for a while. She attributed what she saw to the heat generated by the final fatal explosion. As, in wintry October, the wreckage lay still scattered far and wide across the field, around and in between the broken and burned shreds and shards of mundane material, there had sprung up a glorious bounty of purple crocuses, as though some celestial landscape artist had descended to beautify the former scene of horror.

There is surely no better way to sum up the attitude and character of Ian/Will/Baz than his own words when writing home, beginning in a serious mood and then typically tailing off, as though he is worried that they may sound jingoistic or mawkish:

> Nothing can profit a man so much as knowing his own reactions when faced with life or death, and working with fine men of a like mind for the sake of a principle. With these essential facts always in the balance, I have had a couple of beers. And hence the rather high-sounding verbiage.

3

George Blackburn

Captain George Gideon Blackburn, CM, MC, Ld'H, Canadian, 4th Field Regiment, Royal Canadian Artillery

Above the open battlefield soars a church steeple, or a windmill, or an ancient watch tower. Aloft and alone there a man watches. Below, the enemy traverses his guns to eliminate this unwelcome intruder who spies upon every most secret manoeuvre.

The generals want answers: where is the enemy? What is he doing? What are his intentions? What problems await us across this terrain? What is happening behind the German front line?

Bevies of officers, sporting the red flashes of the staff, can, no doubt, assemble available intelligence, draw maps, pencil graphic sketches, hang up wall charts, work out an analysis, state options, send for RAF aerial photographs, interrogate prisoners or proffer educated guesses. But these are estimates, not answers. And time is passing.

But the generals know that there is one who can shed light on the whole affair. Yet to shed daylight a window is needed. And it must be elevated, far above the normal habitat of marching armies, above the confusing wraiths of smoke and mist and gun flashes, standing clear of the frequent snow flurries. High and exposed, itself a prime target for the enemy's guns. This is Holland: a windmill surely? It is 21 January 1945. The taciturn Canadian, Simonds, and the affable Briton, Horrocks, two of the most distinguished field commanders in Northwest Europe, climb the giddy steps inside the windmill, the isolated sanctum of a mere subaltern, George Blackburn, an artillery Forward Observation Officer (FOO) who has survived so long where so many have perished.

One of the most vital battles of the war must now be fought across this terrain. After eliminating the German army in Normandy, after the wild advance across the whole of France and Belgium, after the temporary disappointment of Arnhem, the Allies have reached the Siegfried Line, the symbol and bulwark of German resistance against those who wish to penetrate into the sacred Fatherland. Nature itself has loaned a hand in producing formidable defensive barriers, for on the skyline rise

George Blackburn survived to compose and campaign.
(Courtesy of Kim Taylor-Galway)

two vast, dense forests, the Hochwald and the Reichwald, which must be captured by the Allies. There the snow lies, as yet smooth and serene, as George Blackburn remembered:

> Across the silent white valley, dotted here and there with lifeless farmhouses, the dark evergreen mass of the Hochwald frowns down from its ridge; mysterious and formidable, so dense and easily fortified that it forms the lower bastion of the Siegfried Line.

As long ago as 9 November 1944, George Blackburn had discovered this unrivalled vantage point at Groesbeek, a windmill high and stark amid its surroundings but brutally exposed to any enemy anger. During two-and-a-half months, whilst friend and foe endured the winter storms and massed for major action, the lone FOO had preserved his perilous observation post. He had become familiar with the vital landscape beyond and learned the furtive secrets of the forces which moved thereon.

Now the two lieutenant generals join the young artillery observer in studying and assessing what they see spread wide before them, every aspect so clear in the crisp air. Strangely, George later found the lesser ranks, with their insistent need to capture and comprehend every detail of the view, more intimidating than the imperturbable generals:

When company commanders returned with their platoon commanders, maps were marked with razor-sharp pencils. Huddling over their maps before the window of your mill with their subalterns not speaking for minutes on end, they peered out at the ground they knew they'd have to cross, where every fold in the ground could turn out to be of ultimate consequence to their lives and to the lives of their men. They would sometimes ask, in a quiet voice, barely above a whisper, questions like 'Is that a ditch out there, running left at 11 o'clock from that last glider with the broken tail?'

What George does not say is that those tough, experienced infantry commanders were instinctively subdued, lowering their voices and keeping down, because for them it was a daunting experience to be up in an exposed tower, plain to enemy view, deluged from time to time by German bullets and shells. But it took a lot of enemy wrath to radically damage or demolish substantial weathered buildings like Dutch windmills; and no amount of enemy ire would drive the FOO from his windmill.

By this stage of the war George, and his fellow FOOs, were not merely viewers and messengers. Nor was it their only option to send out a map reference so that various grades of artillery command, colonels and brigadiers, could then plan and order a shoot. A new system enabled the FOOs, across a wide artillery wireless network, to state a simple but precise map reference and then utter one of three key words. On the word "Mike", a preselected group of 24 guns would immediately fire at the target. On the word "Uncle", 72 guns would respond. On "Victor", a total of 216 guns would automatically fire. Thus, George calculated, a mere lieutenant or captain FOO could manage an instant artillery concentration "beyond the wildest dreams of even field marshals and five star generals of other nations or generations".

When he landed in Normandy in early July 1944, 27-year-old George Blackburn had been well trained in the functions of his role but was still a neophyte in the realities of battle. He had to learn quickly, as did everyone who walked upright on the earth: infantry, artillery, signals, engineers; there was always the imminent need to dig fast and dig deep into the reluctant Normandy earth, as the deadly batches of 'Moaning Minnie' rockets descended without warning.

There were few open vistas, such as the view towards the Hochwald. Much of Normandy was the *bocage* of small farms with vast hedges where the tallest tree must be the observer's all too exposed eyrie. But no Normandy tree top was beyond the spray of fire from a *Spandau* machine gun, and a single high-explosive shot from a *Panzer* could bring down the whole tree and the incumbent with it. In the more open country, such as the notorious Verrieres Ridge, the *via dolorosa* of Canadian infantry, the Allied observer was forced to look perpetually southwards and uphill into the eye of the brilliant summer sun. Therefore a carelessly tilted pair of binoculars could twinkle traitorous messages to the enemy up above, bringing down instant retribution upon the offender.

George quickly found that, for him and his men, sleep was a major problem:

You're surrendering to the sweetest of sleeps when Jerry starts lobbing over something of very large calibre. You can hear one coming from a long way off, growing louder and louder, sounding remarkably like a bus coming towards you at high speed. Then, just as the sound suggests it's going by, it lands with a wicked flash and a horrendous roar, sifting sand from the bunker ceiling. There's a plaintive cry of 'Stretcher!'.

He continued: "Every chance you get, regardless of where you are, you sleep, usually sitting up leaning against something, seldom stretching out flat, always fully clothed with your boots on. Your body aches arthritically for sleep." George even had nightmares about falling asleep and causing casualties among his own infantry by not alerting his own guns in the event of a sudden enemy attack.

Much as he was personally overawed by the immensity of the barrages fired in Normandy, George had believed that those of the First World War must have been of an intensity that would never be encountered in his war. He was surprised to find that this was not so. He cites an artillery authority who calculated that during the infamous fighting around Passchendaele in 1917 Canadian guns fired 78.8 rounds per gun per day over 18 days. At Verrieres from 20-27 July 1944, the same Canadian regiments averaged 385 rounds per gun per day.

Whilst such a weight of shells gave the infantry an advantage all the time the barrage lasted, George was very sensitive to the dangers and discomfort which his own advancing infantry comrades suffered as they tried to step on the heels of wide-ranging explosions *en masse*:

> While common sense tells you that those crashing orange and black flashes are a safe distance ahead, it seems as though you are running right at them as you feel their hot breath and are enveloped in a continuous reverberating roar. There is vicious cracking and sizzling overhead as the earth before you flashes and spouts with furious overlapping thunderbolts.

The work of the FOO was not all great barrages and tall windmill views. Some FOO action was more akin to the hand-to-hand role of the infantry. At Merxem, in the outlying areas of Antwerp, George was accompanying Major Bob Suckling of the Royal Regiment of Canada to obtain a view from a row of cottages which formed the front line. Somewhere beyond, a German self-propelled 88mm gun had begun to demolish the backs of the cottages, which looked out on enemy positions, in order to deny the Royals the advantage of that view.

George and Major Suckling found an open front door and dashed up into the back bedroom. And behold! There was the 88 well within range. But the German gunner was intent on knocking down the Royals' cottages one by one, getting ever closer and closer to the room they were in. George quickly calculated the precise location of the gun, intent on accuracy amid the panic. His wireless operator was still in the street out front. George dashed into the front bedroom, opened the window and shouted down the coordinates, adding, "and, for God's sake, tell them to hurry!" Pause. Silence. Crash! The bedroom next door had its wall shattered by the 88's latest shot. The room where the two Canadians sweated had to be next for demolition. Hurry the guns!

Then a double event occurred. The Canadian barrage descended bang on the 88, just as Major Suckling yelled, "They're coming!" A number of German *Panzers* had risen out of a fold in the ground, launching a counterattack, but had driven straight into the chaos and destruction of the breaking big gun thunderstorm ordered by George.

Even the back bedroom was luxury compared to some of a FOO's viewing points. On one occasion George and his operator Mel used a pigpen, which made an adequate observation point if one ignored having to share the space with the pigs still snuffling there.

Whilst in the area of Merxem, George had what might be called 'a bravery check'. On his own, entering another cottage and seeking a spying point from upstairs, George disturbed a figure sleeping under a mound of blankets. It might still be a misplaced *Panzergrenadier* with a gun; or it might simply be a vagrant. However, at George's touch, the face of a pretty young girl emerged from the blankets. She was a Resistance nurse who had gone forward to tend Belgian and Dutch Resistance fighters who had preceded the Allies into Antwerp. She was armed only with a bottle of iodine and a few bandages.

In some way the subject of music was broached, George himself being a composer. The Belgian girl told how she and her friends regularly listened to the BBC, specifically to keep up with the 'Top of the Pops' of the time. They would then pass on the newest songs, often disparaging of Hitler and his regime, to other friends to sing publicly in defiance of the Nazis. Even listening to the BBC could be seen as a capital offence and the Gestapo were constantly trying to catch those who dared listen in. "These are the real heroes," thought George, the unarmed but undaunted Resisters.

Whilst the name George Blackburn would one day become famous for writing his trilogy from the perspective of one regiment of 25-pdr guns, there were other independent witnesses who attested to George's skill and bravery, among them the Royal Regiment of Canada. Within long-distance sight of the Royals' front-line posts, regularly at midday, with true Teutonic precision, a German platoon made its way over the street and across an open space beyond, towards their cookhouse which was out of sight. A Royals' scribe noted:

> One day Capt. George Blackburn, a FOO, very casually began to register his guns on the gap which the Germans crossed. The following day, just before noon, he called for his target. When the unsuspecting Germans appeared in Green Street, Blackburn shouted 'Fire!' and eight guns pumped shells into the midst of the unfortunate enemy platoon.

In no way did the young captain's sensitivities become blurred or callous during his long exposure to the worst of war. He was still capable of significant emotions. There was foreboding, if not actual fear: "When you peered across the canal for the first time into Merxem, you knew that one day you would have to accompany an infantry attack to clear it of the enemy. Still, as the moment approaches, you are filled with dread."

There was horror to be dealt with. Having just pushed a soldier's brains back into his head, George was called to tend the wounds of Harold Wienes. He recalled: "The man had seen a civilian carrying an unexploded phosphorous bomb and had taken the bomb from him, whereupon the bomb exploded. It covered him with globules of burning phosphorous which could neither be extinguished nor detached from the skin."

There was sympathy too, especially towards the end of war when old men and boys were forced into the defenders' front line without adequate equipment or training. George encountered a white-haired elderly German who had been a bank manager before being rushed from his bank into the last lines of defence.

There was even humour. George and Bob Suckling, now in Merxem, decided to run down the backs of houses, rather than along the main street, in order to gain time. They found that, even in the midst of battle, the wives of Merxem had been doing their laundry and the two soldiers were caught up in line upon line of drying washing, sheets, shirts, towels and underwear that entangled them in their blundering haste. They paused for a moment to disentangle and laugh at themselves.

The basics of humanity were maintained. A scrawny hen had been captured with a view to fattening it for an eventual banquet. However, the artillerymen noticed that the bird had an almost preternatural instinct for danger, able to warn not only of imminent threat but also the direction from which it came. So the hen was given its own box on a vehicle and honoured as "our great Air Raid Warden". Found dead after a bombing raid, it was ceremonially buried under a grave marker.

There was still the appreciation of beauty. He told of being rowed across a canal with other soldiers, "paddling over the still water, glowing blood red from the stunning sunset, with only the gentle sound of dipping paddles and gurgling waters breaking the silence of the balmy spring evening, it is as though there are no Germans anywhere within miles".

Once the Allies had crossed the Rhine and were dashing eastwards, and while the Russian Army rolled towards Berlin from the east, enthusiasm began to wane in some units. The end of war was clearly now so near that exhausted men tended to avoid undue risks. Some commanders sought to lift morale by emphasising that only small battles remained to be fought. George Blackburn, with his crew of three assistants, had fought 'small battles' all the way from D Day onward, even if they were interspersed with some of the greatest barrages of all time. It was at this time of small battles, a month before the war's end, that George's supreme moment of battle arrived.

The importance of George Blackburn's epic stand is succinctly revealed in Canadian newspaper headlines of the time: 'Toronto's Royal Regiment wins gateway to North Holland', and 'A push over turned into a grim struggle to remain'. Beyond Arnhem, the Twente Canal was the most important barrier to the Allied advance toward the ultimate objectives of the towns of Zwolle and Groningen, whose capture would mean that Holland was totally liberated.

The Royals were briefed on 2 April 1945 to take the Twente bridge or, failing that, to cross the canal and defend the bridgehead until the Royal Engineers could erect a new bridge. Throughout the Low Countries the German tactic had been to mine each successive bridge and then blow it up as the first Allied troops drew near. The crews in the leading Allied tanks learned to duck when about 50 yards short of a bridge. And so it happened at the Twente Canal.

The Royals must therefore cross in canvas assault boats and defend the lodgement until vehicles could drive over a new Bailey Bridge. By this stage of the war there was no continuous German defence perimeter. Their effective tactic was to wait for an Allied advance and then quickly mass troops at the vital location so that briefly the defenders could have a numerical superiority over the Allied vanguard. Thus George found himself in a boat on a balmy evening which appeared to be far from any warfare. Landing on the far side of the canal, he and company commander Bob Suckling were able to walk half a mile forward and, close to the hamlet of Boschhouk, set up a defence based on a railway line embankment. So far it seemed to be a 'push over'.

The FOO had established his post in a substantial house with an integral tower, within which a circular staircase gave opportunities to view from several windows. It was on the second evening in the gloaming that George saw a new wave of German infantry, supported by tanks, attack the embankment, isolate and wipe out the defending platoon and head towards his refuge; 75mm cannon shots from the *Panzers* had already smashed into the staircase walls above and below George's favoured window.

As night and the infiltrating enemy advanced together, everything descended into a chaotic pandemonium of noise and flashing lights. With the house outflanked on two sides, George reached the last resort of calling down a barrage on his own location. First he ordered his crew, including operator Mel Squissato, into a crawl space under the house. There, aware that German infantry might be within yards, he used a brief torchlight glimpse to check and memorise the map reference of the house. He then covered the entrance to the crawl space and hurried back to the entrance hall. Calling headquarters, he gave the coordinates and the order "Fire until told to stop". He himself headed for the cellar, but could only reach the cellar steps as the cellar was crowded with civilians, including screaming children.

There were machine-gun bursts, tank engines, angry yells, agonised screams, Allied shells raining down and masonry crashing, crearting a thunder echoing and re-echoing boomerang fashion. The world seemed to be disintegrating. It was vital to switch off the barrage, so George crawled through the entrance hall to his large radio set, which was on the floor just inside the front door. Suddenly there was a tremendous crash and blinding flash of a tank shot, which for a moment totally confused the FOO. He then realised that this was not a shot from some distance away but the actual muzzle flash from the 75mm gun of a *Panzer* halted just feet away from the doorway. George knew that in the darkness no *Panzer* would be there unless supported by infantry who, at this moment, could be entering the house. Tense moments followed whilst George scrabbled for his microphone in the darkness amid the wreckage on the floor.

At the peak moment of anticipation, a dark figure appeared in the doorway. George wrenched out his revolver and made to fire, but first risked a whisper: "Who goes there?"

In the split second before the trigger could be pulled, the answer came: "Squissato". It was Gunner Mel Squissato, the radio operator, who had decided, against orders and taking terrible risks, to quit the crawl space and offer to help with the radio transmissions. George's outstanding recollection was of the brave operator crouching by the radio, relaying orders, as broken shards of glass and plaster rained down on him. After the war, George prepared for Mel a replica miniature Military Cross emblem, as he considered that Mel should have been equally decorated for his actions.

Then the barrage was switched off. The artillery commander's overriding orders had been that a barrage should not continue indefinitely because the FOO might have been killed and could not countermand his own original order. Confusion still reigned, with the brilliant gun flashes making the succeeding darkness even more impenetrable. Only after ranging his guns around the gardens and fields in a calculated searching tactic did George realise that the *Panzer* was no longer firing. The imperious barrage had driven the enemy infantry to retire and, deprived of its foot support, the *Panzer* on its own in the darkness was in jeopardy. It had withdrawn.

Dawn broke to a sudden quietness as the crafty German lead troops had pulled back, no doubt retreating to the next defensive line. His heroics over two nights would eventually bring George a Military Cross, but there was an earlier much-appreciated prize. Attracted by a seductive smell of bacon and eggs from the civilians in the cellar, on the way down he was distracted by discovering an ample store of wines and spirits. From the cellar a woman shouted, "Help yourself!" With bottles of German brandy and Scotch whisky under his arms, George was the most popular victor among his fellow officers from the Royals that night.

After events at the Twente Canal the war moved into what George, as a musician, might have termed *molto diminuendo*. When it was all over, some soldiers felt a sense of bereavement on abandoning the vehicles which had become almost an extension of their own bodies. Cartoonists depicted tank soldiers shooting their steeds, as at the end of ancient wars. Watching the end of war ceremonial parade, George encapsulated that feeling succinctly:

> As the first gun rolls by, chuckling and clinking on its limber hook, there's a growing awareness of how deeply these cold, steel machines have endeared themselves to you. It's as though you're saying goodbye to old friends. Can it be right for a man to look with affection on killing machines? But as you stare at those passing guns you decide that a man would truly be perverted if today he was unable to feel gratitude for those trustworthy weapons that unquestionably saved the lives of many, many men, including your own.

George Blackburn's achievements and survival as a FOO are all the more remarkable when his problems of enlistment are considered. He applied to both the Royal Canadian Navy and the Air Force but was turned down because of extremely poor eyesight. His son, Ron, said that George "made an incredible effort to join". Rumour has it that when being examined for the Army he memorized the eye chart. George needed to use binoculars more than the average FOO. However, some FOOs, proud of their keen eyesight, eschewed the use of binoculars and suffered because of this. It was calculated that, on average, a FOO might survive only 11 minutes in action. George's stint from July 1944 to May 1945 was a record.

Returning from the war, George resumed his civilian trade as a journalist, but instead of disappearing into the depths of some editorial sanctum he became Director of Information for the Federal Department of Labour. However, his talents led him into multifarious activities and achievements. He produced the longest-running radio show in Canada, he was a playwright, film script writer, composer, poet, pianist and anti-discrimination campaigner. To crown it all, in the 1990s he produced his trilogy of war memoirs, among the finest of their genre, more instructive than Remarque, more harrowing than Sassoon, with titles *The Guns of Normandy*, *The Guns of Victory* and *Where the Hell are the Guns?*. Nowhere does he specify which of his actions merited the Military Cross. He struck a new vein of memoir description by writing in the second person so that the reader finds themself down in the trench or up in the windmill as though they were the FOO themself, experiencing at first-hand each minute's tense apprehension and reaction to danger.

With the same vigour that George exerted in his incredible effort to join, he applied himself to peacetime pursuits. He had no training in music, although he could invent a tune. He taught himself to play the piano, painfully, finger by finger. He worked out how to transfer his ideas to the blank staves on sheets of music manuscript. His award-winning plays were performed throughout Canada and the United Kingdom.

Granddaughter Kim Taylor-Galway thought his music was cathartic, helping him to deal with the inevitable mental regurgitation of violent and bloody scenes from the battles. His compositions were also influenced by his campaigning zeal. He wrote and produced a celebrated musical play, *A Day to Remember*, whose songs resonated with the public and which appeared to laud the opening of the St Lawrence Seaway. On closer acquaintance it is a cry against the evils which may attend the expropriation of property. In 1917, George had been born in the village of Wales; but the village and his home had then been expropriated, demolished and submerged in order to construct that same seaway. *A Day to Remember* was staged for two successive summers in a specially designed tent theatre.

Commenting on his commitment to reform, granddaughter Kim felt that, as she came to awareness of wider issues in her youth, her grandfather found her to be a rather disheartening 'litmus'. Through her he was gauging the awareness of modern youth regarding the sacrifices made by people of similar age in the Second World War. He was angered by his findings, saying: "It is intolerable that hundreds of thousands of Canadian teenagers should remain completely unaware of what Canadian youth endured for humankind during those awful three months in Normandy in 1944, that they have been taught nothing of consequence about the war in their schools."

Kim also noted "my grandfather's outrage at how historians' accounts seemed to depict the Canadians as advancing slowly, completely neglecting to offer the fuller picture of these battles being courageously carried out by men not only consumed by fatigue but also … suffering … dysentery, lice, sand fleas and the fear that each moment could well be their last, and STILL offering themselves to fight".

A proud family man, George was devoted to his wife, Grace, and their generosity was known to all. George was famous for always 'picking up the tab' when out at restaurants with friends At their family festive table at Christmas there was always at least one seat reserved for someone who had no family. Of Grace's death he wrote: "All favour and purpose of life has vanished. By her belief in me she created MY belief in myself to do things I didn't think possible." After her passing he was rarely heard to play the piano again.

Of his masterpiece, the trilogy, George said: "Any reader looking for adventure must look elsewhere … I was fully aware that, if misery and fear failed to dominate my documentation, it would be in danger of becoming chauvinistic and therefore false." In a remarkable open letter to Canadian youth for the 60th anniversary of D Day in 2006, he quotes from his own books the very horror of war which dispels any sense of it being an admirable adventure:

> On the way here you passed through zones of foul odours, readily identifiable as coming from the rotting flesh of unburied dead horses and cows … But here, throughout the night, the air is filled with a most peculiarly repulsive odour you have never smelled before … you can hardly keep from gagging. Come daylight you discover the source: decaying bodies of men are everywhere.

Did George, like other sensitive warriors, suffer from post-battle trauma? A clue may lie in an obscure note he wrote: "And bad dreams pursued many for years – some up to the present." George was deeply moved, not only by the sufferings of his own countrymen, but also the very young and very old enemy soldiers at the last who were not really capable of defending themselves in battle. Gary McKay, the son of one of George's artillery comrades, remembers George commenting on the horrific bombing of Canadian and Polish troops by their own aircraft. He said it still haunted him years later, watching his comrades running in all directions and being blown up. No doubt those large, capable fingers, exploring the extreme ranges of a piano, were driven by thoughts too terrible and complicated to enunciate; finding a way to peace because, as Kim says, music for him was cathartic.

Her summing-up of her grandfather is obviously inspired by their relationship, but is confirmed by the opinion of all of us who knew and admired him. She says:

> My grandfather was the most shining example of what it means to be an officer and a gentleman. Rich with emotion, empathy for others, passion for fairness and equality, and a creative genius, this inspirational man remains a hero in the eyes of not just his family but the many who knew him.

That opinion is endorsed by George's radio operator, Mel Squissato: "We had quite a few adventures, some very rough times. The bond between us was stronger than brothers. You felt that he cared about us."

4

John Bridge

Lieutenant-Commander John Bridge, GC, GM and bar, British, Royal Naval Volunteer Reserve

Soldiers, sailors, airmen might all expect to become enemy targets at varying ranges, far and near, and, for some, hand to hand. John Bridge, however, was required to cuddle right up to the infernal machine, and lay his ear upon the beating heart of Death itself.

On D Day, just off Juno Beach, the destroyer HMS *Wrestler* struck a mine and was reduced to scrap. Later, off Sword Beach, the destroyer HMS *Swift* also struck a mine which broke her in two and sank her. Further out at sea, the huge battleship HMS *Warspite* hit a mine and suffered damage which could never be fully repaired. If a mine could do that to an armoured steel leviathan, what would it do to a man made of mere flesh and blood who mishandled it?

That crafty old Desert Fox, General Rommel, in charge of Germany's Atlantic Wall defences, had planted a deadly jungle along the foreshore of the Normandy beaches; a labyrinth of iron rods and wooden stakes, interwoven with rusting barbed wire, and festooned with fatal booby traps, some visible but others not. Under the lapping tide were more lethal traps, reaching out into deeper waters with an unseen belts of mines, detonating by various methods. The lead troops of the disembarkation would have to find and follow narrow avenues through the jungle, some opened by mine-clearing machinery, some by the wearying infantry method of prod, probe and proceed. Once avenues were opened up, the rest of the jungle could be left, to be cleared as time and labour allowed.

But in one area of the beaches there was no time to spare: minutes mattered. The genius of Churchill and the generals had envisaged two huge man-made harbours, and a pipeline under the ocean (PLUTO). The gigantic reinforced concrete sections of Mulberry quays and their Gooseberry breakwaters, 1½ million tons of material, were already on board ships waiting to be brought in to land and be constructed without delay. In the selected port area of Arromanches, it was thus imperative that

John Bridge at a VC and GC memorial event.
(Courtesy of Sue Gordon-Williams)

all of Rommel's clever devices be found and rendered harmless. That needed the clev-
erest scientific mind and most skilful fingers to deal with unusual objects which had
no 'Instructions for use' labels attached, and the ideal man for the task was obviously
John Bridge, master defuser of explosive devices.

Without delay Bridge arrived to carry out his vital work, as he had been doing
since 1940. He had already been awarded the George Cross, the George Medal and
bar. Another bomb disposal officer on the D Day beaches, Lieutenant P.D. Friend,
GM, said of Bridge: "[He had] possibly as much experience as anyone. Very sound
and reliable."

It was this reputation which later caused him to be stripped to his underpants,
immersed up to his chin in the murky, swirling waters of the River Waal, feeling with
his toes for an unexploded torpedo device. The torpedo was similar to one which had
already blown a 60ft gap in the roadway of the great bridge at Nijmegen, and had
thereby put in peril tens of thousands of Allied soldiers around Arnhem.

Bridge later portrayed the entire episode as being unusual and intriguing, without even counting the act of searching for the bomb. On 29 September 1944 he had been summoned as he was getting ready for bed and instructed to hurry to Brussels, taking with him only what tools he could carry. In an attempt to shorten the war, Montgomery had planned an airborne assault on Arnhem. This required ground forces to rush from the Eindhoven area towards Arnhem via the Nijmegen bridge to link up with the furthest forward airborne troops. For 40 miles the Allies held only the one main road, with the Germans still dug in on both sides. Bridge was to fly low along that narrow corridor in a twin-engined RAF Avro Anson.

"It was an unforgettable experience," he recalled. "We flew at under 100 feet the whole length of the corridor. The tops of the church spires seemed higher than us. The cows dashed frantically, trying to get away from the frightening noise."

Upon landing, a staff car sped him to a tent under a tree. At the tent entrance, standing waiting, was the unmistakable tall figure of Lieutenant General Brian Horrocks, who commanded the advancing corps. The general's hand was thrust forward for a handshake rather than a formal salute. Horrocks' first concern was to ask if Bridge was hungry and to order sandwiches whilst the young naval lieutenant learned the details of his task. The renowned general had moved a whole corps 75 miles in a day and yet he found the time to concern himself with the needs of one soldier.

The next unforgettable event provided evidence of the ingenuity and bravery of the enemy. A team of German frogmen, including one who had swum against the British in the 1936 Olympics, had contrived to paddle downstream carrying armed devices which, in spite of hostile fire, they placed under bridges. The Nijmegen railway bridge had been rendered unserviceable, and at the roadway bridge a device had already done its devastating work. But another still lurked invisible, deep in the water under the bridge. Had it merely failed to explode, or was it fitted with some new fiendish firing system which would cause it to emulate its twin if disturbed, blasting both the remains of the bridge and the human intruder?

Rowing out into the river and climbing down by the bridge pier, bomb disposal officer Bridge eased into the water, feeling gently with his toes. This was a method he had evolved, having found that toes can be as sensitive and agile as fingers. He pushed down farther, to waist level, then chest level and finally lip level. His toes then made contact. Remarkably but wisely, the young officer then paused, feeling around in the murk "to learn as much as possible about the object". Long experience had enabled Bridge to prepare a 'strop', a gadget like a wire noose. Again using his toes, with the dexterity of an average man using his fingers to lace up his shoes, he grappled and caught the still invisible torpedo, a device with the potential to trigger an earthquake under the damaged bridge. Then, holding the guide wire between two toes, he made his noose fast to a heavy-duty wire let down by Royal Engineers from the bridge above. All this was conceived and carried out on an invisible object down in the murk whilst Bridge's aching arms, relying on the bridge girders, maintained him against the rushing waters.

The soldiers had erected a pulley and brought a half-track vehicle to pull the device up out of the water. Bridge went ashore to superintend the lifting. An assault boat had been brought into position. Bridge shouted: "Heave away your half-track! Lift this thing!" Then, as the torpedo-like device was swayed into the assault boat, he coolly rowed out again to try to disarm and disassemble the menace. So far, so good. But either by design or maybe through damage or rusting, when he tried to loosen the locking ring it jammed. The mantra of the Armed Forces is 'Use only the tools designed for the job'. In this case the designed tools did not work, so he had to attack the dumb death machine using a basic hammer and chisel, fully aware that, with some devices, the slightest outside concussion was enough to set off the firing mechanism. Bridge's comment on completing the task was simply: "That's it. Job done!"

However, John Bridge could not have survived and succeeded without exercising the utmost diligence in analysing and recording every task he undertook, building up a documentary resource to support his own scientific reasoning. One of his three daughters, Susan, remembers: "He was a very methodical and analytical man. He made a comprehensive record of hundreds of timing devices he defused, the methods of firing and the mechanical working of the devices he was called upon to work on throughout his naval career. These notes are still used today."

An unfortunate angle on the Nijmegen operation was that, although the action could have been considered for the exceptional award of a bar to the George Cross, the naval captain in overall command of the operation decided astoundingly, according to Susan, "not to recommend him ... as he already had his quota".

Everything about this quiet man demanded terms like 'unforgettable' and 'remarkable', but perhaps the most amazing factor was related to his preparation and training, or lack of, for such tasks. A 25-year-old school teacher with a BSc in Physics (which would have had little if any reference to defusing bombs), he was interviewed for service on 4 June 1940. Commissioned into the RNVR on 13 June, he was given a short week's familiarization course on German bombs, collected his uniform, which by then was ready at Austin Reeds gents outfitters, and within five more days was defusing his first unexploded bomb without supervision. The enemy were constantly experimenting with and employing new fuses and firing systems found in no book of instructions. Following on from his first success, it was often Bridge who encountered, analysed and defused one or other enemy innovation cunningly designed to despatch the person interfering with the device.

The Germans had always excelled in the development of mines, and in 1920 had set up a mine warfare research and development command. For D Day, in addition to contact, magnetic and acoustic mines, they introduced pressure mines. These had been held back from use to avoid any Allied attempt to identify and counter the new system before the pivotal moment of the disembarkation. Much of the defuser's work was also concerned with unexploded aerial bombs, presenting yet another variety of lethal conundrums.

John Bridge's first award for valour, the George Medal, had been gained for an action back in September 1940. This was in the Plymouth area, where he was in charge of a bomb disposal squad. He was called to attend to a bomb suspected of being fitted with a delayed action fuse. It would be a tense race against time, as ever needing to avoid the error-producing factor of haste, but it was a race which he won. His next award was the King's Commendation for Brave Conduct, this time received for dealing with no less than 15 bombs, one of which was lying in a particularly dangerous position in Devonport Dockyard. It proved to be a double-fused bomb and the stereotypical 'ticking bomb', whose clock could be heard on close inspection. Bridge knew that his main clock-stopper tool could set off the special defensive fuse in the bomb, so he was forced to resort to a process lasting a full hour during the application of a liquid element. It seemed an eternity of inaction until the clock stopper could be brought into play. But even then the ticking did not stop. Undeterred, Bridge carefully unscrewed the entire fuse device so that the bomb could be taken on to nearby Dartmoor and exploded.

Very soon afterwards he became the first serviceman to gain a bar to the George Medal with another incredible feat of both mental and physical stamina. A bomb had fallen into the sluice between two docks at Falmouth so that neither dock could be used. Bridge needed to climb down, clinging to steel girders, for some 35ft. There he was tightly enclosed, trapped, with no way of escape as he examined the device. He observed a hole in the bomb casing. He unscrewed the base plug of the bomb and inserted a cable into it and out through the hole. With this improvised sling through the bomb, he then had another perilous climb back up the girders, guiding the hanging bomb until, above ground level, he could defuse it.

A posting to Simonstown Naval Base in South Africa enabled Lieutenant Bridge to train as a deep sea diver with regulation helmet and pump. It was also a welcome interlude before perhaps his biggest challenge of all, helping prepare for the invasion of Italy from Sicily.

Arriving at Messina harbour in August 1943, Bridge was greeted by two horrifying pieces of news. The harbour was infested by depth charges fitted with a firing device not previously encountered, and the initial disposal squad of seven, examining one such depth charge, had set off an enormous explosion which killed five of the team and badly wounded the other two. Yet it was crucial for the invasion of mainland Italy that the harbour be cleared without delay.

The citation for Bridge's George Cross is emphatic in its commendation: "For the most conspicuous and prolonged bravery and contempt of death in clearing Messina Harbour of depth charges". It also explains the strategic importance of the act: "This enabled the invasion forces to cross the Straits of Messina in far greater numbers and a day earlier than had been planned, something which proved most valuable during the follow-up operation." (*London Gazette*, 20 June 1944)

The war in the Mediterranean had reached a vital stage in the overall plan to destroy Axis power in the region. Since 1939 British and then Allied troops had been struggling to clear the coast of North Africa and open up the Mediterranean to Allied amphibious forces. The capture of Tunis had opened the way to Sicily. Now the grand plan espoused by Churchill and Roosevelt at the Casablanca Conference was possible of achievement. This was to strike at what Churchill termed "the soft underbelly" of the Axis, storming up the length of Italy into Austria and causing Hitler to divert precious resources from the two major fronts, that facing the Russians advancing from the east and the other along the Atlantic Wall in occupied Europe where the Allies were expected to launch a major cross-Channel assault.

With Sicily as its start line, the aim of the invasion of Italy was to land at three places on the mainland leg, sites which might be described as the shin (Salerno), the toe pad (opposite Messina) and around the Achilles tendon (Taranto). The obvious first move would be the short sea hop from Messina across to the toe of Italy. The straits are so narrow that Messina harbour was in full view of German artillery on the far shore. Any team working in Messina harbour would therefore be in double jeopardy, facing the danger of direct hits from the large-calibre German guns or a spontaneous explosion of the extensive mines in and around the harbour.

Although not a person to flaunt his own achievements, John Bridge was, in later years, persuaded to add detail to the bare formal words of his citations, particularly in a debriefing by Julie Land for the Second World War Experience Centre. Bridge immediately perceived that, in addition to the unknown quantity of mines hidden in the waters of the harbour itself, many more such devices were piled on the quays, in warehouses and elsewhere around the port. The mystery devices, whose key had first to be sought, were particularly difficult to investigate because the mines were stored in bundles lashed together by steel wire, as were others under the water. To each such bundle were attached two metal cylinders, which could possibly be to deter any attempt to disassemble the clutch, making it perilous to detach one item for investigation.

The two survivors of the previous ill-fated disposal crew were able to pass on basic information about what they had been trying to do, but Bridge had first to carry out a complete reconnaissance, of the situation beneath the harbour waters and of the various stocks of mines and other explosives. The possibility of a mass chain reaction to any lesser explosion was a horrific consideration. Conditions under water in the harbour were appalling, with little visibility, so everything had to be done by touch alone. Meanwhile, throughout the four or five days of the team's work, enemy guns were firing at frequent but irregular intervals directly into the harbour.

On 30 August, Bridge started diving, having identified 40 mines under water. He remembered: "I was the only one diving. I had an assistant and several men working above water. My longest spell was one of 20 hours. I did not suffer any particular discomfort and never got tired. I left that until afterwards." The risk to all his team was such that two other members, who were required to handle the unknown devices, were awarded the George Medal.

The method selected to deal with the mines was to use a tiny controlled explosion, a minimal charge sufficient to cut and separate the steel wire binding the various elements of a bundle together, without activating whatever malignant mechanism could be hidden there. Hooks were attached, again depending on sensitivity and skill of touch in the murky water. A lifting apparatus then carefully raised and transferred each item on to the wharf. It was thus possible, with reduced risk but constant need for care, to probe into the mystery cylinders, learn their functions and disarm them. The team was now able to proceed further with the task of disarming what proved to be more than 200 explosive devices of various types. The comment of Bridge's immediate commander on this occasion was that he "had never before had the fortune to be associated with such cool and sustained bravery as Lieutenant Bridge displayed during the ten days of the operation".

The enemy guns were still firing but Allied naval forces were able to sail into the main Messina harbour once wharfs had been cleared of all sources of danger. This enabled the loading of troops, vehicles and stores much more rapidly and efficient-lythan would otherwise have been possible. On 3 September the invasion fleet left Messina and landed successfully on Italy's toe, thereafter advancing rapidly to link up with landings at Salerno 300 miles to the north. On 8 September the Italian government surrendered, removing an entire army from the forces which the Axis had at their disposal.

John Bridge's bravery deserved a happy little footnote. His action took place in August and September 1943. The award was processed through the normal channels and gazetted in June 1944. However, the investiture could not take place until 16 March 1945. Felicitously, John had just married Jean (née Patterson) when he paraded at Buckingham Palace to receive his George Cross from King George VI, the monarch who himself had instituted the award in 1940. Accompanying John to the pomp and majesty of the occasion, his wife remarked: "It was a sort of extended honeymoon."

Ironically, the distinction between the Victoria Cross and the George Cross is that the latter award is designated as gained by an act 'not in the face of the enemy'. A man hugging an enemy depth charge of immeasurable explosive potential, whilst being bombarded by heavy artillery across the Straits of Messina, might have thought himself to be very much 'in the face of the enemy'. However, the George Cross has its own resonance in that neither can the winner normally fire back.

Bridge's undoubted athleticism and mental calmness must have owed much to his upbringing in a farming community, having been born in rural Culcheth, now part of Warrington. His daughter, Susan, draws the picture of John as the family knew him.

> My Dad came from a rural background, making do and mending, learning to be practical, getting on with the daily chores and routines on a farm. He was always helping out at home. He was protective of his sisters. He had a determination to better himself, so gained a place at university (the only one in the family to do so at the time). Also, having a scientific education, he wanted to put that to good use.

Being of a pacific, perhaps even pacifist turn of mind, when war broke out John felt drawn to some kind of activity which might save lives rather than destroy them. During the great blitz on British cities, about a tenth of all bombs dropped by the *Luftwaffe* failed to explode. These now lay about in or under the cities and were a terrible menace to the civilians who continued to dwell there. John therefore volunteered for bomb disposal duties. As mentioned, he was rushed into action almost immediately and was spared the prolonged and sometimes brutal service introduction, familiarly known as 'square bashing', aimed at instilling a rigid discipline, or even a killer instinct, into raw recruits. Bridge brought his own discipline to the war.

Susan takes up her father's story again at the war's end. "He was very proud of the fact that all the men working for him were volunteers and he was never short of them, even considering their dangerous work," she says. "And none of his men were injured while working for him. He valued loyalty and a strong sense of duty."

Even though he was far from a militaristic frame of mind, she adds, "he admired strong leaders with compassion, quoting the encounter with General Horrocks before the bridge at Nijmegen: the General was concerned that after my Dad's journey he was given something to eat despite the urgency of his mission."

Moving on to later days, Susan records that John "had a taste for adventure, training in South Africa as a diver, or towing the family caravan across the Pyrenees, or travelling to exotic places around the world in retirement".

Whilst he particularly enjoyed fell walking, he equally relished more quiet pursuits. Susan says:

> He kept two allotments, one for vegetables and the other for my Mum to grow flowers. They took great pride in producing fruit, vegetables and flowers which they distributed among many friends and neighbours. Typically he systematically recorded goodness knows how many pounds of raspberries, broad beans and sweet peas, allocating them to a 'goodie box' for distribution.

Having enlisted from his schoolmaster's position at Firth Park Grammar School, John Bridge returned to the same school but eventually moved on to an administrative role, becoming Director of Education for Sunderland in 1966.

His continuing social commitment is illustrated by two aspects of his later career. Susan says he became deeply involved in Remembrance events: "He loved ceremonies and had a tremendous sense of occasion but was always modest, even when he was in the limelight." This is confirmed by another friend who shared with John many Remembrance events in Sunderland, Arthur C. Lockyer, MBE:

> I had the honour of meeting Lieutenant Commander Bridge many times and found him to be a most courteous, highly intelligent and quite private man. Although he was well aware of the distinction and singularity of his gallantry awards he was very modest about his achievements. He must be one of the very few service personnel who knew that the success or failure of their actions would have a direct impact on the direction and progress of the war, such as his courageous work at Messina harbour and also at Nijmegen Bridge in 1944, for which latter fearless and undaunted work he received no formal recognition.

Arising out of what Susan describes as "his very strong sense of decency and fair play", and his detestation of inequality and injustice, he was most proud to be one of the instigators of the purchase of Derwent Hill in the Lake District to enable disadvantaged children to have an active holiday, learning practical skills.

Indeed, Derwent Hill stands as a continuing and still developing memorial to John Bridge, GC, GM and bar, as he would have wished. It has extended beyond its somewhat limited beginnings and now caters not only for colleges and youth groups but also for businesses and other organisations, offering adventure training, including John's own favourites, hill walking and canyoning. During the financial year 2017-18 it was used by 4,270 people, including 3,438 youths.

John seems to have lived a serene life after the war, but no doubt would have suffered with reflections and dreams about some of the sights he saw. However, he was probably spared the worst aspects of war-related Post Traumatic Stress Disorder as avoiding the two main causes of the syndrome. He would not have experienced the guilt of having been a trained killer, but rather would feel justified by having saved many lives, most of them unknown to him. Furthermore, because he never lost one of the volunteer crews who assisted him, neither would there have been the guilt associated with a fatal bullet or explosive charge choosing to kill one of his comrades rather than himself.

Daughter Susan states that: "He really believed that he had led a charmed life." In his bomb disposal role there is no doubt that his survival and achievements owed much to his mental acuity and physical agility. However, when pressed about his achievements and survival, his opinion may not accord with the view of those who study his actions from afar. Yet John Bridge is surely entitled to his particular opinion, which adds an interesting contribution to the whole debate on the nature of bravery. He insisted:

No matter what anyone says, at the end of the day the role played by luck is a very important factor. I remember when I was going down for a dive at Messina I thought 'this is it, this is the testing point. But I will come out alive because there are far too many people praying for me.' I can't explain why I was so lucky and some weren't. That is the nature of luck. And I had it.

Alongside luck, however, was the ability to think more laterally, or guess more cogently and outflank whatever extraordinarily complex and malignant device might be invented to thwart him: surely he was of the breed of the chess master rather than of a roulette player.

5

Robert Cain

Major Robert Henry Cain, VC, TD, Manx, 2nd South Staffordshires (Air Landing)

Overwhelmed, outnumbered, surrounded, isolated, exhausted, guns out of ammunition, at least there remains a decent razor; thus to shave, dust off, square the shoulders and march tall, turning tribulation unto triumph.

If earth were ever invaded by aliens from a remote planet, bearing weapons of superhuman ferocity, it is to be hoped that there would be warriors like Robert Cain who, through sheer stubbornness and calculated belligerence, would overcome the superiority of the infernal machines.

This may appear to be a rather frivolous introduction to a serious theme, but it is relevant to Cain's heroics at Arnhem in September 1944. On the battlefield the weapons available did not unduly favour one side over the other. In small arms the Germans might have had a slight advantage (*Schmeisser* against Sten), but no more. Of the workaday tanks, the Sherman and the *Panzer* IV were fair competitors. And if the heavy gun barrages of the Allies surpassed anything the enemy could muster, the constant niggle of the omnipresent *Nebelwerfers* tended to even the score. Only in one respect was there a kind of alien indestructible presence which struck almost atavistic fear into infantrymen and tank crews alike: the German Tiger tank. Hitherto this 54-ton grinding, rumbling, armoured-steel mobile fortress had prowled about the battlefield unchallenged. Even the Sherman Firefly, its 17-pdr gun more than equal now in firepower, still needed to hide from the monster which could blast through the Sherman's modest armour at 2,000 yards.

In the debacle of Arnhem it was difficult to keep an accurate count, but it is probable that Cain personally, and with whatever imperfect or inappropriate tools were available, knocked out four Tigers, as well as several other large fighting vehicles. It was as near to hand-to-hand fighting, man against leviathan, as could possibly be imagined. Yet at first glance he was hardly the youthful tearaway who might be expected to perform Herculean physical and mental feats: he was a quiet and modest man and already 'old', or at least 'elderly', by front-line measures.

Robert Cain, clean-shaven at the most desperate
hour. (Courtesy of Francie Clarkson)

Five awards of the Victoria Cross were made for valour at Arnhem. The average age of the other winners was 25: Cain was already 35. The four other recipients, Lance Sergeant J.D. Baskeyfield, Captain L.E. Queripel, Lieutenant J. Grayburn and Flight Lieutenant L.D.S.A. Lord, did not live to tell the tale. Cain did survive, but for the rest of his life he rarely told the tale.

His elder daughter, Rosemary, knew about the award of the Victoria Cross, the medal having been donated to the Staffordshire Regiment Museum. However, daughter Francie, 17 years younger than Rosemary, was unaware of her father's full heroism until after his death. Then, aged 13, she found an old suitcase full of newspaper cuttings and photos which revealed the whole story.

Cain was unique in being the only Manxman to win the VC, his country's highest honour. He was born in Shanghai, the son of Manx parents, but educated in the Isle of Man. His civilian occupation was that of an oil company executive. At age 19 he joined the Territorial Army and on enlisting for war service in 1940 was commissioned into the Royal Northumberland Fusiliers. By 1944 he was commanding B Company of the 2nd South Staffordshires. Having already seen action in Sicily, he and they were now destined for Arnhem.

The story of Arnhem, popularised by the book and film as 'A Bridge too Far' but officially designated Operation *Market Garden*, is well known. British and Polish airborne troops were to establish a bridgehead over the Lower Rhine at Arnhem and hold it until the main ground forces south of Eindhoven could complete the last 60-mile lap of the long advance that had begun in Normandy on 6 June. It was an audacious plan but hopes for success were partially founded on the facile assumption that the German Army, shattered around Falaise in Normandy as recently as late August, would not yet have had time to reorganise. Things went wrong from the start.

Firstly, unbeknown to the Allies, two of the best surviving formations in the German Army, the 9th *Hohenstaufen* and 10th *Frundberg SS Panzer* Divisions, were in the Arnhem area resting. Secondly, as the first gliders descended, no less a commander than Walter Model, C in C, Army Group B, was sitting eating his lunch under the flight paths. Known as the 'Lion of Defence' for his tactical skills, the Field Marshal's first instinctive reaction, on seeing a few enemy gliders, was that it was merely a small raid aiming to eliminate him personally. Thirdly, there were grave errors in the choice of landing sites at Arnhem. The lead troops were expected to complete a fast march of 8 miles from the landing zones towards the bridge, a task which could have been possible only if there was virtually no opposition on the way, rather than an elite, well-armed force. Finally, there were faults in the equipment employed, particularly in the matter of communications, and in the chain of command.

In Cain's case, departing on the first daily lift-off, the tow rope between the tug plane and his glider became entangled and they had to return to base, being delayed then until the second lift which could not be arranged until the next day. Once the relatively lightly armed air landing and parachute troops had landed they were violently attacked by elite battle groups of all arms. From 18-21 September, only Lieutenant Colonel John Frost's small group reached the Arnhem bridge, this force being too weak to capture the bridge. They were forced to surrender once surrounded and having completely run out of ammunition.

The initial task of the South Staffordshires was to advance from the landing zone to the main Arnhem bridge, it being assumed that German resistance would be weak. In fact it was the South Staffordshires who were soon outnumbered by the quickly assembled defenders. The airborne men were armed only with the infantry's light weapons: machine-guns, PIAT mortars, rifles and grenades. They encountered experienced German troops furnished with heavy artillery, *Nebelwerfers* and tanks. Many good defensive positions were available to the Germans in houses and woods. Consequently losses were high, but the South Staffordshires pushed on until their numbers were insufficient to assemble an attack. Now the enemy took the offensive, virtually surrounding the remaining infantry. In a hand-to-hand confrontation, Major Cain and a few others were able to fight their way out of the initial trap.

Cain now found himself commanding about 100 survivors. He was ordered to attack and hold a piece of high ground called Den Brink. He led a bayonet charge up the slope, driving the Germans away. However, when Cain's men tried to dig in, they found that the interlaced roots of the trees made digging impossible. They were forced to lie exposed to the enemy's withering fire. The only way to avoid total annihilation was to withdraw back down the slope and find softer earth into which they could dig slit trenches.

The cumulative effect was that, after such severe fighting, Cain was able to assemble only two small platoons out of the survivors of his entire battalion. They, with other survivors, guarded an isolated area around Oosterbeek, with a flank on the river but not connected to Arnhem town or the crucial bridge. They hardly realised that they were trapped in this enclave until any order was given to evacuate the entire surviving airborne force. Even then they would have to cross a stretch of river where no bridges were available. No contingency plans had been made for such an eventuality.

Cain had seen hundreds of his battalion comrades killed, wounded or taken prisoner and was angrily awaiting the opportunity for revenge. It came on 21 September when a Tiger tank was reported to have forced its way to where Cain had stationed himself, lying flat beside a building in order to steady and aim his PIAT mortar. A lieutenant had climbed up inside the building as a lookout.

The only weapon available to Cain was the PIAT, which while ostensibly an anti-tank weapon had proven inefficient and clumsy. Simply to cock the apparatus it was necessary to up-end it, stand on the base plate and, by force, pull the cocking handle against an extremely strong spring. Then, after a bomb had been inserted into the open slot, the unwieldy weapon must be aimed, using primitive sights. Waiting until the tank was only 20 yards away, Cain's first shot exploded plumb under the Tiger but did no harm at all to the tank. The big tank gun instantly flamed a response. The shell, 15in long, weighing 20lb, trailing tracer fire and travelling at 2,700ft a second, missed Cain by inches but smashed into the building, killing the lieutenant and bringing down masonry and rubble upon Cain.

The tank's machine gunner wounded but did not disable Cain, who managed to reload and fire time and again until several shots had struck the tank and immobilised it. A second armoured giant then smashed its way through the gardens. Cain loaded and fired once more, but the bomb exploded whilst still in the PIAT, splattering him with tiny pieces of shrapnel and temporarily blinding him.

Disorientated but still shouting orders, he was hustled away into shelter to be treated. Cain emphatically refused morphia, saying he was not sufficiently wounded. Gradually his sight returned. One of his men remembered the ghostly sight of Cain returning to the fray, his face blackened and peppered with the marks of tiny shards of metal. In response to Cain's frantic calls, a 75mm anti-tank gun had been brought up and with it they destroyed the second *Panzer*.

One of the tanks involved was described as a Tiger. Another was a monster which, although not as heavy as a Tiger, could, at close quarters, look as menacing as the bigger tank. This was the *Sturmgeschütz III* assault gun. The Tiger, with its traversing turret, at least gave some indication of a fallible human presence within it. Lacking a turret, the 'StuG', had a blank, flat superstructure, its long 75mm gun able to smash armour plating at 2,000 yards. Seeing it approach, a lesser man than Cain would have sought immediate cover.

There followed another four days of similar challenges, the brain and athleticism of British fighting men pitted against the brute but ponderous might of the tanks and assault guns. The only advantage the men had was a result of the enemy's difficulties of manoeuvring a huge tracked vehicle with a long projecting gun amid thick woods and high garden hedges. Seeing Cain's boldness and several successes, his small contingent of survivors rallied to the task. One painted a picture of this valiant figure "wounded, bandaged, dirty, dishevelled", but driven on by anger. Another queried why this man could not say "I've done enough already" and pull back into a safer position. Cain had continued firing the thunderous PIAT so much that his eardrums burst. He fought with shreds of bandage stuck in his ears.

It almost seemed as though Cain had some hypnotic power over the German armour. The next day three tanks in turn attacked his position, but each time he broke cover, positioned himself in the open and fired at the tank, hurling a continual barrage of shots from his puny, undependable PIAT. Yet enough bombs struck home to scare off each of the tanks. A crew within a tank cannot fully assess what effect frequent explosions on the outside may mean. Any hit could have engulfed the tank in flames, fuelled by petrol, oil and ammunition. It is also not easy for a tank, with its ponderous turret traverse, to hunt down a single mobile figure. A contemptuous withdrawal might be the tank commander's choice. Cain was aware that he had this one potential trump card in the otherwise weak hand dealt to him.

The actions of Cain have more than once been written of as though they occurred almost continuously during a relatively short period. His glider came in to land on 18 September and he was still fighting furiously on 25 September, the actions described above spread over that time. It was an extended period of constantly erupting battle during which he continued to suffer from wounding and deafness, insisting against medical advice on remaining in his forward position.

It is physically and militarily impossible for soldiers to fight continuously throughout such a period. Ammunition must be replenished, guns cleaned and deeper trenches dug, the tree roots making the latter a particular problem. Platoons must also be reorganised, wounds bound up, food eaten and short bursts of sleep crammed in.

On the German side, the experienced and highly competent Field Marshal Model knew that whilst he had the 9th and 10th *Panzer* Divisions available, there were no trained German soldiers to spare. After the second day at Arnhem, the Allied airborne force was cut off and scattered, with no rescue imminent. The German tactics were therefore probing attacks and discreet advances; knowing the skill and élan of the opposing airborne troops, there was no indiscriminate sacrifice of irreplaceable men and materiel.

The resistance of men like Cain, as well as the reputation of the British and Polish airborne soldiers, meant that the Germans always approached them with some measure of caution. Other soldiers were displaying equal resilience and gallantry. Lieutenant Grayson had, for two days, defended a tactically vital house near the bridge against all arms until he was killed. Lance Sergeant Baskeyfield had taken on a Tiger tank and more than one *StuG*, destroying them at point-blank range with an exposed 6-pdr gun before he too was killed. Captain Queripel had charged and destroyed a strongpoint defended by an anti-tank gun and two machine guns. He also was killed. Other soldiers in lesser moments of opportunity reinforced the warning message to the German attackers.

Cain thus continued, responding to whichever more senior officer was within range. Major General 'Roy' Urquhart, GOC of the 1st Airborne Division and ostensibly in command, had lost overall communication contact and control; Brigadier John Hackett (commanding the 4th Parachute Brigade) and Brigadier Philip Hicks (1st Airlanding Brigade) were extemporising in different ways; and less senior commanders continually gathered what remnants they could and tried to continue the fight with whatever weapons were to hand.

On 24 September a brief truce was arranged to allow for the collection, treatment and evacuation of the wounded, in the case of the British and Poles all as prisoners. On the resumption of hostilities, another Tiger appeared within Cain's view. He had earlier seen an untended 6-pdr anti-tank gun. Running to find it, he was joined by an artillery gunner. They manhandled the gun into position, loaded, sighted carefully on the approaching Tiger and fired. The giant tank was disabled, the crew piling out and retreating. Cain tried to continue using the gun, but discovered that its recoil system had been put out of action. It could not be fired again.

On 25 September the Germans attacked in force a final time, using flamethrowers and self-propelled guns as well as probing infantry. With the 6-pdr useless and no ammunition left for PIATs, it seemed there remained no weapon capable of dealing with heavily armoured vehicles. Undaunted and ingenious, Cain reverted to the most improbable method of all, a 2-in mortar. This was a lighter weapon than the PIAT, a small tube normally set firmly on the ground, pointing upwards to launch a small bomb gracefully into the air, thence to descend on to the target, normally infantrymen. The piece was loaded simply by dropping the bomb on to the spigot within the slender tube, which was simple enough when rooted firmly to the ground and with no vital need for pinpoint aiming.

Now Cain was forced to carry the mortar under his arm, firing from the hip, clumsily feeding the bombs one by one into the tube. There was no way of taking precise aim at a target. He was like a cricketer trying to defend his wicket whilst his bat was still tucked under his arm. But the small bombs sailed in the direction of the enemy, exploding among them with sufficient anger to force the Germans back. They were unlikely either to have been trained to respond to such a method or even to imagine any sane enemy coming at them in such a fashion.

At about this time, Major General Urquhart sent a despairing telegram to Lieutenant General Frederick 'Boy' Browning, commander of I Airborne Corps, who was back at headquarters: "All ranks now exhausted. Lack of rations, water, ammunition and weapons, with high officer casualty rate. Even slight enemy offensive action may cause complete disintegration."

It is unfortunate that he did not interpose the word "further" between "even" and "slight"; Robert Cain could have advised him that there had been more than "slight" offensive actions already.

The inevitable reply from Browning was to effect a silent evacuation of all remaining force across the river that night. This would be a hazardous undertaking as, not having been foreseen, the supply of boats was inadequate. Some of the troops were so weary and disillusioned that they could not make the great physical and psychological effort to find their way to and cross a wide, rushing river in darkness to unknown terrain on the far bank. The Germans would eventually take over 6,000 Allied prisoners at Arnhem.

Major Cain's concept of leadership did not include slinking away in defeat. He and his men had fought courageously and had inflicted on the enemy losses beyond what could have been imagined. Their daring had gained minor but inspiring victories amid a major military catastrophe. They would go out as true soldiers, proud of what they had achieved. Cain managed to find a razor and give himself time to shave, encouraging the men around him to do the same and to dust down as well as possible. He then led them to the river, if not in parade order, then as a disciplined group still capable of fighting if needs be. When a watching brigadier commented on Cain's smartness, the major replied simply: "I was well brought up, sir!"

However, Cain's problems were not yet at an end. He was ordered, with his dwindling number of survivors, to form the rearguard defending the crossing point from which assault boats would ferry the troops during the night. All went well until it was the turn of Cain's tiny rearguard to cross quickly before the Germans realised what was happening.

But there were no boats waiting for them; none had returned to pick them up. With desperation about to set in, some floating wreckage was observed in midstream. They swam out to find it was a damaged boat, but in just sufficient condition to carry them across the river. There were no oars, rifles having to be employed as paddles. Yet compared to facing a Tiger face-to-face, such impediments were little more than minor embarrassments. Not a man was lost as they crossed to safety.

The citation for the award of Cain's Victoria Cross was headed: "To Captain (temporary Major) Robert Henry Cain (129484). The Royal Northumberland Fusiliers (attd. The South Staffordshire Regiment) (1 Airborne Division) (Salcombe, Devon)." It describes the battle at length. Two statements highlight the significance of his achievements beyond basic statistical implications. The first is the official citation:

> The Germans made repeated attempts to break into the company position by infiltration and had they succeeded in doing so the whole situation of the Airborne Troops would have been jeopardised. Major Cain showed superb gallantry. His powers of endurance and leadership were the admiration of all his fellow officers and stories of his valour were being constantly exchanged amongst the troops. His coolness and courage under incessant fire could not be surpassed.

Cain's own assessment of his actions was always more critical and pithy. Commenting on his wounds from the explosion in his own PIAT he said: "I was shouting like a hooligan. I shouted to somebody to get onto the PIAT because there was another tank behind. I blubbered and yelled and used some very colourful language. They dragged me off to the aid post." The impression he made on others was very different. Admiration was expressed by one of his soldiers who noticed blood streaming down Cain's face and uniform, not from one of his bullet or shrapnel wounds but as the result of his eardrums bursting. When the major behaved with such disdain for pain, lesser soldiers felt impelled to imitate him.

The British and Polish units involved at Arnhem were left so depleted that there would need to be a considerable time of reinforcement and reorganisation. But it was Cain's destiny to be involved in continuing action after the official VE Day. The Allies had long nursed fears that fanatics loyal to Hitler would refuse to accept an official cessation of hostilities, even with their Führer dead. There were thoughts of guerrilla-style 'werewolves' operating in the hills around Hitler's eyrie at Berchtesgaden. It was thought that some fanatics might also remain in the wild mountains of Norway and carry on the fight there.

On 11 May 1945, as part of the Airlanding Brigade in Operation *Doomsday*, Cain landed in Oslo. Cooperating with the Norwegian Resistance, the South Staffordshires and other units ensured that all German troops in Norway surrendered without further fighting of any significance. The brigade stayed there until the end of August. Just before the end of the year, Cain left the Army with the honorary rank of major and returned to the oil industry.

He might have looked forward to the idyllic life of a top oil executive in the tropics, all exotic sea beaches and sundowners. In fact he became involved in the transition of the British Empire into the Commonwealth of Nations. In West Africa he was elected a member of the House of Representatives. As a member of the legislature he assisted in the setting up of the new independent country of Nigeria. He also did voluntary work with the Red Cross and VSO. He returned to the Isle of Man for his retirement.

Daughter Francie sums up his character vividly: "He was a warm, convivial and kind man with a great sense of humour. He nearly always wore a jacket and tie. Only in the garden or on the beach would he wear an Airtex shirt or roll up his sleeves."

Her words are reflected in the testimony of one of Cain's contemporaries, Jack Reynolds, MC: "He was very kind. He had a great sense of humour. He always bought the drinks." Whilst Reynolds spoke as of equal rank, George Ashington, looking up from the ranks to the giddy heights of field officer, stated: "You didn't have to be frightened of him. You could go and ask him anything and he would listen."

A more recent commentator, Jack Daly, adds: "I must confess to having a particular admiration for this Victoria Cross winner. There is something so completely normal and modest about his life before and after the VC that it shatters the myth that all VC winners are supermen." In spite of his collar and tie civilian persona, Robert Cain was, however, a superman for a week in September 1944.

His sense of humour has been referred to, and daughter Francie illustrates it with an example of his practical jokes. He was building a swimming pool to his own design as he "didn't want a blue symmetrical eyesore in the garden". A small higher pool fed water down through a rockery to the main pool. Robert's sister donated a garden gnome, holding a fishing line, which would sit and fish in the upper pool. Soon the gnome disappeared. It reappeared from time to time in many unlikely places, such as fishing in the sister's bathroom loo on Christmas Day, appearing on the holiday beach after being hidden in a suitcase, and angling from the roof of the sister's flat. Explanations were neither given nor requested.

Francie continues:

> He loved gardening, charity work and crosswords. He did *The Times* crossword every day and in retirement he would complete it before getting out of bed ('teas-made' conveniently by the bedside) every morning. Above all, he loved

animals and we had Corgi dogs and Siamese cats. I only saw my Dad cry twice; once watching Churchill's funeral on TV and when his dog Tiger was killed on the road.

This reference to the dog Tiger raises intriguing questions. Did the name 'Tiger' consciously or unconsciously link back to the horrific days among the trees at Oosterbeek? Did this naming arise as a sublimation of those terrible dreams of wartime atrocities which so many veterans suffered, often for long periods after the war? Did his reluctance to talk about the war with daughters Francie and Rosemary, or flaunt his medals, signify a deliberate attempt to banish lurking thoughts about so many horrific moments in battle?

In those days of more formal dress, the British stiff upper lip was an essential norm of behaviour. Nobody exhibited it better than Robert Cain, who could play practical jokes with fishing gnomes and do *The Times* crossword before breakfast, yet would face out a Tiger tank at 20 yards, wielding a totally inadequate weapon whilst bleeding from multiple wounds; and find time to shave decently whilst an entire major military operation was crumbling about him, with no boats available to ferry him across the river.

But then he came from the ancient Nordic traditions of Orry the Dane, who, according to the Isle of Man national anthem, "in Mannin did reign".

6

Ken Cardy

Staff Sergeant Ken Cardy, DCM, British, Royal Mechanical and Electrical Engineers

He is the AA man, the RAC man, the Green Flag recovery man, in front of the very front line if need be. But, unlike the military medic wearing his Red Cross, he, the ARV man, will not expect to enjoy immunity from the enemy's guns.

An ugly, unlovable beast is the ARV (Armoured Recovery Vehicle), a mere armoured steel hulk with no pretentions to finesse, a lumbering monster deprived of its turret. A complete tank has at least some design intentions, with its traversing turret sitting proud and its potent gun protruding well forward with intent. The Sherman, with its rounded dome outline, maybe even evokes in more imaginative minds some intimations of Byzantium or Samarkand. But not the ARV.

However, if your tank has just liberated a Dutch village street, halted on the objective and the roadside has collapsed, and the tank with its human contents has toppled over into a deep Dutch dyke? Then there is nothing more beautiful in this world than, within a brief minute or two, the almost angelic apparition of the ARV up above, lifting you and yours from the miry clay. And then the ARV crew, in total disdain of that *Spandau* machine gun sniggering away somewhere ahead, lighting cigarettes and discussing how to right your tank, using the heavy-duty winch on the ARV.

The rescue crew would be commanded by someone such as Ken Cardy, wearing the black beret with that unfamiliar REME badge. It is the early autumn of 1944, and two years ago the Royal Mechanical and Electrical Engineers did not even exist. In the Second World War soldier's father's war it would have been the familiar Royal Engineers and Royal Corps of Signals who would be doing such tasks. It was not until 1 October 1942 that the REME was formed to provide a breed of super-technicians who worked mainly in workshops but were also attached to line regiments, on call for the roadside accident or to rescue abandoned, knocked-out vehicles. Because from August 1944 onwards the Allies were mainly advancing and the Germans retreating, it meant that each German *Panzer* knocked out was a total loss. But on the Allied side the ARVs could rescue damaged vehicles and in many cases rehabilitate them immediately for further service.

Ken Cardy, REME trail-blazer and Ford innovator. (Courtesy of Cardy family, Linda and Christine)

Diminutive Staff Sergeant Ken Cardy of the REME was attached to the giants of the 2nd Battalion, Welsh Guards, serving as part of an armoured reconnaissance unit. Ken's story underlines the importance of opportunity as fate shuffles the cards to select those destined for highest honours.

Much of a REME NCO's duties would be confined to reasonably safe workshops. But there were still many moments of risk to life and limb for those whose duties called them to the front line or near it. Ken's adopted battalion had already experienced the catastrophic 'Death Ride of the Armoured Divisions', Operation *Goodwood*, south-west of Caen in Normandy in July 1944. A Guards tank officer fighting nearby, Robert Boscawen, described the scene into which the ARV must drive:

> Beyond the railways the horizon was covered with burning tanks … twenty … a whole squadron, burning in one field alone. More were hidden behind the black smoke of others brewing up, whilst still others were still being hit and bursting into flames. A number of men were crawling towards us through the corn.

At such moments ARV crews might be required to also act as emergency medics and ambulances.

Another infrequent but dangerous element in the balance of forces was that the *Luftwaffe* was not, as sometimes implied by commentators, totally absent from the skies. Ken Cardy, like many others, suffered an unwelcome 1945 New Year's greeting recorded in his diary: "31st Dec overnight stop on an airfield north of Maastricht.

1st Jan '45 a bright morning. Suddenly the air shattered with jet aircraft – German! About a squadron and shooting. Several tanks struck. Luckily [firing] only machine gun ammo and not cannon. All over in a flash. New type of planes." That morning, for Operation *Bodenplatte*, the *Luftwaffe* had assembled nearly 1,000 planes and at 0920 hours on that New Year's Day had attacked 16 Allied airfields where many personnel were still struggling with hangovers.

A slower but equally hazardous death trap awaited tanks crossing unknown terrain. Tank publicity tends to portray the tracked vehicles ploughing through all types of obstacles on the proving grounds at Bovington. But tank tracks have one fatal fault: in a certain type of mud, as they delve deep seeking firm ground, they can dig themselves further and further into a grave. Again the ARV has to come forward to the point of peril and its crew must dismount to secure tows or cables to rescue the sinking 30-ton vehicle. The ARV itself could become trapped. Ken remembered such an event during Operation *Veritable* in February 1945:

> As the first troop was crossing over what appeared good ground, it turned out to be a bog, thick, gluey and they were all bogged down. We went to the rescue … and got bogged down too. The CO arrived … and he went down. With the help of an artillery tractor, our pulley block and the longest cable, we got out, caked in mud.

Such incidents might have brought a little humour to the routine of war, but not if the leading tank had been stalking enemy *Panzers* or guns, and was now stalled and sinking in full view of those guns.

Later battles did not reach the massed wrath of Normandy. But immensity is not to be confused with intensity. In Normandy the average German soldier was simply carrying out his duty with no emotional attachment to, or passion for, the French countryside. Once the Allies had reached the German border, the enemy fought in smaller formations but were now much more passionately defending their Fatherland, fighting for their homes, their families, as well as their own lives. They often had recourse to more desperate and vicious tactics.

The Germans were now laying mines too deep to be detected. Ken recalled: "They were primed so that one or more tanks or vehicles could pass over them, but a later vehicle would trigger the explosion. They were also booby trapping the ways that the infantry had to go." Another comrade, Peter White of the King's Own Scottish Borderers, added: "The enemy secreted with devilish cunning explosives with an anti-lifting device under his own or our dead or even wounded men. They boobytrapped vehicles, door handles, WC chains and so on."

Whilst Ken's ARV was intended to rescue other vehicles, it was also prone, as in the mud episode, to the kind of accident to which clumsy heavy-tracked vehicles were vulnerable. Ken had vivid recollections of crossing the fast-flowing River Rhine over a temporary bridge structure which, with fractions of an inch to spare on either side, demanded the commander's and driver's utmost concentration and dexterity:

We crossed the bridge to the usual yahooing by the Paras and Commandos along the way. As we hit the seeming fragile bridge it bucked and swayed like a ship at sea. We had even been issued with blown up life jackets for the crossing. More than one vehicle had taken the plunge. Beyond the river the devastation was chronic, not a building standing, telephone and electric cables all over the place. Mines everywhere, not buried, just lying around. A narrow route had been cleared by the REs but death literally lay around on the ground for the careless driver.

Ken experienced many routine risks, dangers and escapes which were common to all. Unexpectedly the door of opportunity into the hierarchy of bravery opened for him a chance not encountered by most REME NCOs in the north-west European theatre of operations. In Normandy a tank battalion could find itself leapfrogging along a single road, with other units on parallel roads. Now, nearing the end of battles, the Allied armoured divisions were, as Ken noted, "off the leash" and fanning out, widely dispersed into vast territories, having been ordered to "bash on regardless" towards Berlin. In the lead, he said, the Household Cavalry "used their armoured cars like sports cars, always driving flat out, that was their defence really because the fastest vehicle is the hardest for the enemy guns to hit".

The effect of all this was that squadrons were well separated, with few if any reserves left behind at Regimental HQ where the ARV awaited developments. Ken Cardy was now about to undergo trial by fire twice in quick succession. The dangers of fire at sea are well recognised, but it might be thought that a land-based armoured steel hulk would not be exposed to that level of risk. However, a stranded tank might still have most of its capacity of 150 litres of high-octane fuel remaining, plus a large stock of high explosives. Any white-hot shot or splinter piercing the fuel tanks or ammunition racks could cause the instant eruption of flame so well known to tank men. The vehicle also inevitably carried other incendiary triggers, such as oil, signal flares, ammunition and assorted debris. The resultant inferno could cause the entire massive 30-ton structure to glow orange like an incandescent light bulb. Tank commanders would thus normally approach any sign of tank fire with the greatest of caution.

It was now 9 April 1945, some 77 months of Britain's war already fought out and only one month left before VE Day. The Guards Armoured Division had reached the area of Osnabruck in Lower Saxony. Ken's immediate colleagues were approaching Menslage, a village with medieval-style half-timbered buildings and a population of about 2,500. Operating as the Recce unit of the division, the 2nd Battalion Welsh Guards, rather than concentrating its forces, had spread out, probing like the fingers of a hand stretched wide, until the fingers recoiled into a fist to punch at the enemy's weakest link.

Ken's ARV, named *Atlas*, was tailing a Cromwell tank moving cautiously towards Menslage. In open country this road would be under enemy observation. Inevitably shells began to slam down on the roadway; not the comparatively light 'Moaning Minnies', so deadly to the infantry, but heavy shells fired by large-calibre guns. A moment later a shell crashed into the Cromwell, sparking instant flames. The crew instinctively bailed out. As they did so, another shell exploded in the road, wounding or confusing the escaping crew members. Falling or staggering, they were prey to continuing blasts, each of which could fling razor-sharp shards of shrapnel in every direction. A jeep was coming along the road behind the ARV. Ken stopped the jeep, ran into the road, supported or lifted the bailed-out crew into the jeep, and ordered the driver to turn around and "Get to the medics fast!" The jeep driver needed no encouragement and roared away back down the road.

The REME NCO was left briefly standing in the road. This was, for a tank man, the moment of leaping over a precipice: to run for one's life, or to move forward cautiously and investigate. There were flickering flames and billowing smoke, but as yet no violent explosion within the Cromwell. Was it the blanket rolls and boxes on the flat rear deck of the tank which were burning, a combination of spills of oil and other flammables in the turret or a triggering of a devastating reaction from the ammunition within?

With no time for contemplation, Ken sprints back to the ARV, grabs a fire extinguisher and returns to the Cromwell. He knows he only has seconds to spare as he furiously pumps foam into the flames, stemming and dousing them. The Germans, no doubt having seen the smoke, switch off their barrage. There is silence. The blackened Cromwell stands immune, surrounded by a halo of purple-grey smoke and steam. Surprisingly, it appears that a little cleaning and a few simple repairs will put the tank back on the road again. Indeed, with a new crew on board, it is made ready for further action the very next day.

With singed overalls, Ken Cardy then takes ARV *Atlas* back to RHQ to await any further call out. The British artillery barrage moves ahead of the tanks, setting fire to old properties with dry wooden beams. Parts of Menslage become a flashing, exploding bonfire. The blackness of night frames and exacerbates the dazzling conflagration close to hand. Ken and his crew wait while the wireless set on *Atlas* chatters away with messages from far and near.

Suddenly a clear voice breaks through with a familiar code sign, appealing for support. It is the gunner on a Cromwell well forward in the village itself. Gunners do not normally hog the airways, but this one is desperate. His tank has been hit, The commander and operator are wounded and the engine is out of action. There is no power in the turret traverse, so the gunner is able to fire only within a narrow arc, winding the turret by hand. There is no way of reversing out: it is a blazing inferno to the rear. The enemy in front have him in their sights. He needs immediate help.

Ken knows that there are no other tanks available in reserve. The normal tactic would be for another tank, with its 75mm cannon firing high-explosive shells and armour-piercing shot, to go forward past the disabled one and defend it. This would allow the ARV time to try to tow it away. In the absence of an available tank, Ken calls the colonel, volunteering to take *Atlas* forward into the growing firestorm and find out what can be done to rescue the tank or its crew. The ARV has only a single machine gun for protection against whatever weapons may be battering the disabled tank. In the moment of extreme emergency, the colonel approves Ken's idea, but counsels: "Take great care! Be ready to pull out!" The ARV heads towards the fiercest concentration of fire, some of it descending in massive explosions from heavy enemy artillery or spraying out from amid burning buildings.

It becomes obvious that the marooned Cromwell lies somewhere beyond an epicentre where fires from two opposite houses embrace across the street. There is no other way through. As *Atlas* appears to swim in a sea of flame, it is possible to distinguish the disabled Cromwell close to a farm, also on fire, merging with further flashes from the Cromwell's own gun blasts and incoming enemy tracer. Ken's own words best describe what happened next:

> Traversing his turret around by hand the gunner had no power for hydraulics. But he was loosing off the big gun a couple of times and also machine gunning. Jim England and I baled [*sic*] out and started getting crossed cables attached. Using the tank's infantry phone [in the vehicle's side wall] I said 'We are towing you back.' He replied 'Get under cover. You are under observation. That's what we are shooting at.'
>
> Shells were falling all around. One fell on a large shed and blew it to pieces. We were showered by wood and dead chickens and blood and feathers. I shouted to Jim to get back into the ARV. How we never got hit I will never understand. Anyway we took up the slack and started towing.

He makes it sound so simple. Towing a car with both vehicles reversing is a fairly simple task, given the turning versatility of the car's wheels. Tanks are more clumsy vehicles, tending to slew and jerk. Towing a tank in reverse needs ample space for error, and there was virtually no space between the fires through which *Atlas* had to drag the reluctant deadweight of the wounded Cromwell.

The citation for Ken Cardy's Distinguished Conduct Medal is unusually insistent on one aspect of the two rescue events. It says: "By this cool and gallant action, and by showing such a very great devotion to duty, he had saved two tanks for the battalion at a time when it was extremely short of vehicles."

The priorities of the commanders seem obvious. Yet for Ken, whilst pleased to have indeed rescued two valuable Cromwells, the most important outcome of his adventures was the rescue of two tank crews, good comrades who must otherwise have perished.

The DCM was promulgated much later after due process. However, for Ken, his crew and a few friends an even more pleasant immediate celebration was a sumptuous chicken dinner. Whilst mounting up on *Atlas* after fixing the towing lines, the ever cool Ken had paused a moment amid the turmoil and slung on to the back plates of the ARV more dead chickens to join those which had been blown there by the blast. The dinner compensated for the gruesome task of cleansing body and overalls of the loathsome mess caused by a chicken shed exploding at short range.

The Distinguished Conduct Medal is no longer awarded, having been superseded by the Conspicuous Gallantry Cross in 1992. During the Second World War the Distinguished Service Order (DSO) was available only to officers, whilst the DCM was the equivalent award to 'Other Ranks'. The DCM preceded in seniority of foundation even the Victoria Cross itself, having been introduced during the Crimean War two years before the VC. The recommendation for the award is also of interest, demonstrating the extent of vetting and supervision which went into such an award. Army Form W.3121, making the recommendation for '6025124 Sgt Kenneth Francis Cardy', had to be and was signed personally by his battalion commander (a lieutenant colonel), his brigade commander (brigadier), his divisional commander (major general), his corps commander (lieutenant general), his army commander (general) and finally by the Commander in Chief, Field Marshal Bernard Law Montgomery.

Even in war, life, especially with the Guards, was not always dirt and danger. The battalion's fearsome sergeant major, 6ft 6in tall and well known in peacetime ceremonial parades, had formed an attachment with the rather frail 5ft 4in REME sergeant. Attached personnel were not always welcomed in elite units, but in the inverted way of military affection the RSM referred to Ken as "my 'orrible little REME man".

One day, with the battalion's tanks all in action, a signal went out for all remaining personnel to parade. Ken went along to discover that what was planned was a ceremonial parade. Like the Highlanders with their kilts and bagpipes, the Guards carried in their echelon ceremonial dress in case of being called for formal duties. However, when Ken was arrayed in a guardsman's outfit a quick piece of nipping and tucking had to be undertaken to fit him into the standard uniform. Fortunately, once beautifully arrayed, Ken was happy to find that the Welsh Guards' parade formation did not involve any complicated marching, such as for Trooping of the Colours. They were only to serve as background colour for photographers and film cameramen for one of the famous parades at which Montgomery handed out medals and cigarettes, and then made an impassioned publicity speech to the assembled press corps.

Ken was later also amused when the Guards were preparing for a great Victory Parade. Not content with only applying a new coat of paint to each tank, a team of welders was going around filling in shot holes and other battle damage which some units might have deemed to be honourable scars of war. For the Guards, not even such scars could be allowed to mar parade perfection.

The near approach of victory brought no remission for the fighting men. By 18 April 1945, all hoped that they would make it through to the end. It was too late in the war to die now. But fate declared otherwise as the battalion approached its last defended village, Visselhovede in Lower Saxony. Ken would never forget the name:

> Jim England, Lewis and myself had got out for a stretch and a smoke. Jim Mills was standing on his seat, half in, half out, all of us, side by side. Three shots rang out. One shot clipped my epaulet. One spun on the visor in front of Jim Mills. But Jim England had dropped like a stone. Of course we had all dropped down, but Jim was pumping out blood. Some Scots Guards stopped and we told them we had been sniped at. They ran forward and blasted the nearby tree tops and out fell three snipers.
>
> The large barn beside us was burning and by its light we dug a grave. We rolled Jim in his blanket, said a prayer and buried him. We had just finished patting it down, put the cross in, when Padre Payne arrived in his jeep. He said,

'Is he a Catholic?' I said 'Yes!' He said 'Take him out again, please. I will take him to a Catholic centre.' So with big lumps in our throats we lifted Jim out again and on to the jeep stretcher. And that was the last we saw of our mate who had been with us throughout the battles.

The final days of the war were a confusion of 30-ton tanks trying to make their way through crowds of refugees and wandering disarmed German soldiers. Amid it all Ken,

> had a fascinating chat with some *Volkssturm* [militia comprising mainly the young and elderly] prisoners who had all served in the First World War and had a great respect for 'Tommy'. They told us why they had been anxious to surrender. It was because of the Hitler Youth squads: if the *Volk* didn't toe the line they were reported to the nearest *Gestapo*, the swines that they were. It was disconcerting to see the familiar field grey uniforms standing idly in fields and farmyards, watching us pass by. Freed Russians were roaming about all night and we expected some trouble, but all went well.

The ceasefire brought an immediate change of tasks for Ken, by now a staff sergeant. After trundling all the way from the Normandy beaches to Germany in a clumsy ARV, he was transferred to the luxury and speedy delights of a two-seater, 10hp open-top Adler car – definitely not standard British Army issue!. He was given free roaming rights to anywhere within 50 miles of Cologne. Armed, and accompanied by an interpreter, he was to requisition civilian trucks needed to transport supplies for the hundreds of thousands of displaced people who were now coming within the responsibilities of the occupying troops. Ken had to oversee the commandeered lorries being delivered daily to the Daimler Benz works. During the war much road transport in Germany had been adapted for wood-burning power, small cubes of pinewood being fed into a firebox to produce a resin gas. Now they all had to revert back to petrol or diesel.

As the Welsh Guards reverted to an infantry formation, Ken was posted, under the nominal command of a major, to organise the 21st Army Group Training School for Armoured Recovery at Sennelager. Simultaneously, battlefields were being cleared of abandoned military vehicles which were destined for recycling as scrap iron. Ken was fascinated by the variety of adaptations of fighting vehicles made by both sides during the war. It occurred to him that some of the variants, once destroyed, would never again be seen. Future generations would be deprived of items of huge historic interest. He therefore suggested to the major that an example of each variant vehicle or gun be retained in a vast hangar at Sennelager with a view to their being used some day as formal museum pieces. The idea was approved and put into practice, producing a unique collection which might never have been saved for posterity.

Ken Cardy's foresight and ingenuity served him equally well in civilian life. Working for the Ford motor company from 1960, he quickly made a mark with his ideas, under Ford's staff suggestion scheme, for improvements on the production line.

He developed a method for shortening the static part of the seat belt which brought him, in addition to a cash reward, a new Ford Capri. He then went on to develop a new way of sealing diesel pumps after they had been calibrated, which earned him a new Ford Escort.

Another wartime trait that remained with him was the ability to discern danger and react promptly. Many years after the war, he was walking beside the River Crouch near Hullbridge in Essex. A woman and her grandson were splashing about in the water in an ungainly way. Ken quickly realised that they were stuck in a mud bank, unable to tear themselves loose. Meanwhile, the rapid Crouch tide was coming in fast. He immediately rushed to the spot and hauled both grandmother and boy out of the lethal trap and up to safety on the solid paving.

Ken's daughters, Linda and Christine, say that he was not much involved in physical sports but was still a very active man, being part of the Ford Rally Team for the 1964 Monaco Rally. He was no stay-at-home recluse, caravanning with his wife, Lily, for long periods in Europe and taking an active interest in Ipswich Town Football Club. However, any further sporting interest, such as snooker and motor cycle racing, he enjoyed vicariously through the medium of TV. He also enjoyed the beat of military bands, but otherwise his daughters describe his musical taste as "Silence is golden".

The ability to sit in silence without giving offence when in company is an unusual trait, but one close friend remembers that Ken seemed to have a reserve of calmness and contentment which allowed companionship without chatting incessantly. Indeed, Ken visited one veterans club where drinking was excessive and the influence of alcohol led to men boasting of war feats and describing incidents which Ken knew to be impossible. He did not visit that club again.

As a boy, Ken had once been allowed to have a pet fox. In retirement he did not revert to keeping such an animal but, especially after snow, would prowl the park and woods looking for animal footprints, particularly the fox's. He was also an avid bird-watcher. Above all his family remember his interest in the work and activities of his children, grandchildren and great-grandchildren. He enjoyed frequent family events and was regarded as "the fount of all knowledge", especially in respect to cars.

He remained skilled and ingenious, for among his last interests, in his 90s, was the construction of a functional camping trailer assembled from an old tent plus other bits and pieces. He vigorously lobbied the local authorities to have a shelter put up at the local bus stop, and also enjoyed sowing a wild flower garden in the rural spaces around the chalet where he lived in his last days.

Compared to his burly wartime Welsh Guards comrades, Ken was a man of limited physical stature but of considerable mental acuity, able to respond to the challenges of war and peace and often exceed the ordinary claims of duty.

At the time of D Day his REME badge was still unfamiliar to many soldiers, the corps having been founded less than two years previously. Ken was one of the founding race of REME sergeants who set markers for a corps that was to grow into one of the outstanding military units of the 21st century. And in a sense Ken's DCM was the historic marker for personal service and commitment by members of all ranks of a remarkable corps.

7

Ted Chapman

Corporal (post-war CSM, TA) Edward Thomas Chapman, VC, BEM, British, 3rd Monmouthshires

Cymru am byth! Where has he gone? – the warrior of mighty impulse and immediate action? Up the Wye, fly fishing, waiting for the trout to rise, or out in the field, patiently tending a pregnant pony.

Does history repeat itself? In the year 9AD, at the *Teutoberger Wald*, or thereabouts – where Corporal Edward 'Ted' Chapman found himself almost 2,000 years later – was fought what has been described as one of the most decisive battles in world history. It was a total disaster for the Roman attackers.

Under Emperor Augustus, Imperial Rome ruled almost all of what is now called Europe. Only an alliance of 50 wild Germanic tribes, who lived beyond the *Wald* (forest), resisted. Notable Roman general Publius Quintilius Varus was sent with three legions, the heavy armour of the day, to vanquish the tribes and extend the Roman Empire to the far north, completing domination of the continent. Quintilius, as he was generally known, had already carved himself a niche in Biblical history, having, when Governor of Syria, destroyed Jerusalem following a rebellion and crucified 2,000 Jews. He then issued an edict that everyone must return to their town of origin in order to be taxed, thus causing the birth of Jesus to take place at Bethlehem instead of Nazareth.

The hitherto invincible imperial infantry, shields interlinked – the Tiger tanks of the time, if you like – expected to roll over the uncivilised forest people. But faced by an ingenious Germanic tactician, Arminius, and strung out in the treacherous bogs and dense forests, the Romans were surrounded, overwhelmed and annihilated. Varus committed suicide. The Roman Empire's expansion to the north ended, and the *Teutoberger Wald* became a place of national pride and inspiration for the German race, possibly even more emotive than British scenes of battle such as Hastings, Dunkirk or Arnhem.

Edward Chapman, from Bren gun to fishing rod. (Courtesy of the
Trustees of the Regimental Museum of The Royal Welsh, Brecon)

Moving on to 1945, another mighty force was assembling to drive the Germanic
race off the sacred *Wald* and open the way into the armour-accessible plains towards
the east. The responsibility for this new attack was being handed to Major General
'Pip' Roberts and his 11th Armoured Division, of the Charging Bull badge. Would
history repeat itself? Would this be another *Teutoberger Wald* disaster for unduly
confident attackers? The 11th Armoured might have had some reason for dismay.

Although this was late in the war and the German armies were considerably
depleted, a modern-day equivalent of Arminius had assembled on the *Wald* a truly
elite force of instructors and cadets from the *Kriegsschule*, the officer training college
in Hannover. They had been immersed in their eight-week general officer training
before moving to their chosen arm of service: infantry, tanks or artillery. They were
mainly graduates from the fanatical Hitler Youth movement. Now they were to
defend the steep, sacred Teutoberger ridge. There could, at the time, be no German
unit more skilled, ruthless and dedicated to the Nazi cause than this elite selection.
There were also few defensive positions more likely to frustrate attackers, especially
when, over the centuries, this same battlefield had become for its inhabitants a symbol
of the supposed superiority of the Germanic over the Latin races.

The 11th Armoured knew full well about ridges, to its cost. South of Caen there
was another ridge around Bourguébus and Verrières. There the 11th, with two other
armoured divisions, had been sent, driving across open plains under the sights of the

German guns up on the ridge. In the early shambles of Operation *Goodwood*, some tank units had lost more than 50 percent of their strength. But whereas that gentle ridge enticingly offered open farmlands up which tanks could eventually drive and conquer, here the *Teutoberger Wald*, rising in steep crests to more than 1,000ft, was clothed tightly in thick forests through which no tank could move. So this, as distinct from the tank-intensive *Goodwood* plan, was to be an infantry-only attack.

Opening the way into Germany there was, as yet, only one bridge available across the wide Dortmund to Emms canal. From that bridge a road ran to Ibbenburren across the *Teutoberger Wald*. The view from the defenders' fastness on the ridge dominated the canal bridge and the road forward. To assault those wooded slopes, the 1st Herefords and 3rd Monmouthshires – two of the few units which had actually achieved their objective nine months earlier during *Goodwood* – were chosen. Amid all the tank chaos on the first day of *Goodwood*, these two infantry battalions had successfully cleared the villages of Cuverville and Demouville, suffering few casualties while taking many prisoners. On 1 April 1945, April Fool's Day and also Easter Sunday, the Herefords advanced to clear the way up to the tree line. This they achieved, but found it impossible to occupy the ridges. The result of their assault was a warning of perils to come for the Monmouthshires next day. There were at least four worrying factors.

Firstly, so closely packed were the trees and so dense the undergrowth in between, that there was no possibility of any kind of line abreast formation or of units maintaining visual contact during the advance. Progress would have to be by individual, isolated, 'Indian file' probes.

Secondly, the skills of the defenders and the incline of the *Wald* meant that the German cadets could use virtual guerrilla tactics. A tight group could crash down through the forest, momentarily overwhelming and furiously punishing the scant forward troops of the advance, then retire before themselves suffering excessive losses. The defenders could thus outnumber the attackers at the spearpoint of any advance, which must be confined to the width of a narrow track.

Thirdly, the Herefords had counted exceptional losses due to friendly fire. Allied artillery shells aimed at points high on the ridge had hit treetops directly over the heads of the advancing units and caused mayhem. This was one of the most demoralising experiences which hard-pressed front-line troops could be called upon to endure, so-called 'friendly fire'. There was no way of hitting back at one's own guns.

Finally, because of the tree cover, like a thick mat spread overhead, wireless communication was unreliable and at times impossible. The use of runners was confined to the few tracks. Hand or other signals relying on sight were impossible in the dense thickets. The relatively junior officer or NCO in front would have to take more senior decisions promptly.

To further harass the Monmouthshires, the night of 1 April brought a great rainstorm which caused misery to the infantry perched on the steep slopes. As one private said with grim humour: "Nothing makes a foot soldier more fed up and miserable than rain, running down your neck, forming puddles in which to stand at the bottom of your trench, and soaking your boots and socks. Many were the groans of 'I only put these clean socks on three weeks ago'."

So on 2 April, in an attempt to dislodge the Germans from the top of the ridge, the Monmouthshires set off, line ahead, up separate tortuous paths and deer tracks, cautiously awaiting the first response from a fanatical enemy. Commanding one section is Corporal Ted Chapman, physically no heavyweight figure but lithe and endowed with the powerful muscles of a coal miner.

The file of climbing men is hit by a storm of fire. Men fall or throw themselves to the ground. In a brief pause, Chapman orders his few survivors to tend and evacuate the wounded. He himself grabs the Bren gun and, standing tall, sprays the forest with a torrent of bullets that drives the enemy back under cover. He then charges forward to scatter the enemy further up the ridge. His company, mostly unseen across the hillside, has been hit hard and lost many men. On his winding path, Chapman rallies his section and then dashes up the hill again, firing furiously. The enemy slowly retire and then make another rush. With casualties mounting, the Monmouthshire's CO sends out an order to return to the start line. No message reaches Chapman: he and his small cohort are alone on the upper slopes of the ridge.

He continues to carry and fire the Bren. This is not an easily portable gun like the Sten or *Schmeisser*, which are light and facile to handle. It is a 23lb dead weight of metal, the effect of which doubles or trebles as the gun fires, recoils and kicks in the hands of the gunner. An incident from the previous day illustrates the difficulty of continually firing a Bren from the hip. Droves of *Luftwaffe* planes had swept down on the attackers. One angry private had raised a Bren gun and was firing vertically up at the planes. After a brief while it was noticeable that his muscles refused to support the strain. The muzzle of the Bren slowly fell, until the gun, now almost horizontal, was wrenched from his grasp to prevent him shooting his comrades.

Because of the rapid rate of fire typical of the Bren, Chapman is running out of ammunition. He shouts down the track for more to be sent up. In the meantime he displays a remarkable feat of skill and physical power. He knows that if he were to lie down on his chest, the normal practice for firing, with his head higher than the gun, his posterior would be high enough for snipers to hit him with ease. Instead, he throws himself down on his back in a dip in the track, lifts the heavy gun over his chest and continues to fire short bursts over his shoulder. The enemy pauses briefly, possibly somewhat bewildered. This was not something they had been taught in training and would require another tactic to deal with. More ammo arrives for the Bren. Almost as though in response, the defenders, slithering like snakes through the undergrowth, mount an assault from multiple hiding places. They shower many hand grenades through the trees, hoping to smoke Chapman out. Surrounded by bursting bombs, he retaliates by leaping up and rushing forward again, the reliable and accurate Bren mowing down those who choose to continue the close fight. Again the astonished cadets give ground to this menacing figure. One man against a college-load of cadets, to whom battles are not supposed to develop like this.

The corporal is not to know that, in the confusion of narrow paths and congested forest, one enemy group has already penetrated far below and got through to battalion headquarters. Lieutenant Colonel W.P. Sweetman himself has had to seize a Bren gun and, rallying drivers, cooks and slightly wounded men, fight off these zealous young warriors. The cadets know they are the last hope of the Fatherland, fighting on such an historic and symbolic battlefield, the heirs of Arminius the unconquerable.

But the battle noises are diminishing, Chapman observes through the trees the body of a British officer lying prone. It can only be his company commander, Captain V. Mountfield. With the situation static, the enemy quiescent and his section well hidden in the undergrowth, the corporal pushes his way through to the officer, who is unconscious but still breathing. Using his miner's muscles to the full, he picks up the captain in a fireman's lift and begins to plough down through the scrub towards medical help. A sniper's bullet rips into his thigh. Another bullet thumps somewhere on his back, causing a stumble but not penetrating his body. Battalion headquarters is there ahead and a busy medical officer comes to help. Chapman gently unloads his burden. The awful truth then dawns: the thump of that unseen bullet! Mountford has been shot dead by a sniper whilst over Chapman's shoulder.

Colonel Sweetman tells the wounded corporal that he has done enough. But Chapman insists on returning to his section. That is his right as a soldier whilst he can walk and shoot. For another two hours he is back at the high point of the Monmouthshires' attack while the battle positions are stabilised, ready for a final leap to the crest of the *Teutoberger Wald*. A tired enemy agrees to a temporary ceasefire in order to collect and tend the wounded, and decently straighten the dead.

The battalion's report recorded:

> The attack disorganised the enemy and forced him to withdraw. In the Teutoburgerwald [*sic*] the battalion's losses were the heaviest it ever suffered. The task which it had been allotted took an infantry brigade three days of hard fighting to achieve. The battalion could be proud of its attempt to dislodge a superior and determined enemy.

On 13 July 1945, the award of a Victoria Cross to 4080657 Corporal Edward Thomas Chapman was gazetted, with emphasis on several points of this heroic episode:

> [The Teutoberger Wald was] defended by a battalion of German officer cadets and their instructors, all of them picked men and fanatical Nazis ... his company was ordered to withdraw but Corporal Chapman and his men were still left in their advanced position, as the order could not be got forward to them, He had nearly run out of ammunition. Shouting to his section for more bandoliers, he dropped into a fold in the ground and covered those bringing up the ammunition by lying on his back and firing the Bren gun over his shoulder.

This last fact obviously impressed the reporting officer as being unusual enough to emphasize in the *London Gazette* pages.

The *Gazette* concluded:

> Throughout the action Corporal Chapman displayed outstanding gallantry and superb courage. Single-handed he repelled the attacks of well-led determined

troops and gave his battalion time to reorganise on a vital piece of ground over-looking the only bridge across the canal. This magnificent bravery played a very large part in the capture of this vital ridge and in the successful development of subsequent operations.

By 1 April 1945 the battalion had already lost more than 1,000 casualties during the campaign from Normandy onwards. On 2 April it lost another 100. Not having enough fit 'rifles' to man a position, it was withdrawn from the front line for reorgani-sation, being replaced by the Cheshires, so the battalion did not have the satisfaction of completing the conquest of the historic *Wald*.

Ted Chapman's level of bravery was far removed from mere reckless bravado or mindless fury. The various experiences of previous actions foment and synthesize within the mind of the soldier. They form the basis for future disciplined actions which may appear to have taken place without due thought. There were aspects of the battle which, if not directly favouring Chapman, at least equalized the odds on the day.

As long as he could support the Bren in a firing position he was at an advantage against the numerous Germans coming down the hill, who would be armed with rifles and bayonets or *Schmeissers*. These latter, the MP40s, were manual machine guns, roughly equivalent to the British Sten, and would not have anywhere near the stopping power of the Bren. The tactic of shooting whilst standing tall, whilst poten-tially fatal, could also cause confusion in the minds of the enemy. It was one thing to attack a machine gun fixed in a trench and, in one sense, a 'sitting duck'. It was quite another to be aggressively attacked by a mobile man wielding that machine gun. To some extent a gun crew static in a slit trench sent out a message that they were vulner-able. But an attacker could himself feel extremely vulnerable when the machine gun, in powerful hands, was charging at him personally. The close clustering of trees also deprived the Germans higher up the ridge of a clear, wide arc of fire through which the Monmouthshires would have to cross.

It is likely that Chapman's first charge was almost instinctive and, having seen those in front of him wounded, would be super-charged by mounting fury. But over the several hours of the combat there was ample time for him to review his decisions and opt for a more passive defensive tactic. Certainly he positively resisted a legiti-mate indication by his colonel that he should withdraw from the fight and have his wound properly treated. At that point he had already done enough to be counted as an extraordinary hero.

As he ordered the realignment of his battalion, the colonel could have sent another corporal up the hill to take over the isolated section. It was at this point that the utmost loyalty of the soldier drove Chapman to refuse the easy option. The remnant of his men, just four or five of them, were still on the hill. They had no clear idea as to how the battle was progressing or how they might extricate themselves safely. They were his section, his devoted family, his sheep lost without the shepherd and at the mercy of ravening wolves. There would be no glory in going back up the hill; the snipers' bullets would be just as accurate and lethal. What the civilian world could never understand was this indissoluble tie, almost an umbilical cord between a leader and the led in the minimum unit of an army, but the tightest emotional link in the whole of a life's experience. The calm decision to go back up the slopes was no less heroic and commendable than the original belligerent charge.

The closeness and ruthlessness of the fighting must have left a lasting impression on Ted Chapman's mind, although it is not clear whether he suffered long-term traumatic stress. He must have had recurring sensations of such horrific moments as feeling the impact on the sniper's bullets on himself and the wounded captain, exacerbated by the later realisation that one of the bullets was killing not him but the helpless man he carried. Such things were rarely spoken of at the time. But niece Nanette learned from her father – Ted's brother, Dick – of another incident which must have returned to haunt him upon his return to normal life. She recalls:

> Ted rarely talked about the war, although my father, Dick, asked him many times as a young boy. Only once, Ted told him that it had been 'terrible'. Ted said that one day he and a comrade were in a trench being held down by a German machine gun. The gun stopped firing and his comrade looked up to see what was happening. The machine gun started to fire again and blew his friend's head off, and it landed at Ted's feet. What horrors such memories provoke in the darkest hours of a night can hardly be imagined.

Up to D Day, Ted Chapman had trained with his second battalion, 2nd Monmouthshires, in 160th Infantry Brigade of the 53rd Welsh Division. It was with the same battalion that he crossed to Normandy in June 1944, being involved in hard fighting on the Odon and at the closing of the Falaise Gap. Casualties had been severe, Ted himself being wounded. A and B Companies temporarily had to be amalgamated. Upon release from hospital, Ted was posted to 3rd Monmouthshires, 159th Infantry Brigade, 11th Armoured Division. The division advanced swiftly for 400 miles through Holland into Germany. The war was coming to a close. It was remarkable that a man should take such risks as Ted did on the *Wald*, when his battalion was actually fighting the last battle of its long war. Many would have been more cautious, coasting along that last lap to the golden prize of peace.

Everything about Ted's later life tends to provide evidence of a quiet, thoughtful man, not the least militaristic. His wartime record, however, suggests a firm sense of duty and patriotism. It may have been this that led him to continue to serve his country in a khaki uniform as the Cold War evolved and fresh dangers threatened Britain. But now it would be with the Territorial forces, still the Monmouthshires, rather than the regular Army. Enlisting in 1947, he proved to be an effective and inspirational NCO and later rose to Company Sergeant Major. When discharge in 1957 he was judged to have made a substantial contribution to the improved efficiency of his unit and was awarded the British Empire Medal for his service with the Territorials. His BEM citation stated that "his company has grown in stature, having him on its strength".

Ted Chapman was born in 1920 in Pontlottyn, a colliery village at the top end the Rhymney Valley (now part of Caerphilly). Both his grandfather and father were miners. Although he also commenced work down the mine, he dissuaded other younger family members from that employment. He was haunted by the memory of his grandfather being killed when the pit cage in which he was descending crashed to the bottom of the shaft. Ted met his future wife Rhoda, an Irish girl, in Newry during the war, and they married in 1942.

With the war ended, Ted chose not to return to mining, moving on to engineering work with a stint on the railways. For the greater part of his subsequent working life he was involved in nylon spinning with ICI at Pontypool. Some indication of his general character and disposition are provided by his two great interests as he progressed far beyond the grim bondage of a small mining community of the 1930s.

The first interest was in fishing. Niece Nanette remembers:

> In his early years he enjoyed fishing for pike. After the war, my father remembers rowing him around Llangorse Lake, maybe over a hundred times, to fish. Later on Ted turned to trout fishing in the local reservoirs and in some of the best South Wales rivers, always with a fly rod. He was joined by his wife, Rhoda, who took up fishing with as much enthusiasm as well.

The couple also went on fishing holidays as far afield as Scotland and Iceland.

Brother Dick sums up Ted's character:

> Ted was a quiet unassuming man, who was never one to tell a joke but always had a ready smile. He was not religious or showed any interest in politics or social affairs. It was rare for him to lose his temper; he was not well built but nevertheless, if extremely provoked, was not a person to be crossed. He liked to read, in particular books about science fiction and space odyssey novels, and his favourite film was *War of the Worlds* made in the 1950s.

All this was far removed from the wartime reality of *Schmeissers*, Brens and stick grenades.

Ted's other great passion was horses. His father, Evan, had been an excellent horseman and regular competitor at events like the Waun Fair near Dowlais Top. Ted himself eventually became a great friend of Sir Harry Llewellyn, then the world's champion horseman at gymkhanas and show jumping events. This may have prompted Ted to take an interest in equine affairs, especially the more docile line of ponies.

He began to breed ponies and became one of the founder members of the Welsh Mountain Pony Association. He registered with the Welsh Pony and Cob Society, entering three sections, using Ynyswen as a prefix to his ponies' names. He seemed to favour the Welsh Mountain pony, a breed not exceeding 12 hands or 121.9cm. At one time he was running 30 mares and two stallions on 50 acres near Ynyswen. The breeding of ponies requires patience and tranquillity quite equal to that demanded by fly fishing.

Mention of registering brings to mind another type of registering. Ted, who desired only to escape from the mines, enlisted in 1940. If he had been born in 1924 he could have registered with his peers in 1942 for national service, which by that date was compulsory for 18-year-olds. Under the then lottery system of posting, he might well have been sent back down the mines for his war service, instead of wearing the khaki uniform. Such was the fate of many 18-year-olds, termed the 'Bevin Boys' after Ernest Bevin, the Minister for Labour and National Service. Who then could have been the hero of the Teutoberger Wald?

For the service which he did render, Ted Chapman was honoured in 2010 by the setting up of a Memorial Garden in Pontlottyn, his birthplace.

A clear picture emerges of this man, abandoning his earlier fights with pike, now patiently waiting for the trout to rise, and even more patiently and gently counting the months for a mare to foal. As he waited by Llandegfedd reservoir, what thoughts might come to him of battle horrors, and the thump of a bullet into a man dying upon his shoulders?

As he surveyed the steep wooded cliffs of some Welsh *Wald*, like Mynydd Du or even the ridge behind Ynyswen, would his mind regurgitate scenes of a steep *Wald* through thronging trees and clinging undergrowth, deafened by the thudding of Bren and *Schmeissers*, and the wild cries of frustrated Nazi cadets as one man alone stood tall to frustrate their charge down the sacred scene of that ancient epic battle?

For centuries the *Teutoberger Wald* had been a symbol of the supposed superiority of the Germanic races over the Latin peoples, but then there appeared a Welshman.

8

Bill Close

Major William Herbert Close, MC and bar, British, 3rd Royal Tank Regiment

Year after year after year, tank after tank after tank blows up under him, all a part of a learning process which would enlighten the next generation of tank soldiers.

If a novelist wished to write an improbable story about the experiences of a tank soldier in the Second World War, he need look no farther than Bill Close for his model. And he might find the story already partly written in Bill's own precise, detailed but often humorous prose.

He escaped across the sea three times as the enemy net closed around him and threatened to incarcerate him for the rest of the war. On two of those occasions he formed and guided a mixed squad of lost soldiers back to base. One time he hijacked a fishing boat, the *Popeii Veronica*, for a long sea journey and, when fuel ran short, chopped up the superstructure to keep the boilers working: pure Jules Verne adventures, it might seem.

Where the average tankie might desperately hope that he could bail out two or three times, but not four or five, and avoid cremation within the vehicle, this man bailed out no less than 11 times and yet still pursued the enemy. He rose through the ranks from private to major. The two bravery awards he earned should have been at least four. At the close of the war, his further service was curtailed only because there were other officers more senior who returned from soft jobs to take over command as the bullets ceased to fly. Jules Verne could hardly have hoped to persuade readers to believe such a saga; and there was much more to his war service than this.

It can be argued that Major Bill Close's most heroic exploit was one for which no award was made. It took place throughout the two days of calamitous chaos called Operation *Goodwood*, on 18-19 July 1944, as the Allies tried to fight their way out of the Normandy bridgehead. As part of 11th Armoured Division, Bill's unit, the 3rd Royal Tank Regiment (3RTR), together with the 23rd Hussars and 2nd Fife and Forfar Yeomanry, were tasked to make a left-hand sweep around the ruined city of Caen and then cross the level open *Plaine Sud*. This would bring the tanks east to west, totally exposed to the enemy's more powerful guns hidden along the gentle

Bill Close, tank escapologist and academic apologist.
(Courtesy of the Tank Museum, Bovington)

slopes of Bourguébus Ridge to the south. High Command having failed to supply the requisite infantry support for such a venture, the tanks were like a boxer with one arm tied behind his back, fighting an invisible man.

Bill, commanding his squadron of 19 Shermans, recorded that:

> As we approached Grentheville I could see the crews of enemy anti-tank guns feverishly swinging their weapons towards us. *Nebelwerfer* bombs howled over-head. Woompf! A Sherman right next to me burst into flames and two more were ablaze within minutes. Hatches flew open and more crews came tumbling out to roll in the corn [to douse the flames].

More than one of the crew members would probably have been physically on fire.

There followed a lull as the squadron crawled cautiously towards its objectives, villages on the lower slope. The German gunners were not wasting ammunition on long shots when the targets continued to approach and loom larger. Then, Bill recalled:

500 yards from the two villages all hell broke loose and we came under intense fire from all directions. Immediately tanks in all three squadrons were hit, bursting into flames with crew tumbling out and the corn burning all around. Burning tank crews bailed out and rolled in agony on the ground. Wham! Crash! My own tank was hit and a stentorian yell emanated from down below: 'Bail out, sir!'

Close sprinted to another tank which appeared to be intact, but found it was already immobilised and empty. He ran on to a Troop corporal's tank which was still mobile and took command of the squadron from that vehicle. A small dip appeared in the ground ahead, enough to hide the tank hull-down and enable the gunner to fire back at the enemy. That at least gave them the satisfaction of knocking out two anti-tank guns, but the three regiments had lost massively. They went to ground for the night, Bill's tank in a small quarry, others behind a railway embankment. A few replacement tanks arrived, together with the precious lorries to replenish ammunition and petrol.

Compared to the previous day's long-haul attack, on the morning of 19 July the two objectives, Hubert-Folie and Bras, were well in sight. The first mad charge carried Bill's squadron within 400 yards of outlying houses, but then the killing began again as the mighty Tiger and Panther tanks opened up, together with other guns hidden in the woods.

The squadron's Firefly tanks, with their larger 17-pdr guns, were the equal of the Panthers when they could locate them. A battle of attrition developed, the British attackers always suffering greater losses but the German defenders losing vital tanks which they were unable to replace in the prolific way the Allies could. By 1600 hours, when it was decided that a concerted effort must occupy Bras, Bill's squadron was down to only five tanks, and other squadrons even less. Tanks of Bill's squadron were still burning or smouldering around him:

As I moved forward out of my shelter, with an almighty crash the tank shuddered and crunched to a halt. I bailed out with my operator and gunner. An 88mm shell had gone straight through the front of the tank, killing the driver and co-driver outright. I dashed over to my nearest tank, commanded by Troop Sergeant Freddie Dale. He very reluctantly got out and I took command from his tank.

The Germans then began withdrawing up the ridge. Bras was occupied, with 300 *panzergrenadiers* as casualties or taken prisoner. At 1900 hours the colonel called an 'O' group (order group), coordinating one final thrust into Hubert-Folie. As the colonel talked, a shell landed in the middle of the group and the three officers next to Bill were blown to bits. He survived to command his last three tanks, together with Rifle Brigade infantry and Fife and Forfar Yeomanry survivors, into Hubert-Folie. The village was still only halfway up the ridge but it became a vital lodgement.

American industry could quickly replace nearly 400 lost tanks. Questions would later be asked as to the wastage of trained crews. Post Offices in Britain would be sending out sheaves of yellow telegram envelopes informing loved ones of those killed in action. Bill's extraordinary actions were regarded as simply 'in the line of duty'.

During the confused three-division action at Bourguébus Ridge, a mere major was a pawn on the vast chess board of battle. But just weeks later, on the road to Amiens, Bill suddenly found himself to be at least a bishop or castle on that chess board. His squadron was to be the spearhead and he would have effective command of the immediate action. Colonels and generals would have to wait in the dark, literally, for this was to be a gallop by night. Bill's tanks would be unable to see beyond their own headlights. The attack would also be tactically in the dark, as there was no intelligence of the fleeing enemy. Around Falaise, a day or two previously, two German armies had been virtually destroyed. But the German command was adept at summoning reserves and forming lethal *KG* battle groups, counter-attacking where least expected. The rain poured down. There was no moonlight or starlight to aid the spearhead, which was far beyond the reach of any searchlights producing 'Monty's Moonlight' by reflection from the clouds.

The Allies were now committed to a great advance towards the German border. A vital point would be the bridges across the Somme at Amiens. A crossing must be forced and any German resistance there forestalled. There was 20 miles to go as Lieutenant Johnny Langdon's Sherman roared off in front, Bill's three tanks right behind, blind in the darkness. After several miles a crossroads was reached, where a ghostly column of horse-drawn enemy artillery blocked the road. Crashing through them, on they went with the squadron following. A Volkswagen German staff car was smashed past, then an enemy tank surprised. Three shots from just 20 yards caused a massive explosion, and on the squadron roared.

Three miles from Amiens, Bill halted and assembled the squadron, only to find that the supporting troops had been left far behind. Just ten tanks and 70 riflemen were with him. They pressed on regardless. Dawn's light allowed them to spot targets, fire, score and bash on. French Resistance fighters appeared in the streets, guiding the tanks. Locals spoke of 4,000 German troops in the town. Realising they had to keep the initiative and count on surprise, Bill's tiny spearhead force blazes forward straight on to the bridge. Lieutenant Bill Yates' lead troop races over the bridge, securing lodgement.

The Germans then employed a tactic which would become well known on the canals and rivers of the Low Countries in the weeks and months ahead. As Bill Close's own tank approaches the bridge, a remotely controlled explosion collapses it into the river. The Resistance men mention another smaller bridge, barely wide enough for tanks. Again Bill's tanks accelerate through the town, firing bursts of their Brownings. Meanwhile, the troop beyond the bridge has trapped an entire German anti-tank unit in a narrow street and sealed off both ends. As the infantry, finally catching up, arrive, the Amiens bridgehead is consolidated, and the way to Brussels is open. Bill gains the bar to his Military Cross, and Bill Yates also wins the MC.

For 3RTR, the climax of the tumultuous chase across France into Belgium, 386 miles in eight days and the liberation of Antwerp, was the most confused period of all. Bill's role had now reverted to that of a pawn, unable to crucially affect a fatal omission made by the big pieces on the board. Eisenhower, in the remote Supreme Headquarters, was insisting that the port of Antwerp must be brought into action immediately. But Montgomery's eyes were fixed, perhaps fixated, on Arnhem, on crossing the Rhine and invading Germany, not on studying the seaway into Antwerp.

Supplies for the forward troops in Belgium and Holland were still being ferried by lorries from the Mulberry harbours way back in Normandy, after the sea crossing from Southampton. Entire brigades were stranded near Le Havre because of lack of fuel. Even if Montgomery had succeeded at Arnhem, he would not have had sufficient supplies to maximise the victory. Not without Antwerp docks in full flow.

Antwerp, on the short sea route from England, was a huge, active port ready for use, safely occupied by the local Resistance. German troops thereabouts were in total panic, their formations rapidly disintegrating. Bill and other pawns in Antwerp could read the situation, but the big pieces on the chessboard ignored the gambit. This was a case much as if Southampton itself had been liberated but the enemy were still in control of the Solent: no ships would be able to pass. A child could understand it. A port without its seaway is no port at all. Yet the immediate hierarchy of generals and their aides either failed to see or ignored the obvious, whilst Eisenhower fumed. No immediate attempt was made to occupy the Scheldt, the seaway into Antwerp. Allied forces would be hamstrung until deep into the winter for lack of supplies. Many thousands of the Canadian First Army would die in clearing the Scheldt during October and November. Bill would have sharp words to say later in life about the Antwerp seaway, but by then he himself would have become a permanent large piece on the chessboard of post-war analysis and apologetics.

At the time, for Bill personally the liberation of Antwerp was a reward for the countless miles of danger and hurt he had endured, from Calais and the disasters of the 1940 evacuation, through the ignominious British defeats in Greece and Crete, events in Gazala and the Western Desert, and the murderous assaults on Bourguébus Ridge. As Resistance fighters rode 3RTR's tanks, the population of Antwerp emerged in adulation for the liberating troops. Amid the applauding, cheering, kissing masses, it seemed as though the war was over and peace was declared. Bill was working with an infantry company of the Herefords. As he halted on the final objective, the railway station, he could see his own tanks, clustered with Belgian Resistance fighters and civilians, towering in the distance behind him. The company commander of the Herefords, climbing on to Bill's tank, confessed that he could find very few of his men because they had been swallowed up as they advanced into the vast, swirling crowds of enraptured civilians. It felt like while it was not yet 'The End', it presaged a final collapse of the enemy.

But there was still plenty more action to come. Bill, having been feeling ill, was diagnosed with a severe dose of malaria, necessitating three weeks in a UK hospital. Returning to action, he was ijnvolved in crossing the Dortmund to Ems canal and the River Weser. As late as 11 April 1945, approaching the River Aller in northern Germany, Bill was again leaping out of his tank. This time, while not himself bailing out, he was located between two burning Shermans and was hurrying to tend to badly burned comrades, and then to bury the dead.

As Germany surrendered, Bill's sense of humour bubbled to the surface. His squadron encountered a complete *SS* anti-tank battalion, paraded as for inspection, officers in full dress, wanting to surrender. Arrogantly, they stated they would surrender only to an officer of field rank. Bill descended from his tank, his overalls now irredeemably besmirched with oil, mud and burn marks. The immaculate German officer insisted "Only to an officer of field rank!" Bill grinned, assuring him "that I was an officer of field rank and that this was borne out by these seventeen tanks of my squadron with loaded guns now surrounding him".

It was 12 years and many thousands of miles since Bill Close had enlisted at Stamford after an unsuccessful, accident-prone attempt to become a chemist or a dentist. He had badly damaged an expensive dentist's chair and crashed a new delivery bike full speed downhill; his chemist employer at Uppingham, a Mr Bayley, thought that it was a very good idea for him to work off his energies in the Army. Vacancies existed with 3 RTR at Bovington, where Bill found his destiny.

In 1940, as the Allied front in northern France and Belgium collapsed and the evacuation at Dunkirk commenced, 3RTR had landed in Calais. Bill, now a sergeant, was driving a Dingo armoured scout car at the service of the local commander, Brigadier Nicholson. An attempt was made to send supplies from Calais towards Dunkirk. Speeding ahead, Bill encountered some troops having breakfast beside the road, with an anti-tank gun mounted. Realising they were Germans, Bill swore that no Dingo had ever moved faster in reverse gear.

Calais was quickly surrounded by an entire *Panzer* division. Nicholson was ordered to fight as long as possible which, for him, meant no escape, but he gave all surplus troops the opportunity to evacuate, including Dingo drivers. Bill raced to the harbour and managed to jump aboard the last boat leaving, a trawler, which was immediately dive-bombed. Only 250 men of Bill's regiment eventually made it back to England.

There followed a chaotic period when, like other units, 3RTR patrolled the East Anglian coast without tanks. They were equipped only with personal weapons, awaiting a German invasion which never came. New tanks arrived, and Bill was promoted to squadron quartermaster sergeant. Eventually the reinvigorated 3RTR assembled on a boat destined for Greece. Having survived the Dunkirk debacle, they now discovered that British troops in Greece were likewise in a hopeless position, defending a collapsing front following the battle of the Monastir Gap. After a few days of futile but costly intervention, the survivors of 3RTR were ordered to the beaches, where the Royal Navy was carrying out another evacuation. To reach the designated beaches, Bill's group would need to cross the Corinth Canal, passing through territory already occupied by the enemy.

He recalled: "The drill was to move along the roads at night, taking to fields if we saw headlights, which the Germans, not being worried about air attacks, used freely. It was estimated it would take three nights to reach the crossing places on the canal."

Once across the canal they latched on to a much larger party. However, the senior officer in the group was pessimistic, announcing: "There's nothing else to be done. I intend to surrender tomorrow. We can't fight and we can't run. We'll simply go into the bag in an orderly manner. See your men hand in their weapons."

A group of dissenters, led by Bill, preferred a disorderly further trek across unknown ground to try to find a boat of some kind. Bill recorded:

> We spent another four or five days living rough and keeping to the heights. I had a small prismatic compass and a map. When we stopped we took it in turns to mount guard. When we walked someone scouted ahead. According to the map there was a small fishing community between Argos and Paralion Astrous and that was where we made for.

At the tiny village Bill negotiated with the locals the hire of a fishing boat, using Greek *Drachmae* which were part of a squadron payroll he was still carrying. Hurrying on board, they put the benighted shores of Greece behind them. Then, out of the fog, there emerged a British destroyer, HMS *Hotspur*. They climbed aboard up the scramble nets. Suddenly, German dive-bombers descended on the destroyer. It was hit, listed to one side, but continued to make headway. Then came the dreaded announcement, "Damage to the engine room", and the refugee soldiers soon found themselves being decanted on to a beach in Crete.

Crete, too, was attacked and quickly taken over by German paratroopers. Once again Bill set off on a clandestine escape safari with a select multi-national party of soldiers who refused to submit. They came at last to another fishing village, where the partially derelict *Popeii Veronica* was moored, the owner's wife serenely hanging out the washing on the superstructure, all intact as yet. She and her husband were unaware that the rickety crate was about to sail into history. When the old boat ran out of fuel, it was the superstructure which Bill and his comrades chopped up to keep the boiler functioning as they headed for Alexandria.

Bill Close would now experience all the vagaries of tank warfare, bailing out of burning tanks, fighting the very terrain and climate of the Western Desert, tasting victory and defeat, being wounded and losing good comrades. He was commissioned, not with formal OCTU training or trumpets of glory, but simply moving from the sergeant's mess tent into the officer's mess tent somewhere in the desert. Battles followed: Sidi Rezegh, Gazala (and a Military Cross), Alamein, the Mareth Line and Tunis.

Much of the story was repetitive, but always grim and galling:

> We were being hit by all sorts of things and it was difficult to see what was going on. The air stank from the thick cordite fumes and our eyes were red rimmed and streaming. Now and then there would be a terrific thud and the inside filled with dust and sparks as the tank rocked on its bogies.

Even painful wounding was met with a wry humour:

> It was discovered that the ball bearings (from an exploding mine) had made a mess of the back of my head. A single one had hit me in the back, whizzed around the outer lining of the stomach and come out again without doing serious damage. I could look forward to having two navels to contemplate.

Never a 'yes man', Bill was capable of rebellious or imprudent moments. Convalescing from his injuries but bored with the restrictions at the medical centre, he, with a like-minded New Zealander, absconded and went off to a party where liquor of a suspicious strength ran freely. This resulted in a dressing down, as he recorded: "I was called before Brigadier Baker-Baker who lectured me on my responsibilities and gave me a reprimand."

Did this wayward trait influence the eventual official decision not to offer Bill a permanent commission when the war ended? Brigadier Christopher Dunphie, who has written about Operation *Goodwood*, is emphatic on this point: "I hang my head in shame at Bill's treatment after the war. Despite two MCs and two or three MiDs [Mentions in Despatches], several wounds, five years of non-stop battle, he was not considered to be a 'proper officer'. He would have been invaluable at Bovington [the British Army's home for tank warfare training] teaching young officers." It was tantamount to an insult that the War Office should have offered Bill, among other options, a return to warrant officer status.

Bill did eventually come into his own as a civilian analyst of, and speaker about, the events in which he took part. In the meantime he took a peacetime commission with the REME (Royal Electrical and Mechanical Engineers) in the rank of second lieutenant, ending once more as a major. Later, in civilian days, he moved into quieter waters as a school bursar. But throughout this time his fame was established as a teacher of tank tactics. One of his young listeners, now Major (Retd) Colin Hepburn, RTR, says:

> Bill Close was small in stature but a giant among men, quiet spoken, a sharp wit and sense of fun. He had played hockey both for his county and for the Army. He was at ease with us young NCOs. He could talk to anyone. His tales were fascinating. He also presented 'Operation *Goodwood*' with [German Colonel] Hans von Luck who he became firm friends with, even though they had fought against each other and been bitter enemies [during *Goodwood*].

As a young officer, Christopher Dunphie was afraid, when introducing Bill, that his quiet manner might mask his heroism: "I felt he would never have sought to promote his own image. So I made sure to leave people in no doubt that they were about to hear from one of the most outstanding tank commanders in WW2. He was a very special guy."

Bill's daughter, Joanna, recalls:

> Despite his reticence to talk about the war, he thoroughly enjoyed going on the battlefield tours to Normandy. I know, having talked to several young officers who witnessed his talks on these occasions, that he made a great impression on them, both professionally and socially (my father would certainly not be the one to leave a party early or a drink undrunk!).

The soldier who knew Bill as well as anyone, and had followed him up the military ladder, always one rung behind, was Jock Watt, who says:

I followed Bill step by step, corporal to sergeant, RSM to lieutenant. He was a good mixer, easy to talk to, clear word of command, serious when on the job but with a quick sense of humour. Never needed to raise his voice. A loyal friend. He never vaunted or used his rank to get his way.

A very personal memory of Bill is the author's first meeting with him years after the war. The conversation went thus: Bill: "What regiment were you with?" Self: "Northants Yeomanry." Bill: "First or Second?" Self: "First!" Bill: "Oh, good! Didn't think so much of the Second. Colonel was a fool. Didn't take notice of my warning. Went the wrong way and lost a squadron." This referred to just one out of a hundred times when Bill exposed himself selflessly to some terrible fate. During *Goodwood* he had jumped out of his tank and run across the open plain, which was dominated by enemy guns of all calibres firing from three sides, to warn the colonel of another regiment, with whom he had no urgent wireless link, that the colonel's regiment was running into danger. Major Bill Close did not choose to send one of his crew as a runner on so suicidal a mission.

It is to be wondered what impact so many horrific experiences might have had on Bill's mind. He was very clear as to one such event, saying: "It was something I shall never forget." He had led his squadron up to the gates of Belsen, not knowing that it was a concentration camp, a living hell. "The huts were full of almost naked inmates, some dead, some only just alive and pitifully thin. There were bodies everywhere – lying in the small ditches around the huts. The stench was indescribable." For the very professional soldier this must have been even more appalling than seeing death in battle, however wasteful.

Daughter Joanna recalled that her father "was a very modest man and was reluctant to speak about his experiences during the war. I remember one Christmas when he reflected that he didn't feel he was a very nice man and that there were things he had done in the war that he was not proud of." That remark was probably made at least 40 years after the battles, and reflects the enduring mental impact of such events.

Bravery is an unquantifiable, intangible concept. Multiple awards for valour can be a contentious issue, as in the cases of Stan Hollis or John Bridge, who may well have merited even more recognition. Brigadier Dunphie has an interesting view on this point as it affected Bill Close:

> His escape from Calais may not have been exceptional but his escapes from Greece and Crete certainly were. How sad it was that they were not recognised by some award. Many people will not have been aware of his distinguished time as an NCO/WO before he was commissioned. 'Major W.H. Close, MC and bar' sounds fine, but gives no indication that he had come up through the ranks with real distinction. It would open the eyes of many if it read 'Major W.H. Close, MC and bar, MM'.

But as Dunphie also says: "Bill never showed any serious resentment."

After Operation *Goodwood*, with its appalling casualties, morale among tank crews was understandably low. Three long-service sergeants approached Bill asking to be posted away from tank duties as they were no longer mentally capable of carrying on. A period of rest was agreed, and two of the sergeants soon returned to continue as before without further problems. Whatever his inner feelings, Bill Close always seemed to be able to rise above the horrors of the moment and continue where others wilted. Perhaps his dry and sometimes wicked sense of humour helped him in this.

Indeed, he was able to jest:

> Major causes of 'bomb happiness' are the enemy, the weather and the Staff. The first sets out deliberately to make your life a misery, the second is a natural and neutral phenomenon in league with the opposition, and the third is absolutely unpredictable and sometimes seems to possess all the adverse tendencies of the others.

Joanna adds:

> I wouldn't say my father was a great comedian but he was not afraid to laugh at himself. We used to spend family Christmases at a hotel in Bournemouth and invariably, come the fancy dress night, my father would find himself immersed in a box of some description, attempting to recreate a tree or a pack of playing cards.

In peacetime there were still periods of turbulence for Bill Close, such as a divorce which meant estrangement from his three sons. However, with the arrival of grandchildren he was able, with considerable sensitivity, to renew relationships and enjoy becoming a devoted grandfather.

Joanna was born when Bill was 52 years old, and she saw him from a unique angle. She was most impressed by his abilities as a sportsman and his patience in trying to guide her in similar pursuits as she grew up:

> Dad was a great sportsman, playing county level hockey into his late 40s, but also was an all-round athlete, pole vaulting in the days when they landed on sand.
>
> He was also a tremendous shot, a hobby which he carried on into his 80s. When invited to an informal shoot he would out-perform the paying guns. I used to tell him that he wouldn't be invited again as he put them all to shame. He took up bowls on retirement, playing in county competitions. He started playing skittles and consistently held the record for most points scored, as well as most pints drunk, during a season. Although 52 years older, he would play tennis with me, run me through hockey drills in the back garden and take me walking and shooting all year round …
>
> My father was a man of integrity with great charm. It has been a source of immense pride to me and my brothers to know that he is regarded in such high esteem by the wider military family, He, of course, would underplay it all and be incredibly embarrassed by the attention.

9

George Eardley

Sergeant (later CSM) George Harold Eardley, VC, MM, British, King's Shropshire Light Infantry

Slithering through the undergrowth, moving with the skill and stealth of a panther, he could be belligerent and lethal in the heady comradeship of battle, but afterwards bewildered in the purposeless vacuum of peace.

The massed force of two armoured divisions, two infantry divisions, the corps artillery and squadrons of fighters and bombers having failed to force a breach, the fate of the battle now devolved on one lone rifle. Or, more precisely, on one Sten gun and half-a-dozen hand grenades. The objective: to open the only road which can carry the heavy artillery and tanks of the Allies from Holland into Germany. The date: 16 October 1944. It is unfortunate for the enemy that those feeble small arms, the Sten and the Mills, were being handled by 6092111 George Harold Eardley, ranked private acting sergeant, aged 32.

Overloon might be called 'the forgotten battle'. It has not caught the attention of authors and film producers to the extent that Alamein, Arnhem or the Ardennes have. Yet more British soldiers were killed in action at Overloon than at Arnhem or in the Ardennes. Paradoxically, Overloon is also one of the best-remembered Second World War battlefields, as some of the many vehicles knocked out in the battle were retained there to form the basis of a war museum which is now world famous.

Overloon was an offspring of Arnhem. The ground forces rushing from Eindhoven towards Arnhem had opened up only the one major road. The Germans remained entrenched within firing distance on both sides of that road. Allied troops would have to push the northern margin of that corridor towards the Maas around Den Bosch. Other troops would need to clear the country south-east towards the Maas around Venlo. Overloon was the critical site along that southern advance towards Venray and Venlo.

George Eardley had already proved his aptitude for field craft. Enlisting in the Queen's Royal Regiment in May 1940, Eardley was then posted to the 4th King's Shropshire Light Infantry of 159th Infantry Brigade, and in 1944 was sent to

George Eardley comes home triumphantly to Congleton. (Courtesy of the *Chronicle Series*)

Normandy where the 4th King's Shropshire Light Infantry (4KSLI) were part of the 11th Armoured Division. After the long stalemate around Caen, by 1 August the Germans were fighting desperately to prevent their entire Normandy front crumbling and becoming trapped in the catastrophe of the Falaise Pocket. Resistance was particularly heavy at the crucial junction of Le Bény-Bocage.

This was Private Eardley's first battle. Whilst tanks clashed in the open spaces, infantry patrols aimed to infiltrate through the infamous *bocage*, a temperate jungle of thick banks and hedges. The section of which Eardley was a part was feeling its way along under the partial cover of the vast hedges. Those same hedges, with their elevated banks, also provided prime hiding spots for German machine-gun crews. Suddenly the harsh, superfast ripping sound of a *Spandau* machine gun erupted from a few yards ahead, spurting bullets at the section. Eardley flung himself to the ground. Behind him men fell wounded, while others dived for safety. Eardley shrank into the ditch, playing dead.

This is the point when the mind questions itself. A suppressed cough, sneeze or even sniff could bring death at a few yards' range. Was it better to stop breathing, or would the silence itself betray his presence? Was cessation of action more suspicious than actual movement? The *Spandau* gunner might think it too quiet; might decide to fire another burst, deluging the hedgerow, to make sure none of the recumbent bodies came to life again. This was the moment of utter jeopardy.

Then, somewhere to one side, something moved. The *Spandau* gunner swiftly traversed his gun and pulled the trigger. In that brief moment Eardley was leaping to his feet, pulling the pin from a grenade, lobbing the missile, pressing the trigger of his Sten gun, sprinting forward, spraying the gun pit and wiping out the German team, saving himself and his section from total extinction. An immediate Military Medal was Private Eardley's reward for his first-day quickness of thought and action. In the long subsequent chase across France, Belgium and Holland, which 11th Armoured led, the new private continued to prove himself. Thus, by the time 4KSLI neared Overloon, the private was wearing a sergeant's stripes, in the obtuse way the British Army had of temporarily promoting the man who had the skills and resolve but not the seniority.

The eventual aim at Overloon was to open roads through Venlo and Venray to the major crossing place of the River Maas opposite Germany. Some way south of Overloon, the Peel area consisted of peat fields and canals. Tanks sank in the soft earth the moment they had to leave the roads, which were few and narrow. Thus the battle zone had to be compressed northwards into the somewhat more solid terrain of the area between Overloon and Venray. This would focus the advance towards a crossing over the small but vital Loobeek dyke, at which point Acting Sergeant Eardley became involved.

In the quaint 'horsey' world of British headquarters in 1944, the battle of Overloon from 30 September to 18 October was given the military title of Operation *Aintree*, just another racecourse to follow *Epsom*, *Goodwood* and so on, while *Totalize* evoked thoughts of horseracing's Tote. Like *Goodwood*, *Aintree* was to prove the graveyard of many British tanks, the modern-day cavalry. The infantry also lost heavily, with more than 2,500 British soldiers being killed. By 16 October the advance was within rifle-firing distance of the small village of Smakt, where the only road capable of carrying heavy traffic crossed both a main railway line and the Loobeek dyke. There the advance stalled again.

On 16 October, in heavy rain, tanks tried to advance down the road along Pelgrimgasse, which was targeted by German artillery. At the same time, 4KSLI had to find its way across fields, through orchards and, in deep mud, reach the Loobeek. Eardley's section was to cross an open field for about 80 yards and then clear an orchard just short of the Loobeek. The enemy were understood to be tough German paratroopers, armed with the inevitable *Spandaus*. They were able to hide in pits under the fruit trees and hedges, no doubt with snipers up in the branches. This was going to be a muddy as well as a bloody business. One of the main problems for the infantry would be to keep Sten gun and rifle muzzles free of mud every time it was necessary to dive for cover into the squelching ground. In the meantime, the Germans greeted the probing British with their usual showers of 'Moaning Minnie' rockets, falling in clusters which could not be evaded. Apart from the sheer fear of the unknown, it was a miserable day physically for the walking men who had already endured a night of freezing sleet without shelter.

Their bleak night had been further disturbed by memories of a failed attempt across this same ground the previous day. Comrades had been killed and wounded, the attack halted in disillusionment. In the confusion Privates Scott and Savage had been left wounded, lying at the abandoned point of the advance. The order had been given: "Take a German prisoner to go in front of you, and recover the wounded men." There had been further confusion of firing guns, and the German prisoner acting as a shield had been killed. A second attempt was made and did reach the isolated comrades, but by that time both Scott and Savage had died of their wounds. It was a story repeated time and again in such actions.

At H Hour, in the manner of highly trained German soldiers, the defending paratroopers preserve a total silence and lack of movement, patiently waiting for the British infantry to come within range. The Shropshires will have to walk into a death zone of massed bullets surging from each *Spandau* at 20 rounds a second, smashing into them at a muzzle velocity of 800 yards per second. Secure in their gun pits, the Germans wait and watch the tentative enemy movements. The men of 4KSLI edge forward, anxious to spot the slightest movement, or perceive a foreign object amid the green tracery of leaves or a patch of un-natural colour, needing all the while to keep moving forward. They pause, wait and move forward again, treading softly through the clogging, clinging mud – the Germans' ally – as if that might make them invisible.

They are hit by the first hurricane of bullets from a single *Spandau*, invisible at first, then betrayed by its flaming muzzle. The Shropshires throw themselves down, Eardley as quick as any. He looks around: nobody is moving; they might all be dead. The template from Le Bény-Bocage activates in his mind. Should he play dead, or wait, a recumbent target with no chance of the ground opening up and swallowing him, a soft targets for an angry enemy?

Eardley can by now make out the darker mound of the gun pit in among the trees. He takes two grenades from the man behind. Carefully feeling for the safety ring, after a moment's pause he leaps up, pulls the ring and throws the grenade. Firing his Sten, he runs for his life, forward, getting at the Germans. His Sten blazes furiously and the German crew are cut down, lifeless or insensible in their devastated gun pit. His comrades from the Shropshires, following up, are cheering, tensions released having secured the gun pit.

But it is only a mock victory. Their adversaries are the famed *Fallschirmjäger*, highly trained German paratroopers. A supporting *Spandau*, only yards farther on, invisible until now, fills the air with bullets again. Down go the Shropshires again, ducking for cover, but Eardley is up again, charging, swerving, side-stepping like a rugby three-quarter, lobbing grenades, firing his Sten and leaping into the next gun pit. *Spandau* number two and its crew are also immobilised, destroyed by the sheer impetus of the leaping Eardley. Again the lads are following up, this time celebrating more cautiously, but again it is too soon.

Yet a third *Spandau* and its crew are sited in this clever defence complex, further on through the orchard, just before the Loobeek dyke and the railway line. This time Eardley's Shropshire comrades are with him. They spread out, hunting, crawling cautiously. The *Spandau* rages again, but too high, missing its targets. The Germans throw a stick grenade, but it lands too short. The attackers now only have a few yards to go, almost seeing the whites of the Germans' eyes in the filthy masks of faces. Eardley has one last Mills bomb to lob, but his Sten clicks hollow and empty. He quickly changes the magazine and, with finger on trigger, is up, throwing the grenade and firing one final long burst in a last frenetic sprint.

The enemy fire has ceased. "OK to cheer, lads!" shouts Eardley. Tanks are beginning to edge down the road. Other sections, platoons of 4KSLI, rise and slosh forward through the mud. The company commander realigns his troops, signalling for medics. The level crossing is seized and the way ahead is open. The victorious infantrymen are soaked, splattered and saturated in mud, like chocolate parodies of warriors, with almost the only way of distinguishing between enemy and friend being the shape of their helmet. The cheerful, relieved, thankful faces of the victors shepherd the stunned, resentful surviving paratroopers in their similarly mud-caked uniforms.

Amid the sudden jollity, they were not to know that, although the way to Venray was open and the town only a couple of days of fighting distant, the road on to Venlo would be a much longer story. By then, 4KSLI would have been inserted elsewhere in the constant manoeuvres of war.

Exploits such as those of Eardley and the Shropshires raise several questions. How can a frail human body evade and survive such deadly torrents of bullets and shrapnel? How could the almost ramshackle Sten prevail against the sleekly engineered *Spandau*? From the German viewpoint, how could such a mass of bullets miss one man again and again?

There is a photograph of General Montgomery investing Eardley with the ribbon of the Victoria Cross. Monty himself was quite a diminutive man, yet he stands clearly taller than the sergeant. At 5ft 6in and weighing 120lb, Eardley is, in boxing terms, not even a featherweight. But lighter boxers are usually faster and more elusive than heavyweights. He was always, his father reported, good at sports. In the orchards around Smakt, this slender man, moving fast, dodging here and there, would be the most difficult of targets for a machine-gunner firing at ground level from a pit, with the gun tending to thrust upward under intense pressure. The muzzle velocity of the *Spandau* could also prove a problem as the gun heated. The aim could vary, the magazine would run out of bullets and at some point even the barrel had to be changed. There is also the psychological problem for the gunner when the barrage of bullets fails to stop the target and the man, who was an easy, helpless target at 80 yards, is suddenly at point blank range, imminent, indestructible, rampant, poised to kill.

On the attacker's side, the value of the unique, and some might say cheap, combination of Sten and Mills bomb could be lethal. At Smakt, as at Le Bény-Bocage, the lobbed bomb, capable of devastating explosion, shredding into sharp, lethal shrapnel, was a distraction to the gunner trying to maintain a steady aim. The Sten, although with only half the rate of fire of the *Spandau*, could be far more mobile at waist level in the hands of one such as Eardley than a fixed gun down in a pit.

Having said all that, the odds against Eardley's survival must have been at least 100:1 against for the first charge, increasing incrementally thereafter.

Whilst the British units involved had lost heavily at Overloon, their commanders could count on a reasonable supply of reinforcements of suitable age and training to fill the ranks and take promotion, as Eardley himself had done when casualties were suffered in the earlier Normandy campaign. The Germans, however, were rapidly approaching the time when they would be forced to use *Volkssturm*, mainly soldiers above normal military retirement age alongside boys, younger than those who would qualify for the trained *Hitlerjugend* (Hitler Youth) units. They already had 'white bread' units in action, entire divisions of soldiers downgraded because of intestinal ulcers or similar illness. There was a need to conserve resources of manpower. Once the three machine guns had been eliminated in front of Loobeek dyke, there would not have been a sufficient defence force to resist the further British advance across the railway line. The sensible tactic was to move back to the next defensive line further down the road. Whilst still in a foreign country, Holland, the Germans had available wide areas of land over which they could make tactical retreats without undue loss of morale.

In due course the award of the Victoria Cross to Sergeant Eardley was gazetted. However, an intriguing mystery still begs a solution. Eardley was a resident of Congleton in Cheshire and first worked in the print room of the *Congleton Chronicle*. In 2015 the *Chronicle* published a request for any member of the public who had memories of George Eardley to get in touch with the present editor, Jeremy Condliffe, son of the wartime editor who had been Eardley's employer. Within 24 hours two elderly witnesses had responded, saying that they believed Eardley had stolen the Victoria Cross award from another soldier who had really earned it. This same rumour had been investigated by the elder Condliffe as editor just after the war, yet still persisted 70 years later. What basis could there be for such an extraordinary story?

The judgement of the editors, past and present, is that in some way Eardley must have caused offence, real or imagined, to someone locally in order to suffer from such a malicious impugning of his character. It is not relevant here to ask if such an offence existed or what it could have been. What can be addressed is whether it was possible for Eardley, or any other serviceman, to have stolen the credit for an action such as that at Smakt?

The recommendation for the award went through the normal process of checks and authorisation. Anyone who knew the records of Brigadier Jack Churcher of the KSLI or Major General 'Pip' Roberts of the 11th Armoured Division would assume that they would apply an almost agnostic review to a recommendation for so high an award linked to so outrageous an action. There also had to be witnesses of a superior rank. The approach across the Loobeek fields did include orchards and hedges, but this was not the almost impenetrable jungle terrain of the *bocage*, where it might have been possible to commit an act unobserved. At almost all times Eardley would have been within the sight of other sergeants and at least one officer. It is likely that even the battalion colonel was close by: he had been near enough to be giving specific orders during the action.

It is possible therefore that the rumour was related to some local issue at home which arose after the award of the VC. The *Chronicle* editors also pointed out that in no way could Eardley have known that the action would produce a Victoria Cross award, and he would have had no incentive to rob another comrade until the VC had been gazetted. John Condliffe, who as editor knew Eardley well as a former employee, did not believe the rumour to be true. He thought that staid residents of Congleton of the time might have felt that George Eardley's subsequent behaviour did not conform to the stolid standards or style of citizenship which people thought appropriate from a holder of such a high honour.

Be that as it may, the *London Gazette* entry, reflecting the report approved at all levels of command up to Montgomery himself, states among other facts that "fire was so heavy that it appeared impossible for any man to expose himself and remain unscathed ... The destruction of these three posts singlehanded by Sergeant Eardley ... enabled his Platoon to achieve its objective, and in so doing, enabled the success of the whole attack."

Whilst the sergeant would never again have the opportunity to prove in such a way "his outstanding initiative and magnificent bravery", the rest of his war was not without incident and interest. At the period when Arnhem was being assaulted from the air, the huge port of Antwerp had fallen to the Allies but there had been a failure to clear the seaway and enable ships to use the short sea route, linking close to the German frontier. This would have avoided the hundreds of miles of hauling supplies by road from the Normandy beaches. The omission gave the Germans time to reinforce and dig in. The subsequent operations to open the seaway cost thousands of lives and necessitated the virtual sinking of the island of Walcheren; and 4KSLI was present in the latter operation.

During the clearing of the sea route to Antwerp, Eardley's platoon came under sniper fire. Charging forward to eliminate the snipers, they discovered that the building they were entering was a *Wehrmacht* headquarters. Eardley remembered smashing down a door and finding himself face to face with a German general (Daser). There is evidence of a sense of humour in the sergeant's own account of the incident:

> I found myself facing a German General. The General shot at me with his revolver and missed. Instead of shooting back at him I knocked the revolver out of his hand and covered him with my bayonet. He seemed dumbfounded. Then I smashed up his wireless apparatus in case there was a chance of anyone listening to what was going on in the room.

There was nothing of humour about another experience. As the advance into Germany began to speed up, the route led more and more through populated streets. Tank commanders began to suffer excessively from sniper fire; they were easy prey for a sniper with telescopic sights. They could hide by an upper floor window, take a quick shot, often leading to the death of a tank commander, then make a swift exit through the back door of the house. The Shropshires found themselves 'riding shotgun' to the tankies. Two or three riflemen rode behind the turret of a tank, watching out for movement in and around houses, tryimg to get in the first shot, whilst the tank commander and gunner focussed forward.

On one such mission in April 1945, troops were astonished to see German soldiers standing at the side of the road holding large notices which proclaimed, 'Typhus!

Do not dismount from your vehicle! Typhus!' Behind them there was a barrier of straw, soaked with disinfectant. Brigadier Churcher of the Shropshires and the local German commander had agreed a truce to prevent fighting spilling into Belsen concentration camp, with it tens of thousands of inmates, many infected with deadly diseases. The British troops were receiving their first induction into the realities of the Holocaust, the full horror of which most British people, and probably not a few Germans, had been ignorant until now.

Unlike the many British soldiers who, the war successfully ended, had no ambitions but to achieve their demob number, collect their demob suit and go home, George Eardley would continue serving. He would ascend to greater eminence than that of an acting sergeant leading a section of half a dozen men. He soldiered on in several postings, mainly of the instructional variety, being promoted to Company Sergeant Major Eardley, Warrant Officer Class II. The summit of that period was a spell as drill instructor to officer cadets at the Royal Military Academy, Sandhurst, a compliment to his professional abilities.

One who knew him well at that time was Cliff Charlesworth, who was at Arborfield Army Apprentice School from 1947-50. Eardley had been posted to Arborfield from Sandhurst. Cliff comments:

> I got on well with Eardley and liked the guy. He had a sense of humour and, like all highly decorated forces personnel, (or so I have heard), he did not flaunt or boast of his award. Or of his [means of] achieving it. He kept all reference to it secreted away in a chest or drawer under his bed. I did try to broach the subject but he clammed up about it when it was mentioned.

Charlesworth is an acute observer, having spent a lifetime highly qualified in the nursing profession, an expert in mental health. Among his charges in one appointment had been killers confined at Rampton Hospital. He noticed what he called "a dark side" to Eardley. This related to an apparent restlessness, a failure to settle for long in an appointment. Whether this predated the war or whether it was the result of war experiences cannot now be assessed. But it is not unusual in a former soldier. His moments of communion with death in battle, and necessary sudden violent actions, may make it difficult to conform to the often monotonous routine of civilian life and the ingrained behaviour codes of a close community.

A job in the print room of the local paper would certainly not be too attractive to a man who had proved himself in such dangerous adventures. The editor of the time recorded that on one occasion the then Mrs Eardley arrived at the *Chronicle* office in considerable distress. She had not seen her husband for three days and was seeking news of him. It later appeared that his disappearance was the result of succumbing to the calming balm of alcohol, including three nights 'on a bend'. Again this might legitimately be linked to the inability of an untamed spirit to fit back into the tight harness of civilian life.

However, when the sergeant first returned home to Congleton on leave, all was joy and jubilation: brass bands, flags, mayoral receptions, press interviews, processions and street parties. His son, Roy H. Eardley, then aged 5, remembered the wonderful occasions with the family apparently all united and happy. He particularly recalled his father picking him up at the end of the leave "and kissing me good bye with his prickly face. It reminded me of the coconut mat by the front door." In his childhood innocence, Roy preferred the bright colours of the Military Medal ribbon on his father's tunic to the rather sober and drab ribbon of the Victoria Cross.

George Eardley's own memory of the presentation of his award was of chatting to King George VI, who was of a stature to look Eardley directly in the eyes. After the investiture, sherry was being served. Eardley was offered a second glass, which he gratefully accepted. However, the King stated that he himself was restricted to only half a glass as he was "on duty".

The Overloon hero did eventually settle down to civilian mode, although only long after the heartbreak of divorce and separation from the family. Marrying again, he qualified as an electrical engineer and settled into long-term employment with Rolls Royce.

Life can play terrible tricks upon individuals, and George Eardley was to be shocked by an experience far worse than anything he had known during the war, at Le Bény-Bocage, Smakt or Walcheren. There he had emerged with only the minor bruises and lesions of any more fortunate survivor of front-line warfare. Civilian life was to demonstrate that it could deal quite as horrific a blow to flesh and blood, and also to the human mind, as war could.

HRH the Princess Royal was to present new colours to the KSLI on 25 June 1964 in Shrewsbury. Eardley, invited with wife Winifred, set out from Crewe in their Ford Zephyr car. They approached the railway crossing in Nantwich and were correctly passing over between the protective gates when, with no warning, the 6:35 a.m. Plymouth to Manchester express, at full speed, crashed through the closed crossing gates, smashing the Zephyr against a gate post, slamming into an 8-ton milk tanker and carrying that vehicle 100 yards along the line. The tanker driver climbed out virtually unhurt; George and Winifred were not so lucky.

They were both trapped. Winifred was freed first and rushed to hospital, but survived for only three days. George himself was pinned down by a trapped left leg, whilst his right leg was badly fractured. With the car in danger of catching fire, a doctor, who happened to be at the scene, had to amputate George's left leg immediately and without anaesthetic.

George Eardley survived to marry again, and also learned to drive an adapted car. In 1991 he moved back to Congleton, but died within weeks. Forty years earlier, the then editor of the *Congleton Chronicle* had written a long and fascinating article about the VC hero and his problems. It highlighted the contrasts of his career:

> The houses were bedecked with bunting ... as the hero's car thrust its triumphant way through crowds of cheering townspeople ... 'It was a fine piece of work', the King had said ... But where is he now, that hero whom we delighted to honour six years ago? Unfortunate events that subsequently occurred have blotted his name and face from the memory ... In some cases, as in this, the VC

is incapable of conforming to the conventional social pattern. For one reason or another the hero comes to be forgotten.

The hero is not quite forgotten, though, for son Roy was able to inspire a project to erect a statue of Congleton's hero in the main street of his home town in more recent years. He is also remembered at Overloon, where the war museum records his actions in destroying the three machine guns in battle. At one memorial event, the officiating Dutch dignitary shone an unusual light on Eardley's motivation, in case his actions should be thought to be merely self-promoting:

> We all know how he risked everything by destroying three German machine gun posts alone. But that was not all. He also risked his life afterwards in the fact that he later went into enemy lines to bring back several of our dear people who were trapped by the enemy. The memory of so great a soldier will always be in our hearts.

Eardley's own reaction to questions about his bravery were more pithy and down to earth. A Congleton resident, John Knox, once met George Eardley in a southern country pub and asked him: "How did you cope out there facing death like that?"

Eardley replied: "I'm not sure, John, I don't usually talk about it. But I'll tell you this: if I had known that there were three of the b*****s in there, I wouldn't have gone!"

10

Erich Göstl

Panzergrenadier (Schütze) **Erich Göstl, Knight's Cross, Dr iur, Austrian, 6 Company, 1st *SS Panzer* Division *Leibstandarte Adolf Hitler***

An enemy without reproach, his young world suddenly gone dark for ever, a heart-beat from death, handsome never again: in war, firing impossibly; in peace, qualifying improbably.

It was as though *rigor mortis* had fused the forefinger to the trigger so that the gun continued to fire until it ran out of ammunition, the gunner pitifully blinded and effectively dead. Almost abandoned for dead, he was then dragged back roughly into some sort of life.

When returning to civilian life, such heroism, such wounding, would leave the man with a high cliff to scale back towards normality. So he scaled that high cliff, then climbed a far higher mountain further on. This worst of experiences happened at the worst moment of the worst of battles.

It is, admittedly, supremely difficult to compare battles and judge that one is worse than another; or indeed is the worst of them all. Any British infantryman locked in mortal hand-to-hand combat around Tilly-sur-Seulles in June 1944 would have recognised all the trauma of a Canadian infantryman similarly locked in combat outside Tilly-la-Campagne in July 1944. But one unit did make such a judgement. It happened to be what was probably the toughest, proudest and most experienced unit of the German Army, 1st *SS Panzer Leibstandarte Adolf Hitler*. The elite of the elite, 1st *SS Panzer* derived from Hitler's bodyguard of the 1930s, had fought on all sectors and been involved in all aspects of land war. When their veterans gathered in later years to drink a toast to the fallen, they raised their glasses to one special cry: "Tilly!"

In July 1944 they were defending evacuated villages up the long, gentle slope of the ridge known to the British as Bourguébus and to the Canadians as Verrières. One German tank driver, *Sturmmann* Manfred Thorn, observed: "Our defences were two and a half times as strong as our defences had been when fighting the Red Army on

Erich Göstl sent home this signed photograph before his
wounding. (Kind permission of the Peter Mooney Archive)

the Eastern Front." Tank commander Gerhard Stiller also testified as to the intensity
of the combat there:

> I was one of the 'experienced' men in my unit and all of my experience
> until then was to fade [compared] with the events of the next three weeks in
> Tilly which can never be forgotten ... The continued artillery fire, fire from
> offshore ships and air raids, these attacks were more than we could imagine,
> far more! It was a hundred times more than we had ever experienced on the
> Russian Front.

Canadian Major Don Ripley commented: "The casualties were heavy and the battle
results were demoralizing. It was complete chaos. It was a very nasty place to die." The
Calgary Regiment's war diary stated: "It is seemingly impossible for men to live under
such fire but the Hun is like a rat that comes up for more however hard we pound
him." Canadian Corporal Charlie Kipp also reminisced: "Later in the war I took a
German prisoner. He asked me if I had fought at Tilly. I said yes and he said that was
the worst fighting they were ever in."

Into this cauldron of hate, unparalleled in the eyes of the "experienced" soldiers,
entered youths who were fighting their first major campaign. Outstanding among
those, with the lowest rank of *Schütze* (private), was Erich Göstl. In his own language
he might have been described as '*unnachgiebig, unbezwingbar, unzerstörbar*' – iron
willed, indomitable, indestructible. Although only 19 years of age, he had already
won the coveted Iron Cross at two levels, Class I and Class II.

Göstl was born in Vienna on 17 April 1925, the son of a state railway worker who originated from the small town of Niederleis in Lower Austria. His father died in 1928, leaving Erich's mother, Margarethe, to survive on the railway worker's pension. They lived in an apartment in Odeongasse, near the Prater, built on the site of the famous Odeon dance hall of the 1800s which had a floor large enough to take 8,000 dancers at a time.

The epic event of his young life occurred at the age of 12 when German troops 'invaded' and took over Austria on 12 March 1938: the Anschluss. On 15 March, Hitler himself arrived and harangued a massed rally on the Heldenplatz. Within a short while, 70,000 anti-Nazi Viennese citizens had been arrested. It is difficult to know what effect these events would have on a Roman Catholic boy growing up with such historic events occurring literally just around the corner. What could have been the impact of the panoply of garish red and black Nazi banners, the pulsating fanfares of the brass bands and the stamping, reverberating challenge of the serried black jackboots?

A year-and-a-half later, further *Lebensraum* (living space) incursions by Hitler had sparked another world war. Erich Göstl's education continued at the *Oberschule für Jungen* in Vereingasse until, in May 1943, he gained the *Kriegsmatura*, a wartime higher school certificate which would have to be ratified in peacetime. Throughout his school career he had been judged a good student and was outstanding at sports. His ambition had been to become a ski instructor.

Just a year later he was emerging from training as a machine gunner and was posted to 6 Company of 1st *SS Pz*. D Day found his division in reserve north of the Seine, the German High Command still uncertain as to where would be the main thrust of the Allied landings. The division would arrive in Normandy only on D plus 21 and 22.

Before the Tilly-la-Campagne encounter, 1st *SS Pz* was sent into two of the most bitter battles of the Normandy campaign. First it fought the Canadians who were endeavouring to storm across Carpiquet airfield and enter Caen, then it was up against the might of the three British armoured divisions in Operation *Goodwood*.

The rapid-firing MG 42 machine gun was normally operated by a junior NCO, but Erich Göstl had made an immediate impression and although only a *Schütze*, he was in charge of one of the *Spandaus*. According to the rank system he might not be promoted to *Oberschütze* until he had completed six months' service. He would still need another step up to become a *Sturmmann*, or lance corporal Although no full citations appear, he had been awarded the Iron Cross Class 2 on 19 July for a June action at Verson, and the Iron Cross Class 1 on 16 August for his service at Mouen in July. But by 16 August he was nowhere near Normandy and was in no condition to worry too much about awards.

Between the two great armoured thrusts of *Goodwood* (18-20 July) and *Totalize* (7-9 August), the Canadian infantry were handed the thankless task of trying to clear the Bourguébus-Verrières ridge. It proved to be a *via dolorosa* of horrific slaughter. Typical of the period was the fate of the Canadian Black Watch who, not far from Tilly, were tasked to march through a valley raked by enemy fire from three sides. Over 300 men set off, walked the valley, advanced over the hill crest and disappeared; only 18 returned. Tilly witnesed the same kind of fighting to the death by several battalions, and the story of Tilly-la-Campagne is also the story of *Panzergrenadier* Erich Göstl.

Standing part of the way up the slow, straight rise of the national road from Caen to Falaise, Tilly was a prime defence location giving secure shelter to the defender and leaving the attackers totally exposed. To quote a French commentator: "Who owns Tilly owns the Caen to Falaise road." The 'town', even with its own mayor, could better be described as a hamlet, having a population of only 90. It was T-shaped, with the vertical stroke of the T pointing towards Bourguébus, a larger village in plain sight less than a mile away. The transverse stroke of the T held the church, five farms, the mayor's house and garden, a bar and five houses. On one side of the vertical stroke lay some eight houses, with fewer on the other side. One large outlying barn would be the scene of insensate mortal struggles. The farms, built of solid Caen stone, all contained large storage cellars, which would continue to provide refuge for defenders after the worst bombardments, even though the upper structures might have been destroyed. In the mayor's garden, which dominated the necessary approaches from north and east, vast hedges enabled Gerhard Stiller's Mk IV tank and others to remain hidden, picking off any Canadian tank which dared appear on the open countryside outside. Surrounding the village were open fields of corn and potatoes. On the northern side a railway ran towards the iron ore mines and formed a base for machine-gun pits. *Panzergrenadier* Elmar Bonn remembered a small railway building standing at the crossing, but within a day or two of Allied bombardment it had totally disappeared.

The siege of Tilly commenced on 25 July when the Canadian North Novas were the first troops to be sent across the wide open spaces to face the fire of the enemy machine guns. Not until 8 August could an Allied infantry battalion, the Scottish 2nd Seaforth Highlanders, occupy the shattered village, supported by tanks of the 148th Regiment, Royal Armoured Corps.

Survivors left graphic accounts of the horror of the time. Captain Bill Whiteside of the Canadian Argylls said: "What Jerry had done was really very clever. They had cut narrow tracks through the wheat and they would site a machine gun down there. And anybody who wanted to cross, of course, got himself knocked off." Firing one of those guns was Erich Göstl. Another Argyll, Private Whit Smelser, enlarged on that picture: "It's a sort of flat piece of ground almost like a billiard table. You're just sending a bunch of people across an open field and they [the Germans] are over on the edge popping them off. The Colonel said 'This is slaughter'." On the German side, *Untersturmführer* (Lieutenant) Gerhard Stiller commented: "Our orders were 'let them come close' … finally the white flare went up. 'Fire at will!' The tracer trajectories shot out of our ambush positions. For five hundred metres in front of us the terrain turned into hell." Again central to this hurricane of destruction was the unremitting gun of Göstl.

Massive air and land bombardments rained down time and again on the tiny village, reducing it to ruins. All but one or two of the buildings were totally destroyed, which was not entirely to the advantage of the attackers. Most of the buildings were constructed of solid Caen stone. Had the buildings been of burnt brick they might have been reduced to dust, but the Caen stone withstood much more pounding.

Frequent repeated hits might demolish a house or level a wall, but what remained could be an even better low defence rampart with, as it were, ready-made embrasures and loopholes for rifles or machine guns. The wily German defenders, well aware that no attacker could walk in the midst of the Allied barrages, could duck into a deep cider cellar until the shelling ceased.

Erich Göstl and the other three MG 42 gunners of *Untersturmführer* Kurt Sieber's 30-man company were thus afforded options to move gun pits as required, to face whatever angle of attack developed. Canadian Corporal Cliff Brown, who led his company attack, recalled the perils of facing the deadly machine guns:

> We advanced close to the railway. We saw some tanks blown up. The Germans seemed to ignore our barrage. They allowed us to get right into the wheat field, then blazed away with machine guns, mortars and tank high explosives. Men fell all around, some dead, some groaning with wounds, others trying to dig into the earth. I tried to encourage men to fire. I tried a shot myself; but we could not, because to fire it meant raising up a little into the path of their bullets and would give away our position to the machine guns all around.

Corporal Charlie Kipp felt the shame as much as the pain: "We didn't have a chance. We were driven back in complete confusion and the loss of half the company. My company! A terrible beating. My section was just swept away and lost in the dark. I was last man back. I was mad and very disgusted over it all. What hurt was the beating." So it went on for the Canadians: the North Novas, the Essex Scottish, the Lincoln and Wellands, the Royals, the Argylls, the Calgaries, the Stormont, Dundas and Glengary Highlanders, the Fort Garry Horse and so on.

Perhaps the war diary of the North Novas best illustrates the confusion:

> The trenches were filled by shouting Novas survivors who shot and threw grenades like wild men. Soon the night was a bedlam of noise. Enemy guns began shooting from all angles. Machine gun fire came from emplacements in haystacks, from the tin-roofed building, from the orchards, from everywhere. The Germans shouted and yelled as if they were drunk or drugged and the North Novas pitched into them with bomb and butt and bayonet in one of the wildest melees ever staged.

The defenders were equally affected by the confusion, although it had been almost an anti-climax at the start. Tank driver Manfred Thorn, driving into the village for the first time, recorded:

> It was really only a handful of houses. Now and again we saw a dog or a cat listlessly roaming around. We had no idea where we were or what lay in front of us. Then suddenly the name appeared 'Tilly-la-Campagne'. Nothing more than a dot on the map. We asked what we were doing here, in such an unimportant place in the middle of nowhere. How wrong we were!

Within 24 hours Thorn was dismayed by the turn of events:

> Somehow 15 or 16 soldiers from the 3rd North Nova Highlanders had worked
> their way past our infantry and quietly dug in 10 yards away from us on the
> other side of the still intact house wall. We suddenly heard their spade work,
> thinking it was our own infantry. But our tank commander could see over the
> wall and now see the 'soup plate helmets' of the Tommies below.

The situation ended when Thorn drove the tank through the wall and the big gun
came to rest "within inches of them".

Thorn also graphically illustrated the force of the Allied bombardment:

> It was so fierce that although protected in our tanks we sheltered *under* them and
> away from the ear splitting noise inside. It was unbearable. We bit dust every
> time there was an explosion and Mother Earth bounced. Our tanks sprang into
> the air like athletes in a gymnasium. For about three hundred square metres the
> area was turned into an inferno of heavy exploding shells without pause.

It was therefore a considerably reduced garrison which awaited the next Canadian
attack on 4 August. *Schütze* Elmar Bonn's post was in the cellar of the last house on
the right-hand side of the vertical stroke of the T, looking towards Bourguébus. On
the other side of the road, beyond the last house, there was a deep trench which led
away behind the mayor's garden, where the vast hedge provided another rampart.
This trench enabled machine gunners to move and cover attacks from any direction.
The most strategic site for a machine gun facing Bourguébus was at the end of the
trench, opposite and some way forward of Elmar Bonn's cellar; and that was where,
on 4 August, Erich Gostl was placed. He was supported at first by the other three
guns and the 30 survivors of Sieber's company.

Their battalion commander, *Standartenführer* (Colonel) Albert Frey, aptly described
the bombardment with which the Allies preceded the Argylls' attack:

> The enemy started the attack with heavy air bombardment, with many heavy
> four-engined bombers and ground attack aircraft, which lasted for a long time.
> Every artillery and defence strong point, including known foxholes, on our
> side were heavily bombarded and attacked with machine gun fire. After the
> air attack the enemy started with an artillery bombardment of all calibres with
> such an enormous intensity which lasted an incredibly long time. Against this
> inferno every one of us, left alone with God, could only pray and hope that he
> would survive the bombardment.

Gerhard Stiller later wrote of the defender at that moment: "Death is his terror, yet
hope plagues his heart."

Some previous Canadian attacks had been launched suddenly en masse in the
hope of overrunning the defenders. Now the commander of the Canadian Argyll and

Sutherland Highlanders, Lieutenant Colonel J.D. Stewart, planned a more cautious approach from Bourguébus across the Clos Neuf fields. A patrol would go forward to test the defence. A carrier group would attack haystacks forward of the village from which snipers had been picking off unwary men. A strong two-company attack would then follow. Even after so many casualties, the individual Canadian companies were generally still stronger than Sieber's company, and Sieber could not expect reinforcements.

Then occurred an extraordinary event exemplifying the courage and discipline of both sides. Sergeant McClaren's patrol was sent to test the 'prohibition zone'. Again the Argylls were allowed to approach almost as far as the nearest farm. At that point the defenders opened up and the patrol quickly went to ground, disappeared into the corn and withdrew. All except Private Ed Purchase. For some reason, possibly thinking he was saving the lives of his comrades, he continued to walk straight up the main street, firing a Bren gun from his hip. The defenders merely ducked, waited until the Bren ran out of ammunition and then took Purchase prisoner. Respect for the brave!

Next, instructed to get rid of the snipers in the haystacks, Lieutenant Johnson ordered his driver to drive his tracked carrier past the haystacks fast enough to avoid the guns of the *Panzers*. Firing only tracers, he set fire to all the haystacks and eliminated the problem of the snipers.

As the main attack developed cautiously through the cornfields, Elmar Bonn, from his post in the last house on the right, could see the head of Erich Göstl on the other side of the street and some way ahead. The surviving German machine gunners opened up on the furtive movements of the Argylls across the field. Bonn caught sight of Canadians with faces blackened or coloured, their helmets camouflaged by stalks of wheat fixed in nets over the helmets. The full blast of defence guns and mortars slowed the Canadian advance. Lieutenant Gordon Sloane approached near enough to throw grenades at the defenders, but was quickly cut down and killed.

Bonn looked across the street again. In that brief instant he saw Göstl's head jerk backwards and then disappear. Bonn continued firing. He was relieved to see Göstl's head reappear. The Canadian attack slowed, but with men falling on all sides the defenders began to withdraw up the street. Göstl's gun continued to fire from its prominent site. He was staying there too long, still firing, but then there was silence.

What had happened was unbelievable. The Argylls were supported by heavy machine guns of the New Brunswick Rangers firing over their heads, and their own support companies were also supplying flanking fire. In his exposed position, Göstl was hit in the left eye by a bullet. Probably it was that which had jerked his head back and caused him to fall. Partially blinded, he was quickly back at the trigger of his MG 42. His loader and others around him were killed or wounded. Only his machine gun was still firing. Another missile struck his body and he began to bleed profusely. A shell then exploded nearby, sending a jagged sliver of shrapnel which ripped open the side of his face, leaving his cheek hanging loose. A final bullet drilled into the right eye.

Now he could no longer see. But he could hear that the enemy were still advancing, and that that no other MG 42 was firing nearby. He would not be deterred, continuing to fire in the general direction of the enemy guns which he could hear. Loss of blood gradually rendered him deaf and insensible. Unwillingly, the finger eased on the trigger. He fainted away. The gun was out of ammunition.

As the Argylls accepted the inevitable and began to creep back through the corn, Bonn could see his friend lying slumped over his gun with no sign of life. An uneasy silence had descended on the battlefield. With another soldier, Bonn moved carefully across the street, approaching the blood-soaked, inanimate Göstl. They felt sure his gruesome wounds and loss of blood would prove fatal, but at least they could bring him back for a decent burial. Then Bonn's fingers found a pulse. Urgently, fearfully, rather than carefully, they dragged their limp comrade back up the street. By now Göstl was becoming semi-conscious and his groans revealed that "he was suffering horrible pain". Bonn and others lifted him into a tank, where the crew did their best by way of first aid before he was rushed off to the field hospital. Left behind, his comrades shook their heads sadly; they felt there was no way could he survive!

Remarkably, the young gunner was alive and well enough to appreciate, if not to see, the honour when on 11 November 1944 it was announced that he had been awarded the Knight's Cross (*Ritterkreuz*) of the Iron Cross. For a mere *Schütze* to receive this award was more than extraordinary; it was unique. It was the only Knight's Cross ever awarded to such a lowly ranked *Panzergrenadier* during the war. A glance at some of the other awards of the Knight's Cross underlines the rarity of this citation.

The *Ritterkreuz* was normally given only to senior servicemen, and usually to officers, for sustained bravery or achievement over a lengthy period. In some cases it was judged on a points system. For example, at one time a pilot needed to destroy 26 enemy planes to qualify. A U-boat commander might need to sink 100,000 tons of enemy shipping, while a general might win the Knight's Cross for a successful withdrawal from battle. The award had replaced the First World War *Pour Le Merité*, which was available only to officers. Hitler, as a lowly corporal himself, had insisted on a supreme award which would be available to all, irrespective of rank. Nevertheless, more than 500 German generals were awarded the medal. Basic grade Private Göstl's one-day battle was therefore unique.

He learned about the *Ritterkreuz* when recovering from the radical surgery required on his eyes and cheeks. His colonel, Albert Frey, had travelled to the Cernin Palace in Prague, which was being used as a war hospital for the blind. Frey's account paints a rather different picture from that of the machine-gun pit at Tilly. The announcement and presentation were made in the presence of Göstl's fellow patients. Frey observed that all had tears in their eyes as the citation was read out. However, the other patients were so excited by it all that they tried to give the hero a typical military salute by picking him up and throwing him in the air. Unfortunately, as they were all vision impaired, they managed to throw him up but failed to catch him on the descent and he crashed to the ground. However, it all ended in happy laughter, providing a momentary glimpse of a lighter side to a man capable of grim implacability.

One minor question arises as to the failure to use Göstl's story as a prime public relations exercise after the award of the *Ritterkreutze*. The Nazi propaganda machine, managed by Goebbels, usually went into top gear to proclaim and popularise the acts of war heroes. Much exposure was given to 'aces' such as airmen Hartmann and Welter or tank commanders like Wittmann and Barkmann. Photographs of them were made into postcards, which were avidly collected and traded by young fans in much the same way as British schoolboys treasured cigarette cards. But Erich Göstl was not included, in spite of the unique nature of his bravery. No matter how many Hartmann or Wittmann postcards one had collected, it was not possible to swop them for a Göstl. It has been suggested that, because of the Nazis' fascination with the image of the perfect Nordic or Aryan man – tall, blond, unimpaired and unblemished – the mutilated gunner's face, even after reconstruction, was not a fit image for such a concept.

Göstl was discharged from the Army in April 1946. However, for members of the *Waffen SS* this was not like the demobilisation of any ordinary military unit. Because of atrocities committed by various units wearing *SS* badges, the Allies had declared the *SS* to be a criminal organisation and its members subject to investigation for possible war crimes. In the cases of Gerhard Stiller and Manfred Thorn, they were arrested and, while not personally charged with a specific war crime, made subject to 'denazification'. This was a form of detention with re-education. Thorn recounts how former concentration camps were used as holding prisons for former *SS* members. In his case, after a course of interrogation at several centres, he was fined a nominal amount and allowed to return home, if he had a home to return to.

There seems to have been an exception to this treatment in that soldiers of the *Waffen SS* who joined their units from 1943 onwards were regarded as conscripts rather than pro-Nazi volunteers. As such they could be permitted the more prompt demobilization of the ordinary soldier. Göstl therefore returned to Odeongasse in Vienna, taking up residence at apartment 6/5 whilst his mother, his legal guardian, continued to live in the same building at 6/12. As a *Kriegsblinder*, or war-blinded, he had certain financial advantages honoured by the Austrian government, although Austria was now independent of Germany. He later married Ruth, a girl from eastern Germany.

In view of the evil reputation which elements of the *SS* no doubt deserved, it is appropriate to mention certain aspects of the battle at Tilly. It had at times been fought with extreme brutality and almost intoxicated hatred on both sides. Yet at points in the action a common attitude of disciplined respect seems to have survived. The case of Ed Purchase highlights one such moment. There were also truces to enable the wounded to be collected and treated.

There were other glimpses of humanity amid the furore. At a moment when the attackers and defenders became almost intermingled in the darkness, the North Nova's Thomas Douglas fell dead almost in touching distance of Gerhard Stiller. The latter was so impressed by the Canadian's bravery that he removed Douglas's identity discs, handing them to his own Red Cross men with instructions that his burial site be clearly identified at a time when many bodies were buried indiscriminately. Years later, Stiller and Manfred Thorn met Douglas's comrade, Colin Nelson, at Douglas's permanent grave in an act of shared remembrance and reconciliation.

By the time of the academic winter term of 1947, Erich Göstl was well enough to think of preparing for life in the new Austria. Vienna was not the easiest place in which to live and study in 1947. The terms of the Allied occupation of Germany and Austria had divided Vienna into separate zones, each controlled by one of the Allies. There were times of disagreement, confrontation and border closures. In such circumstances a recently rehabilitated soldier with very little sight might be excused for choosing an easy learning path. Instead Göstl chose to climb the steepest of mountains. While he would never realise his boyhood ambition to speed down a Tyrolean mountain as a ski instructor, there were even more ethereal peaks for the mind to conquer.

Göstl decided to study law at the University of Vienna, the toughest test at the most exacting of academic centres. He could count on sterling support from his wife, but to qualify as a lawyer would require years of intense concentration and persistence, as well as a high level of intelligence. Undaunted, Göstl entered the university and began his first course on the History of Law. He emerged triumphantly from the examinations at the end of the academic year in 1948. On 26 June 1949 he took the required state examination in laws, thus qualifying to practice. But he was not yet satisfied.

In November 1951 he took the *Absolutorium*, the completion of all examinations leading up to the Doctorate. There remained only the *vivas*. After approval of a profound thesis written by the student, this was the final contest in which he had to defend himself against a panel of aggressive examiners who would try to destroy the student's arguments. The machine gunner of Tilly would surely not have been too overawed by a jury of judges. Be that as it may, on 3 July 1952, Göstl gained the right to append to his name the coveted *Dr. iur.* He seems then to have been happy to practice quietly as a lawyer until retiring to the beautiful Tyrolean lake resort of Sankt Jakob im Rosental, where he died on 27 October 1990 aged 65.

To climb that mountain and become a Doctor of Law would have been a task challenging enough for a well-funded student with full use of their eyesight and no recent history of mental trauma. Fortunately for Göstl, he seems to have married a woman of similar heroic and self-sacrificing tendencies. Throughout the grinding years of tedious research and endless memorising, Ruth was his helpmate and his spare pair of eyes.

In the silence of the law library or the solitude of a solicitor's office, did Göstl's mind ever revert to Tilly-la-Campagne and hear the unseen guns thudding away again? Or perhaps reflect in terms similar to those written later by his old comrade Schiller? "I am seeing the numbers of young Canadians fallen and wounded in front of the railway crossing at the west end of Tilly. I can only say 'Why…? Wherefore…? For what reason…?' But *that* may have been *then,* but have we all now grown wiser?"

Friends remembered that the supreme machine gunner, like so many of the very bravest, was always taciturn when questioned about his wartime exploits, usually responding with "I was only doing my duty" or "I could not do anything else at the time". *Unbezwingbar* indeed!

11

Ian Hammerton

Captain Ian C. Hammerton, MBE, Croix de Guerre, Ld'H, British, 22nd Dragoons, 79th Armoured Division

They must wait for him, here at the enemy's most lethal trap. None can pass until he, in his monstrous cumbersome machine, comes to plough a safe furrow through for all else to follow.

It was almost like rolling out the red carpet to welcome the D Day troops along the Bernières promenade. Of course there was no actual carpet, but the 22nd Dragoons, or as they preferred to be known the XXII Dragoons, were rendering an even more important service to the men of *la Chaudière* Regiment, foot-slogging on behind. One of the Dragoons' Sherman flails rolled from one end and a second Sherman flail rolled from the other, vast blasts of mines exploding as they battered the ground. As they met in the middle, and continued to widen the strip of safe ground, the following on Canadians poured through unharmed. The infantrymen knew full well that it was better to be safe than sorry: better to wait for the Sherman flails to clear the way than to resort to heroics.

The tank troop leader, Lieutenant Ian Hammerton, shivered in his wet clothes and splashed in his waterlogged boots as he directed the remainder of his five-vehicle troop as they cleared the village street by street, cut barbed wire obstructions and ducked the showers of enemy mortar bombs. The crews worked secure enough inside the great armoured vehicles, manipulating the controls of the ugly but effective mechanical contraptions protruding from the hulls, inventions owing much to the genius of 'Hobo' and his 'Funnies'. For the story of Ian Hammerton is very much the story of Hobo and the 79th.

Ian Hammerton was an enthusiastic soldier, having been an NCO in the Officer Training Corps at school. He was trained in the Royal Tank Regiment (RTR) and then received his commission. His war was continuing smoothly as a troop leader of regular tanks in the XXII Dragoons, awaiting the anticipated invasion of France. Then everything changed overnight. The regiment had assembled to parade in front

Ian Hammerton, sweeping mines and conserving woodlands. (Courtesy of the Hammerton family)

of a certain General Sir Percy Hobart, who called on them to gather round so that they could hear what he had to say.

"Some of you are going away to learn about some new secret equipment," he said. "You must not, under any circumstances, repeat a word of what I have said to anyone: your lives may depend on it." He announced that they were to "sweep away all the mines in front of the advancing army". He departed, leaving the Dragoons astounded and disillusioned. A proud British cavalry unit sweeping mines, he had said, like the dust cart at the Lord Mayor's Show?

Hobart's military ideas had often been seen by higher commanders as eccentric, although the German tank expert General Heinz Guderian avidly studied them and applied them to German tank doctrine with compelling effect. Hobart had even been cold-shouldered out of the Army and had served in the Home Guard before being called back by Churchill. It was only 15 months before D Day that Hobart was given free rein to form the unique 79th Armoured Division and devise novel methods of supporting front-line troops. It would then be necessary to invent new vehicles or machinery, manufacture them from scratch, train troops and work out methods of liaison and command. The 79th would comprise three tank regiments plus a number of Royal Engineer formations. However, a regiment such as the XXII

Dragoons would not now fight as a complete regiment or even a squadron, but in troop lots attached to whatever formation required their services. All vastly complicated within the time frame.

But by D Day, the XXII Dragoons and 1st Lothian and Border Horse had a full complement of mine-sweeping tanks, nicknamed Crabs. The Westminster Dragoons were equipped with flame-throwing tanks, known as Crocodiles. Royal Engineers manned various inventions, such as a tank chassis which was a folding bridge able to span a water obstacle, a tank armed with a huge block-buster petard, another armoured vehicle which could lay carpets for airfield runways, the DD (Duplex Drive) 'swimming tank' and the Buffalo amphibian carrier. These inventions quickly acquired the nickname of 'Hobart's Funnies', and Hobo himself was recognised at last as a genius to be revered. All the 'Funnies' would at one time be lead vehicle in some action or other. Some, especially the flame-throwing Crocodiles, were particularly dangerous to their own crews if there should be any mechanical failure or human error.

Ian Hammerton and his colleagues were issued with the Crab, which might well have featured in a competition for the ugliest vehicle ever allowed on the roads. This was basically the quite shapely Sherman tank with its rounded dome, but now hung about with cumbersome projections.

From the front of the tank projected at a vertical angle the steel jibs holding, and lifting back or lowering forward, a huge rotor. Where the rotor connected to its supports, two spinning wire-cutters were fitted. The rotor held heavy chains which, with the rotor spinning forcefully, would be unleashed to hammer the ground and set off mines. A hydraulic ram raised or lowered the jib. To the rear, the tank was fitted with guiding arms and lamps, and also line markers. The turret still carried its 75mm cannon and .3 calibre Browning machine gun, with an optional .5 calibre Browning on top of the turret and another .3 calibre Browning below at the co-driver's seat.

Commanders quickly discovered that in certain positions of the flailing equipment, the 75mm gun sight was obscured and it was necessary to aim the cannon by the ancient system of peering out through the barrel itself. During flailing action, the turret was traversed to the rear. The vehicle needed the standard Sherman five-man crew, and in the XXII Dragoons each troop consisted of five Crabs. The Crab troop leader could expect much more opportunity to act as an almost independent unit, compared to a normal tank regiment troop teader, as his troop would often be detached from the main body of its squadron and regiment in order to work to the requirements of another formation, often infantry.

For the D Day landings, Lieutenant Hammerton's troop was allocated to a Canadian infantry unit, le Régiment de la Chaudière, from Quebec. The Dragoon tanks were waterproofed to land in 5ft of water. All joints and possible leak areas had been stopped up with thick, black Bostic, a loathsome substance requiring pain and persistence to remove from bruised hands after application. At Gosport in Hampshire, tanks had to be reversed on to LCTs (Landing Craft/Tanks), a ticklish business with only an inch to spare on each side of the tank. It would be easier rolling off. The LCTs joined the vast procession of ships heading out in weather and seas so rough that the Supreme Commander, Dwight D. Eisenhower, contemplated a significant postponement.

Once at sea, Hammerton was permitted to open a sandbag which contained orders, maps and aerial photographs in great detail. He recognised former practice maps, which had carried fictitious names. Now the map Sheet 84 stated the authentic Norman names like Bernières on code name 'Nan' beach. The detail of the maps was impressive, stating not only the location of enemy guns but their individual calibres. There were even photographs, taken by a low-flying Mosquito plane, showing German soldiers looking up as they worked, erecting obstacles on the beach.

Now at last, at 0715 hours, H Hour on D Day, the flash, blast and rolling thunder of immense bombardments dulled the senses of those on board. The ramp of Hammerton's LCT goes down precisely on time, on target, but with a heavy tide swelling in towards the sea wall.

As his Crab runs down the craft's ramp, a lurch of the boat tips the Crab against an underwater obstacle. A mine explodes up against the vehicle, without causing any apparent vital harm. Ahead, two of the AVRE (Assault Vehicle Royal Engineers) Funnies, Churchill tank hulls, armed with huge petards, advance to blast the sea wall and any obstructions. A ramp leading up the wall is closed off by a substantial steel barrier. An AVRE climbs the ramp, slides sideways and tips over. The second AVRE advances, pushing the wrecked comrade up the ramp, hits a mine and is disabled. It remains squatting at the top of the ramp, narrowing the access.

In this emergency, Hammerton has to change plans. Blowing the Cordex waterproof protector on the main gun, he bombards the steel barricade and demolishes it. With the tide rising to its highest, Hammerton orders "Driver, advance!" Nothing happens. The driver reports that the process of freeing the Cordex and using the big gun has loosened the turret ring. Water is pouring in, flooding the engine; they have no power. There is nothing to do but gather essential kit and small arms and evacuate the tank. They are in 5ft of water, and dead bodies, floating amid the anonymous flotsam, bump against the crew as they splash on. Weighed down by clothing and equipment, they claw their way up the ramp. Thus it is that Hammerton stands ashore, water streaming from him, to instruct his four mobile Crabs. He sees in front of him, hanging on a belt of thick barbed wire, a warning from the enemy: *Achtung! Minen!* Mines by the dozen are exploding as the flails plough back and forward on the promenade. As a harbinger of things to come, Hammerton passes a Canadian padre comforting a soldier who is still alive but has had his face blown off by an explosion.

The morning merges into a succession of images. Germans with their hands raised in surrender. A large German shepherd dog chained up outside a house. Two Frenchmen smiling, wanting to shake hands, but there's no time to speak. A call from the Chaudières: there's another minefield outside the village. A Bren carrier upside down, the crew killed underneath. The Crabs sweeping up and down a vast minefield, where amphibious DUKWs arrive carrying mountainous cargoes of supplies to be stocked there.

By midnight on D Day a guard needs to be set as they roll into wet and oily blankets to sleep. The *Luftwaffe* are overhead. Everywhere is so crowded with troops that the enemy bomb-aimers cannot miss. As dawn arrives, a French farmer is pointing and shouting, "*Russes! Russes!*" Surely not Russians? But yes, there is a group of Russian conscripts in German field grey, deserting and surrendering on D+1.

During the days and weeks thereafter, the Funnies were called out, in large or small groups, according to the type of battle being waged and the enemy defences needing to be tackled. For Operation *Goodwood*on 18 July, a large-scale sweep would be required. Soon after D Day, 51st Highland Division, defending the far bank of the River Orne, had laid an extensive minefield to repulse repeated German counter-attacks. Now it was necessary for three armoured divisions to cross that same stretch of land. With some 800 heavy armoured vehicles and many soft vehicles queuing to advance, a single swept lane would not be adequate. The Crabs were exposed to enemy eyes and guns across an open plain, but the drivers cannot put their foot down hard on the accelerator and hope for a quick escape. Ian Hammerton frequently experienced the high tension arising from the slow crawl required for their ground-battering process as they searched out every inch of ground:

> We reach the edge of the minefield and I give the order: 'Start flailing now!' One-and-a-half m.p.h. feels slower than ever. Forward we creep, chains throwing up mud and grass, yard by slow yard, the engine racing and creating a gale through the turret. On and on, so slowly that the Infantry could walk past my tank.

Throughout all the battles, the lanes needed to be precise to the inch. A square foot of untested earth could hide the pressure plate of a mine. By employing 'echelon' flailing, the Crabs attained maximum coverage. One Crab moved ahead, the next following close behind, planting its left track firmly in the marks of the right track of the leader, as though on a single railway track.

There was great frustration when, having swept for ordinary tanks to pass through, nothing happened. Hammerton remembered an occasion when a Guards formation considered the swept lane, although exact to optimum requirements, too narrow and would not move until the flails had carried out yet another sweep. Part of the reason for this, Hammerton observed, was that the flails were "such a new conception, many people were unaware of our existence or capabilities. I am sure we would have been used even more if some infantry commanders had realised our potential and our accuracy." The initial high command coolness towards Hobart and his ideas meant that there was too little time before D Day for massed exercises with the Funnies. Infantry and tank commanders were often only poorly acquainted with these exciting technical options. Haughty infantry colonels did not always appreciate having to be instructed by mere lieutenants in oily overalls on the intricacies of mine-sweeping.

Two later events illustrated both the need for precise, inch-perfect flailing and also German ingenuity in reacting to Allied mine-sweeping efforts. Hammerton watched as Churchill tanks of the 7th RTR filed out on to the clearly marked path made safe by the flails. One tank swerved slightly, its track straying only a yard out of the marked path, and 'BANG!', its track was blown off.

More tragic was an incident which was sparked by good humour. Hammerton's flail had halted beside the beaten pathway and the crew were watching the infantry filing past. Wireless Operator Bob Burden was sitting on the turret drinking tea when men walking past shouted the frequent infantry complaint, "Why do the tankies get better tea than we do?" (the tankies brewed their own tea but from the same ration issue). Bob responded by offering the mockers a drink. Hammerton recalled: "He jumped off the tank with the mug and landed on the path beaten by many hundreds of pairs of marching feet during the last hour or so. There was an explosion, and one of Bob's feet was blown off." The Germans were using mine variants with delayed fuses or with springs which required more or less than the normal weight to set off the fatal explosions.

Not all flail work could be carried out as though in a carefully organised country ploughing competition across tilled fields. Operation *Totalize* on 7 August required the flails to form fours and march as part of columns of 200 or more vehicles. They would advance through the night up the Bourguébus Ridge, smashing through all enemy defences. The normal clouds of dust churned up by tanks was added to the detritus spewed out when flails operated their chains. It became almost impossible to see the rear light of the vehicle ahead. Whilst the normal Sherman was quite agile in its turning motions, the flail version had to account for all the additional accoutrements outside its basic profile. Inevitably accidents happened. XXII Dragoon Captain Wheway, seeking Lieutenant Boal's Crab, found it "sharing an enormous shell hole with three tanks which had fallen in, one on top of the other". Hammerton himself crashed into a deep shell crater in the darkness.

During the flailing procedure, with rotor spinning and chains whirling to mash the earth, the Crab was virtually immune from mines. However, when on the march or shooting as a normal tank it was even more prone to damage. Lieutenant W.J. Boreham recorded the damage suffered when his marching Crab, with all its festooned accoutrements, struck a mine: "One bogie smashed. Leading off suspension damaged. Jib supports smashed. Hydraulic cylinder and piston torn off. Near-side track cracked. Hole in driver's plates."

To Hammerton it was not always the massed, climactic battles which held most terror:

> Sometimes we had to lead an advance down a road and this was possibly more fear-inducing than a full-scale frontal attack. It was the apparent quiet, especially when the road was completely empty. One experienced an uneasy feeling in the stomach. I say the apparent quiet for obviously our ears suffered from the constant background mush and frequent wireless messages. It was a relief to our strained minds to halt, switch off engines and 19 [wireless] set, and just listen … but a more dread sound from somewhere in front was the squeaking clank of enemy tank tracks. It paid us to stop and listen.

By late August, the German army in Normandy had ceased to exist and a unique experience awaited the XXII Dragoons: the siege of Le Havre. After D Day and the storming of the impressive coastal defences, much of the later Normandy campaign was a matter of hurriedly devised strongpoints with the Germans relying as much on counter-attacks as on static defence lines. The great naval base of Le Havre was surrounded by massive permanent defences, with more recent Rommel inventions added. It was even indicated on maps as 'Fortress Le Havre'. This would require a measured assault by an entire army corps in Operation *Astoria*.

The task to flail the extreme left flank of the attack, which was a minefield, was assigned to 1 Troop. Fortunately for Hammerton, several French Resistance fighters appeared and were able, ahead of the battle, to lead him to the site so that he could reconnoitre it at very close range. The approach of the Crabs to their starting point was hardly the most dignified or propitious. It was necessary to cross a very steep hill, and the Crabs, weighed down by their unwieldy, burdensome impedimenta, added to the Sherman's normal 34 tons, failed to make the grade. They were nose-heavy and sank into the sodden ground, having to be rescued and ignominiously towed over the hill by Churchill recovery vehicles.

The location of the minefield required 1Troop to advance whilst firing their guns to drive off defenders before reversing turrets and beginning to flail. Tanks were closed down as far as possible to avoid sniper fire. At a vital moment the canvas gun mantle of the turret machine gun caught fire. Hammerton had to get out and, exposed to whatever imminent peril, wield the fire extinguisher. The Crab still had the Sherman's poorly protected petrol tanks and ammunition racks, and thus its propensity for exploding in a volcano of flame.

Once flailing started, Hammerton said it was the old story of fear challenging patience and fortitude striving against the fear:

> At one-and-a-half miles an hour it seemed to take ages and ages to move. We crawled forward. We flogged on and on … we continued to flail up to Stronghold 1.2. Then anti-climax! Not a single mine had been exploded. But prisoners, dazed by the bombardment and the massed attack, were surrendering by the dozen. At the great naval barracks one shot each from two tanks caused the doors to disgorge an ordered procession of three thousand sailors following a white flag.

Tactics had to vary as the Allies rushed north through France and the Low Countries, and both terrain and weather changed. In mid-October near the Leopold Canal, 1 Troop found itself exposed for miles around, flailing along a high dyke elevated 15ft above flooded fields whilst Canadian infantry sheltered as best they could down the sides of the dyke. An anti-tank gun was disposed of, but the main enemy was mud. Every move of the Crab thrust up clinging mud. Everyone was constantly engaged in cleaning and changing periscopes. All rags having been used, spare overalls were pressed into mud-clearance service. Successfully attaining the objective at the end of the dyke, Hammerton tried to dismount, but his boots failed to find any solid ground beside the tank. Plunging into the mud, he slid all the way down the dyke, landing in the midst of a group of amazed Canadians and their prisoners.

For the tank commander more subtle perils awaited along the way, more insidious than the anti-tank gun or sniper's bullet. When traversing urban streets, the wise commander would order the gunner and co-driver to watch out ahead whilst he himself continually surveyed the full circle view. The Germans were experts at letting one or more enemies pass before taking action from behind. In a remote Dutch town, watching to the rear whilst travelling at a fair speed, boosted by the Sherman's many tons of armour, Hammerton had a sudden presentiment, swivelled, looked to his front and ducked just in time to avoid an approaching telephone line. Innocuous in itself, now strung tight across the street, it could have decapitated him like a wire cutting through cheese. With as much as a 200 percent casualty rate among tank commanders in some units, accidents were almost as much to be feared as wounds from enemy fire.

In another tragic act, Lieutenant Hammerton was to see another of Hobart's Funnies in close action. Late in April 1945, the Dragoons had reached the great German city of Bremen. Their route led to a huge bastion of defended bunkers. At that late stage of the war, a first salvo from the cannons of the Crabs produced white flags from the bunkers. With some humour, Hammerton recounts that at that moment their new CO drove across in front of 1 Troop's guns in his jeep, which "could have resulted in an unfortunate vacancy".

Ahead, a motley jumble of parked railway vans formed another barricade. Two AVREs accompanying the Crabs pushed this blockage aside. This revealed a 6ft high concrete wall on both sides of the street. A massive concrete block had been constructed to seal the gap. 1 Troop fired with armour-piercing and high-explosive shells from their cannons, but only succeeded in chipping the block. Hammerton appealed to the AVREs for help.

One of the AVREs drew up with its great yawning petard pointing at the obstruction. One shot, one tremendous flash, and the concrete block disintegrated. The AVRE courteously waved the Crabs through. However, Hammerton soon discovered that his jib was too wide to pass through the existing gap. The AVRE commander wirelessed to say that he would go forward and widen the gap. The Dragoons watched the 40-ton AVRE Churchill pass through the gap and move on a yard or two:

> There was a colossal explosion. And the forty ton Churchill rose into the air shattered, then crashed down, becoming a mass of scrap iron. A jeep which had nipped in behind the AVRE simply vanished. The road had been mined with a naval mine, 300 pounds or so of explosive, which had set off all the explosives carried inside the AVRE.

Having witnessed the vicissitudes of others, the XXII Dragoons were to suffer their own tragedy even as the war stuttered to an end. On 2 May 1945, pushing through crowds of refugees, they supported the Cameron Highlanders towards the village of Glinde. They had been told that hostilities were about to cease and to proceed with care, which they certainly did. However, with Sergeant Jock Sterling leading, they were fired on by some fanatical German gunner still intent on resisting. Jock's gunner, Trooper Turner, spotted an enemy self-propelled (SP) gun, fired immediately and knocked it out. A high-explosive shell then burst on the Crab's cupola, killing Sergeant Stirling. Following it, a high-velocity shot crashed into and through the turret and out of the other side, killing Trooper Turner. The remainder of 1 Troop responded furiously with armour-piercing, high-explosive and smoke shells. A final enemy shot cut off a telegraph pole, which brought down a tangle of wires around Hammerton's head but without causing major harm.

Angrily, the Crabs and the Highlanders surged forward seeking the remaining SP gun. A high-explosive shot, fired by the Crab alongside, brushed a tree as it left the gun, exploded and deafened Hammerton for several weeks. The infantry major was seen wielding a walking stick as he led his men forward. He quickly returned to say that they had used a PIAT mortar to knock out the other SP. Thus ended the war for the XXII Dragoons. Jock Stirling had been a D Day original Crab commander, had later been seriously wounded and then returned to fight and die another day. If only that advance into Glinde had been three days later!

As war ended and peace began to take a political shape across Europe, the XXII Dragoons witnessed a remarkable contrast in national attitudes. What they saw may have been the first tensing of muscles, the first aggressive banging of shields for the Cold War. They were to occupy the village of Walkenreid in the Harz Mountains and establish a border with the Russian Army.

British cavalry regiments tend to display a certain nonchalance in the face of peril. So at each road crossing of the new border line they placed a simple moveable barbed wire barrier across the road and manned it with a few lurking troopers armed with pistols and lodged in a bell tent. At first there was a massive westward flow of refugees intent on evacuating their own homes to avoid living under the Soviet regime. Then the Russian troops arrived and immediately proceeded to erect formidable barriers. They dug and occupied formal trenches, and were supported by a section of tanks with guns aligned on their erstwhile allies.

The XXII Dragoons, being essentially a wartime formation, would, like yeomanry regiments, soon pass into 'suspended animation'. Ian Hammerton found himself translated into a staff captain at the 43rd Division HQ. It seemed to be a routine administrative post, the most interesting task being reviews of courts martial. However, 43 Div had also been given the unenviable task of organising the trials of the camp commandant and other perpetrators of the Bergen-Belsen concentration camp. This involved Hammerton in processing and reviewing statements by the myriad victims, many of them children, some born inside the camp. This experience affected his attitude to life for ever.

In his spare time, with a few colleagues, he facilitated the setting up of a youth club based on the local Church of Scotland centre, the latter being primarily a canteen for the troops. At the club there were two types of wasted youth which most attracted his sympathy and efforts. Many of the boys had been firmly indoctrinated with all the evil tenets of Nazism and needed help in emerging into a world of totally different mores. There were always young girls needing advice or help with an unwanted pregnancy. This problem was exacerbated when the non-fraternisation orders, which had prohibited Allied troops from consorting with German women, were rescinded. Not every Allied soldier was a moral saint, and numbers of German girls suffered betrayal and desertion. Hammerton and his youth club helpers were fighting against the tide.

Such experiences caused him to muse: "These were certainly the most harrowing experiences of my life. But it was not only Germans who had committed these crimes: many of the concentration camp guards were of other European nationalities too. One wonders if one's own people could have been guilty of similar atrocities in similar circumstances?"

All was not horror and despondency, however. Stationed near Celle, Hammerton found it to be a centre of musical activities where he could extend his knowledge and appreciation by attending concerts of the highest quality. But nothing at Celle compared with a musical event which took place while the war was still being waged a few miles away. At Christmas 1944, the famous Hallé Orchestra gave a concert in the Philips electrical works at Eindhoven. Hammerton revelled in the enjoyment of watching that most charismatic of conductors, John Barbirolli, whilst artillery rumbled in the near distance.

He also made friends at Celle with a German musician who was able to tutor him in his playing of the flute, hitherto no more than a personal diversion. With civilian life now beckoning and a teacher training course available, the flute became a part of his professional career. Qualified as a teacher, he first became music master and then deputy headmaster at his Dartford school. Naturally he was involved in local music circles and, together with his cellist wife, played in the Dartford Symphony Orchestra, whilst himself conducting a youth orchestra. He was also an ardent conservationist and in retirement warden of a particularly beautiful wooded preserve.

Ian Hammerton kept in touch with veterans of his XXII Dragoons and became involved in researching and recording the siege of Le Havre, together with French enthusiasts, setting up the 'Remember Le Havre' Association. Some veterans told him they just wished to forget all about the war. He disagreed strongly, arguing that memories must be preserved in the hope of preventing another such conflict.

The horrific aspects of war made such an impression on him that it is to be wondered how much they preyed on his mind in the years following. He was able to pen some graphic sentences in his emotive book, aptly entitled *Achtung! Minen!*:

> Every combat soldier … carries in his nostrils the acrid smell of cordite, and even more the stench of dead bodies of animals and men. His eyes will ever recall the ghastly sights of split-open tanks, of steel interiors burnt out, of remains of flesh sticking to a half-opened hatchway, of maggots crawling in a seething mass in the remains of comrades with whom he had shared life … He can never forget.

Was Crab Troop Leader Ian Hammerton, often in the lead tank, ever afraid? Yes, as he writes:

> Fear stalks at a soldier's side when he knows he is to be sent into action …
> We countered the fear by light-hearted banter, of course, but also by our high state of morale, our fighting spirit and above all, by our comradeship developed by all those hours, days, weeks, years of training and learning together.

12

Jack Harper

Corporal John William Harper, VC, British, 4th The Hallamshire Battalion, York and Lancaster Regiment, killed in action 29 September 1944

Pandemonium! – a manic dash through torrential fire, the leap of an Olympic hurdler, a patient stroll by the wide canal, a slam of the door ... and this most reticent of actors had entered, crossed the stage, exited ... and is gone for ever.

One report declared that "the lunatics watched the sane men shooting each other, and wondered, 'was this some strange form of entertainment put on by the establishment for their benefit?'"

If the outmoded term 'lunatic' is to be avoided, then the battle certainly was frenetic, bewildering and eccentric. It was the most peculiar and potentially dangerous mission the 'Hallams' had ever been called on to undertake. In effect they were to assault a vast fortress, near Merxplas on the border of Belgium and Holland in late September 1944. Astonishingly, they were forbidden to use almost all the appropriate tools of siege warfare. It would be like trying to crack a coconut using a small pair of nutcrackers.

There was even come confusion at Headquarters as to what lay in their path. Corps HQ described it as 'a factory'. In other documents it was simply 'a depot'. The precise title on the map was hardly more helpful, '*le Dépôt de Mendicité*'. The word 'asylum' was also mentioned, perhaps like the asylum back at home, just a rather large building isolated from other habitation? More relevant to the size of the establishment, but no more enlightening, would have been the full original name of the place, '*Maatschappij van Weldadigheid voor de Zuidelijke Nederlanden*'.

What the Hallams eventually encountered was a huge complex of four-storey buildings, set along a wide avenue wide enough for a tank parade, the entire estate bounded, like a medieval castle, by a moat or dyke and defence wall. The dyke, some 10-12 metres wide, ran for 7km around the complex. Inside were 27km of streets and lanes. Added to this were a chapel, a hospital, a farm, a brickworks and a closed

Jack Harper, the quiet man who roared. (Courtesy of
John Brown, former mayor of Hatfield Woodhouse)

prison. A further impression of the size of the complex can be gained from the fact
that, at its inception and before it was built up, it was planned as a community of 125
smallholding farms for indigent people.

Established in 1822 as a version of the British workhouse, but on a vastly larger
scale, *le Depôt* had seen many uses. In 1938 it was a reception centre for Jews fleeing
the Austrian *Anschluss*. When the Germans arrived in 1940, any Jews who had
remained in residence became incarcerated and were eventually sent to Auschwitz. It
was now populated by up to 6,000 people, 1,740 of them civil prisoners, the remainder
vagrants or mentally ill patients plus numerous staff. They awaited the battle behind
closed doors until the Germans began to let them out during the actual fighting.

If the attackers managed to fight their way into the complex, there could still be
daunting problems. In some of the buildings large dormitories provided space for
40 beds. Long corridors were sub-divided into workrooms or rest areas. In both the
penitentiary and the asylum, cell or ward doors were locked. The brickworks itself
was a confused puzzle of brick stacks. The various sections of the farm were protected
by tall windbreaks.

This veritable fortress with its surrounding canal was holding up the Polish
Armoured Division. As happened throughout the Low Countries, the Germans
demonstrated great expertise at blowing bridges to facilitate a retreat. Tanks,

frustrated by the fallen bridge, had to wait for the infantry to establish a bridgehead over any wide water barrier. The bridge could then be repaired or a temporary Bailey Bridge put in position to enable armour to press on. So the Poles waited, prohibited from shooting their 75mm or 17-pdr guns over the heads of the infantry because of the danger to residents. To accentuate the problem, there would be no heavy air bombardment, no support from dive-bombing Typhoons, no artillery barrage, no mass rockets, not even the larger mortars.

Sergeant (later RSM) Dixie Deans was with 1st Leicesters, who were to advance in tandem with the Hallams. He remembered the astonishment at his colonel's briefing. The largest weapon permitted during the attack would be the light 2-in mortar, and that could only be fired singly at a specific identifiable target. And so, said Sergeant Deans, "this was without doubt the most deadly action we had fought".

If adaptability was called for, then the Hallams had a pedigree. A Sheffield-based battalion, as part of the 49th Division they had spent the early part of the war defending Iceland against a possible attack which never occurred. That freezing mission gave them the distinctive polar bear badge on their sleeves. Then in Normandy they had the unenviable record of spending 36 consecutive days without respite immured in the dense, dark thickets of Tessel Wood, most of the time in virtual eyeball-to-eyeball contact with the enemy; or, as evidenced more than once, within snake-throwing distance. After taking part in the siege and liberation of Le Havre, they found themselves stranded for weeks without transport due to the failure to open up the port of Antwerp. Now there was the hazard of this unknown fortress to be assaulted whilst wielding totally inadequate weaponry.

Geoff Cooper and his platoon comrades of the Hallams' C Company were concerned to know how their new corporal would function in battle. Their Corporal Nelson had been wounded and a Corporal Jack Harper had appeared in his place. He was a fine-looking man, athletic, with the kind of face which seems always ready to smile, enhanced by a neatly trimmed moustache. Cooper found him to be "so casual about things and situations, always calmed it down, as it were. He did not yell like a typical army sergeant". He was a great contrast to Corporal Nelson, Geoff thought, who, if anyone complained or queried, would snap: "Shut up and bloody well get on with it." In contrast, Harper was "like a Mother Hen with the lads". But, Geoff had wondered, when the real close combat started in a confusion of anger and hatred, might the aggressive Nelson have been a better leader than this considerate new man?

To add to the normal confusion in unknown territory, it was ordered that the Leicesters should enter by the 'front door' of le Depôt, whilst the Hallams should find and break in through a 'back door'. It seemed all very easy to visualise, that is until it was realised that they were not actual doors in a single building. What it meant was that the Leicesters would advance along the main road with its normal crossing place over the dyke, whilst the Hallams trekked far to the left to find another way across the canal. For the Hallams, C Company would lead the way under Captain Mike Lonsdale-Cooper, who had won the MC at Tessel Wood. The spearhead platoon under Lieutenant Judge would have Corporal Harper as its senior NCO.

Zero hour was 0530 hours on 29 September. Still in darkness, the Leicesters' attack immediately ran into determined resistance. It was now a month since the annihilation of most of the German army in Normandy. There had been time for the Germans to reorganise their defences in the Low Countries; in fact, an entire fresh battalion had arrived at *le Depôt* just in time to stiffen the resistance.

The Hallams had to walk along a quiet avenue to reach their start line in almost idyllic conditions. However, when they reached that crucial cross on the map, it proved to be a belt of dense forest, just like Tessel Wood. The survivors of the Normandy campaign must have experienced considerable trepidation at the prospect of another Tessel Wood before them. But the undefended woods were merely a waiting point. As first light illuminated their route beyond the trees, it proved to be an even more terrifying challenge. A vast field divided them from their first objective, which could be seen to be a substantial earthen wall, an obvious battlement. But they would need to advance for 300 yards, totally exposed and without any form of shelter, across this featureless but uneven turnip field. There was a clear reluctance on the part of some to move out from the comfortable protection of the trees.

Private Roy Simon, recently returned after wounding in Normandy, waited with a support platoon. He recalled:

> We were in a ditch on the edge of this wood and what happened was Errol Flynn stuff. Lonsdale-Cooper was at the side of me and he said 'Right. Get ready!' and he were looking at his watch. Then all of a sudden he blows his whistle and I gets half out of the ditch and nowt happens. Nobody moves. And he says to me, 'Come on, Simon, you're one of the old lads, show em how 'tis done' and suddenly I were running like the clappers.

Lieutenant Judge had already led his platoon out into the exposed field, where Geoff Cooper found that, "It was weird, with a ground mist, the run across the open ground prior to the asylum – Hell itself! Everything was flying in all directions." A *Spandau* and a clutch of rifles were firing from pits dug in the foot of the earthen wall. Clusters of *Nebelwerfer* rockets came screaming down and exploded. More indirect heavy machine-gun fire from beyond the wall joined in. Geoff thought it was like a hailstorm but with flaming bullets.

A few yards out into the great expanse, Lieutenant Judge was hit in the neck and fell helpless. Roy Simon was knocked unconscious until his senses returned:

> I stood straight up but spun around and fell back, but this Lance Jack caught me. Then I felt this warmth down me back and I said to the Lance Jack 'What's me back like?' He said there were blood coming out. And that the same bullet had passed right through me and hit him in the wrist. And one of the young lads comes running up and he had been shot through both wrists by one bullet as he was taking aim. Shells kept falling in a pattern and bodies were going up all around.

Amid all this, Jack Harper, now leading and in command of the platoon, jogged on and on over the turnips rows. Too far to sprint when loaded down for battle, it was a case of a steady lumbering gallop – run, duck, rise and run again. A hundred yards they went, 200 yards, with men falling left and right. Harper slung grenades at the wall, blazed away with his Sten gun, bellowed and yelled. Suddenly the defenders, now isolated on the exposed side of the wall, broke, vaulted over the wall and ran. Harper jumped on to the wall, still firing. Four of the Germans raised their hands in surrender; others continued to run but were shot down.

Considering the way in which Lieutenant Judge and others were cut down within a few paces of the start line, the success of Jack Harper, Geoff Cooper and one or two others was truly remarkable. It could be that the *Spandau* gunner was somewhat distracted by the extensive width of the field, with an entire company spread across it. The *Spandau*, with its high rate of fire, is inclined to be a spray gun rather than an aimed shot weapon. It may be that the position in front of the tall earthen wall meant that some of the Germans in front of it felt hemmed in and insecure. It is also possible that the German battalion at that point included older or lower-grade men, who were little disposed to hand-to-hand fighting. This is illustrated by the fact of four soldiers surrendering to the lone corporal when they might easily have overwhelmed him. All this does not in any way detract from the daring, persistence and bravery of Harper's platoon, and especially of the man himself.

Reports and the official citation give the impression of a hectic, maniacal charging and firing repeated over and again, almost as though without pause. However, Geoff Cooper remembers at least once when Harper, advancing, employed the stealth of a tiger rather than its leaping savagery. Creeping along a narrow lane, they knew they were close to the Poles and were wary of mistaking Polish helmets for German ones. Harper had turned to Geoff and asked for a couple of extra hand grenades. Then he stood listening intently. In the intermittent moments of battle silence, a voice was distinctly heard saying "Fritz". Harper immediately shouted "Fire!", flung a grenade and charged in the direction of the voice. Within a few seconds, an enemy machine-gun pit had been destroyed.

Meanwhile, Captain Lonsdale-Cooper gathered survivors under the shelter of the near side of the wall before crossing the barrier. German stick grenades were still landing along the edge of the turnip field. The captain indicated that Harper should do something about it. The corporal immediately jumped up on the earth wall again. He saw that enemy soldiers were still lurking around a track which separated the earth wall from the dyke itself. Although now exposed to renewed fire from more than one direction, Harper lobbed grenades and fired Sten gun blasts, driving the nearest Germans further back. Some of the defenders jumped into the dyke and, hampered by battle equipment, tried to swim across. Harper continued to fire at them and then raised his Sten and aimed at any enemy daring to show themselves beyond the dyke.

Remembering the objective of the attack, he went forward to the edge of the dyke and, being acquainted with similar water courses at home, quickly judged that it was too deep to be waded at that point. So it was back over the wall again to report to his company commander. He also contrived to continue covering fire whilst encouraging his men to cross the wall into defensive positions in old gun pits beside the dyke.

Lonsdale-Cooper accepted his corporal's opinion as to the depth of the canal, but wondered whether, failing a footbridge, it might be possible to wade across farther along. Hedges and trees obscured the view along the canal. The dyke itself showed evidence of wartime lack of maintenance. There might be a place where piles of rubble or flotsam would afford somewhere for a man to cross, wading and swimming. Harper considered that, with his knowledge of canals, he was the appropriate person to look for whatever 'back door' access might exist.

At this juncture, Harper was seen by Geoff Cooper to head off along the canal as though on a quiet stroll along an English waterway. To Geoff it was clear that for some way the dyke was too deep for a company to ford. Harper might have to reconnoitre a considerable way, always under deliberate enemy fire. He eventually encountered an outpost of the Leicesters who had already found a ford and were guarding it. Firing, both direct and indirect, was still coming from the main German positions within the complex as Harper made a more rapid return journey along the canal bank.

Remarkably, it appears that he had not been wounded during his extraordinary ventures. He was able to indicate to Lonsdale-Cooper where the ford was to be found. But the corporal had defied the odds for too long. Whilst he and the captain were still talking and surveying the route, a rifle bullet – possibly aimed, possibly a stray – drilled into Harper's head. He collapsed. The battle-hardened captain saw instantly that there was nothing to be done. Harper had died almost immediately.

Geoff Cooper heard voices shouting from gun pit to gun pit. The news which was being shouted shocked him more than anything else during the entire battle: "Corporal Harper's been shot! Our Corporal is dead!" Geoff felt that "it was all very sad. He had done his best but it was just not his luck to live to see his reward." In military terms, a suitable reward there would certainly be.

On 2 January 1945, it was announced that, "The King has been graciously pleased to approve the posthumous award of the Victoria Cross to No. 4751678 Corporal John William Harper." The citation describes *le Depôt* as "a natural defensive position, surrounded by an earthen wall, and then a dyke, strongly held by the enemy". It then confirms that, "The enemy were well dug in and had a perfect field of fire across 300 yards of completely flat and exposed country." It describes the phases of Harper's action in extended detail.

Finally, it sums up the action:

> The success of the battalion in driving the enemy from the wall and back across the dyke must be largely ascribed to the superb self-sacrifice and inspired gallantry of Corporal Harper. His magnificent courage, fearlessness and devotion to duty throughout the battle set a splendid example to his men and had a decisive effect on the course of the operation.

In spite of the official plaudits, Jack Harper was possibly one of the least-lauded heroes of his day. This may be related to his own retiring disposition and the modesty of the family in general, and also to their rural origins. As nephew Gordon Harper points out:

> Personally, I don't believe that his family nor the community ever realised just what an heroic individual John was, and never fully appreciated what being awarded the Victoria Cross really means. It took one of our councillors [John Brown] a few years ago [2002] to set up a fund to honour John in a fitting way [with a memorial stone in his home area].

Obviously, the battle at *le Depôt* did not end with Jack Harper's death. The fighting inside the complex became ever more chaotic, as described by Walter Shea, an anti-tank gunner:

> They'd got there a big civil prison. What they done, they let them out … they'd opened the cages and there were criminally insane people. The prison guards weren't anywhere to be seen. There was two of us with a pistol and a Sten gun going in, but with several of these insane people wandering around, even with our guns we was feeling quite a bit wary of them.

Inevitably, some of the inmates were caught in the crossfire. Sixty-three-year-old prisoner Frans Merrens suddenly found his cell door opened and was able to walk out free. Within seconds of gaining freedom he was struck by a stray bullet – whether British or German is unknown – and killed. Warder August Meeusen, aged 59 and just weeks away from his long-anticipated retirement, was also killed as quickly as the freed prisoner. Irrespective of status, bodies – dead and wounded – lay around: paupers, prisoners, 'lunatics', warders and also Belgian and Dutch hostages held by the Nazis. Many of the German defenders just disappeared, removing tunics as they mingled with the crowd and the battle noises died away into diminishing cries of pain or anguish.

The attackers had lost heavily, especially in the maze of the brickworks. Of the Leicesters, Lieutenant V.F.W. Bidgood won an immediate Military Cross for a similar charge to that of Jack Harper, in Bidgood's case seizing the main crossing over the dyke. More than one of the companies involved ended the day with less than half its complement still fit for service. But the Polish tanks were already rolling past, moving on.

So who was Corporal Harper? John William Harper was born at Hatfield Woodhouse near Doncaster and brought up in country conditions at Slay Pits Lane. He had boisterous brothers – George, Frank, Stan and Pete – and a more timid little sister, Joan. When asked if, amid this noisy family, Jack, as the family preferred to call him, ever became aggressive or rough, Joan replies: "Nay! He were the quietest man you could ever hope to know." She goes on to explain that, because their mother went out to work at the farm, she was often left with piles of dirty dishes and laundry to wash. It was always Jack who left the boyish games and came into the kitchen, where men of those days did not tread, to help her. It was always Jack who, if games became too violent, intervened to shield Joan and calm things down.

Jack left school early with a limited education. He became a peat cutter alongside his father, George, digging and lifting the heavy sodden peat. The Thorne Marshes were the largest area of peat in the country. Peat was still used for fuel and also for animal bedding in large quantities. But the cutting work was poorly paid by the length of the strips of peat cut, these being similar to the rolls of grass used for laying lawns or sports pitches. The heavy work would have improved Jack's physique, although he was already an enthusiastic footballer.

Coincidence enters the story: the Thorne area had been drained many years before by means of canals cut and constructed under the supervision of Cornelius Vermuyden. He had been brought over from the Low Countries to import the knowledge and skills gained in pioneering Dutch and Belgian dykes and waterways such as the moat at *le Depôt*.

Nephew Gordon Harper was a witness to Jack's reputation: "Coming from a rather large family with only the one sister, I do know from her that he was extremely protective towards her and she absolutely adored him. I also believe that she never got over his death during the remainder of her long life."

Jack had known his future wife, Lily Marshall, at school. She lived not far away at Drax. After Jack's death she married again. The son of her second marriage, Kevin, described her as someone full of life and with a great sense of humour. She had also revealed certain skills as a poet at school. Jack and Lily had married and lived at South End, Thorne, with Jack still plying the peat shovel until he enlisted in April 1940.

He carried the same dependable reputation into the Army. Gordon Harper comments: "Personnel who I have spoken to during the passing years state that John was a very quiet individual who tended to keep himself to himself. Should there be any trouble or aggravation come his way, he would walk away rather than become confrontational."

Geoff Cooper enlarged on his comment that Jack could be a 'Mother Hen': "He would make sure you were alright in your dug out, before bedding down for the night (I was only18 years old). He was humorous when the situation called for it. He was a very concerning type. We were his family."

On a more official note, Lonsdale-Cooper, now a major, whilst recovering from a wound received at *le Depôt*, wrote to Lily: "He was a very brave man and the best type of NCO … He was always quietly efficient, always cheerful, and somehow gave everybody a feeling of confidence. We are mourning the death of a very fine man."

For the soldier on campaign in a foreign country, all is strange, alien and often forbidding. The terrain itself may appear to be an enemy, as perhaps for many British soldiers in the Western Desert or the men from Sheffield steel mills confined to the sinister shades of Tessel Wood. But one writer brought up amid the apple orchards and cider works of Herefordshire recounted how he suddenly felt at home and welcomed on driving into an ancient apple orchard in Normandy. This can lead to a sense of belonging, assurance or even false confidence.

What would have been the reaction of Jack Harper as, charging from the woods across the turnip field, he leaped over the wall and found himself on the banks of a dyke, so much like those canals at home? Even amid the fusillade of enemy fire, walking along the bank of the dyke, could there have been a feeling of belonging, reassurance or even confidence? For the soldier there is no nice place to die. But there can be places where fear, anger and hatred are tempered by a sensation of empathy with Nature.

Strangely, perhaps the most striking tribute to Jack's personality was a very personal matter pertaining to Lily's second marriage, as noted by her son Kevin. Jack had given Lily a gold locket which she wore permanently around her neck. After Jack's death, when Lily felt that she could move into a second marriage, it was to a new husband who also knew and respected Jack. To the new husband's great credit, he agreed that Lily must continue permanently to wear the locket, which held a small image of Jack.

By a remarkable coincidence, when at school, the then Lily Marshall of Rusholm Grange, Drax, had to write a poem around an 'In Memoriam' theme. She chose to write about 'the little Red Poppy' and its significance. The poem is prescient almost to the point of being eerie, and might well serve as an epitaph to Jack Harper, VC. It includes these haunting lines:

> The earth, once so fair, is now tinged with red
>   on the battlefields grim with the slain.
> There gently you lift up your proud little head
>   that perhaps wears a bright crimson stain,
> the blood of a soldier who lies by your side,
>   a cannon ball mark on his head,
> Slowly bend over him, kiss the cold form;
>   he has joined the great ranks of the dead.

13

Aleksander Jarzembowski

WO1 Aleksander Leon Jarzembowski, alias Manka, *Legiony Polskie* Cross, Polish, 2nd Armoured Regiment, 1st Polish Armoured Division

An odyssey across three decades of battle, from the chaos of disintegrating empires to the Nazi surrender at Wilhelmshaven, but then, for the Standard Bearer, "daleko do domu" (a long way home) meant no way home at all from perfidious Albion.

The story of Aleksander Jarzembowski is closely intertwined with the history of Free Poland, and especially with the saga of the 1st Polish Armoured Division. It is also a reminder of the remarkable contributions made to Allied naval, air and land successes by thousands of Polish exiles who fought from a British base in the Second World War. Those contributions are now widely recognised, but the gratitude which should have been extended to those heroes at the end of the war was grievously lacking.

In September 1939, two days before Britain and France declared war on Germany, Jarzembowski's unit was already fighting the *Panzers*. He was already 22 years into his service record of more than 28 years, of which nine years and 10 months were spent on active service in the face of one foe or another. Over 28 years he was wounded three times, interned twice, evacuated twice and deprived of citizenship twice, all due to fluctuating political and military situations. His use of the alias, Sergeant Manka, typifies the complications of his life journey.

He was born in 1902 at Poznan. He and his father's generation were engulfed in the chaos of the disintegrating empires of Austria-Hungary and Russia, plus three partitions of Poland, and the surprise of a rampant 1914 Germany stumbling to a 1918 defeat. Even when fighting for independence there was bitterness because liberation movements were sometimes in conflict among themselves. Internecine strife was particularly savage in the era when Red Russia fought White Russia. Aleksander's grandfather fought for Germany at Sedan but, as German nationals, his father and brother were interned by the Russians. So confused did events prove that at one time

Aleksander Jarzembowski at peace after 30 embattled years.
(Courtesy of Janus Jarzembowski)

the young soldier Aleksander had a whimsical vision of suddenly finding himself fighting his own father hand-to-hand on some remote battlefield.

However, when he was aged 10, there was a period of relative calm. His father, Edmund, was a *maitre d'hôtel* in Warsaw, married to Janina, daughter of a restaurateur. The boy was sent to Szyling, a good high school. Soon, at the school, he was introduced to the subversive liberation movement which used schoolboys as couriers. Aleksander thrilled to the challenge. After one particularly hazardous mission he was considered for a military award. But he was still too young to be officially a soldier and qualify for a medal. His superiors compensated by awarding him the highest boy scout badge available.

In 1916 he volunteered for the Pilsudski Legion, fighting at that time as a brigade on the German side against Russia. However, the Germans ordained that all the Polish legionnaires should swear an oath of allegiance to the Kaiser. When they refused, the Legion was surrounded and interned. The frail-looking Aleksander, only 5ft 6-in tall and 148lb at full maturity, seemed too small a boy to be a soldier and the guards expelled him from the camp. He moved from farm to farm, once sleeping in a coffin, until returning home, where he immediately enlisted again.

At this point he was furnished with false documents in the name of Manka. This was in part due to the vicious nature of the liberation struggles. If a member of a family was known to be fighting 'on the other side', the remainder of the family might become the subjects of cruel retribution. Posted to the 1st Infantry Regiment, he was wounded at Sadowa. Whilst in hospital he learned that he had been promoted to sergeant at the age of 17. But his Polish liberation army was poorly equipped for major battles. They were forced to use six different types of rifle made in six different countries, each with its particular type of ammunition. The great initial hopes and advances of the liberation army into Ukraine were then shattered by the new Red Army. The White Russians had been defeated. Now, enjoying endless supplies of manpower, the Bolsheviks moved in full force to drive the Poles all the long way back to Warsaw. Only then could the Poles rally and overcome the Russian thrust. Sergeant Manka was again wounded during this time.

Always a fervent Roman Catholic, Manka sought solace in religion at the worst of times. Like British troops in 1914, he had his own variation of the Angel of Mons apparition. On one occasion his section was cut off and surrounded in a wood, where they dug in for the night. The position seemed hopeless; morning must mean surrender or slaughter. Manka went aside a while to pray and have a smoke. Suddenly, out of the total darkness, the moon arose and shone brilliantly on a large cloud in the perfect shape of a guardian angel. Manka felt safe and reassured. Next morning reinforcements arrived.

With international treaties signed and Poland's independence assured, Manka was able to return to his true name of Jarzembowski and continue to serve as a regular soldier, becoming an instructor in both infantry and armoured units in Lublin. He was able to marry Albin Boberska Olga, a girl from Bukovina, now in Ukraine, and raise a family of two sons and a daughter.

It was too good to last. On 1 September 1939, the full weight of Germany's novel *blitzkrieg* burst across the Polish frontier. The by now Sergeant Major Aleksander Jarzembowski fought with his regiment as part of the 10th Cavalry Brigade under the command of Colonel Stanislaw Maczek, a Professor of Philosophy in peacetime. Overwhelming in numbers, the German Army was also far more powerful in armour. Maczek's men had at that their disposal, as a main strike force, only seven small 5-ton Vickers tanks armed only with a machine gun. The main German *Panzer* was the Mark III, weighing 15 tons and mounting a 50mm cannon. The disparity between the Polish tanks and the German *Panzers* was thus more than twice that between Shermans and Tigers in Normandy in 1944.

As the Polish Army slowly retreated, Maczek worked out his own tactics, stating that they were "drawing the enemy into gorges and defiles in which he will be unable to deploy his troops … He will fight us with individual fingers and not with his whole fist … and [we] bite back with short sorties." Any thought of miraculous intervention which the Poles might have nursed were dispelled when, after 17 days of desperate Polish defence, the Russians also invaded Poland from the Polish Army's rear. Europe's two largest battle-ready armies quickly pinched out the smaller nation.

Maczek was ordered to evacuate his brigade and seek to continue the fight elsewhere. So on 19 September 1940, the 10th Cavalry Brigade, having lost a third of its strength, crossed the border of Poland into Hungary and Romania. For Jarzembowski this meant another period of internment in Romania, where the authorities were basically sympathetic to the Poles. Then came an easy escape, a journey through Yugoslavia and Greece, a ship to Marseilles and finally joining up again with his brigade in France. The brigade was already assembling and being equipped with French uniforms and much more powerful French armoured vehicles.

If Sergeant Major Jarzembowksi/Manka had not already had enough disappointments and disillusionment for one lifetime, worse was to come. The great French Army and the British Expeditionary Force proved as helpless in the face of *blitzkrieg* as Poland had been. Following the evacuation at Dunkirk, the Polish Brigade completed assembly just in time to assist in the hopeless defence of Paris. Then Maczek again displayed his tactical ability by conducting a steady defensive retreat of the Polish Brigade as far as Dijon. There the Poles again found themselves almost surrounded, and again the order came to disperse and find another base from which to fight for Poland.

On the night of 23 June 1940, Aleksander Jarzembowski was on board a Polish liner-turned-troopship, the *Sobieski*, bound from Bayonne to Plymouth. The next stop for Maczek's men was in Scotland, where this time the unit would be issued with British uniforms and equipment. By now Polish exiles were finding their way to Britain from many areas of the world, all ready to volunteer for active service. It became possible to enlarge the former 10th Cavalry nucleus to the size of a full armoured division, with Stanislaw Maczek as its major general. Training was completed by D Day in June 1944, and the men of the 1st Polish Armoured Division waited impatiently for their great moment of vengeance against the German Army which had humiliated their country in two world wars. Aleksander was now regimental sergeant major (RSM)/warrant officer class 1 (WO1) of the 2nd Armoured Regiment, which was under the command of Colonel Stanislaw Koszutski and equipped with Sherman tanks. But there was to be a frustrating wait until 8 August before they fired their first shots in anger.

By this date the Americans had broken out of the Normandy beachhead area and were encircling the German left flank. If the British and Canadians could capture the dominant Bourguébus Ridge south of Caen, their armour might race on past Falaise to meet the Americans and close a trap on all the German forces in Normandy. Throughout the night of 7 August, Allied armoured columns stormed the ridge. By dawn the 1st Northamptonshire Yeomanry and 1st Black Watch had liberated the strategically vital crest village of Saint Aignan-de-Cramesnil. The Poles were scheduled to pass through the forward troops at midday. As the first Polish tankies drove through the ranks of the English armoured troops, berets were waved and cheers sounded above the noise of Sherman engines. But the heady cup of comradeship and vengeance proved to contain sour wine.

Several unplanned occurrences marred Polish hopes of any immediate triumph. An aerial bombardment by USAAF heavy bombers should have facilitated the advance of the front-line troops from Saint Aignan. Instead, some of the bombers dropped their fatal loads on Allied supply columns and headquarters echelons, among them the Poles. There is nothing more demoralising to the front-line soldier than to be the subject of 'friendly fire', especially when it comes in the form of devastating attacks from the air.

On the ground, the Allies captured the Bourguébus heights and the German infantry was in disarray. However, just behind this location lurked perhaps the finest armoured unit on the German side, the fanatical 12th *SS Panzer Hitlerjugend*. That elite division was under orders to move west in an attempt to check the precipitous American advance around Mortain. The *Hitlerjugend* veteran commander, Kurt Meyer, known to his men as *Panzermeyer*, aware that an Allied attack past Bourguébus might be imminent, had decided to ignore Hitler's orders and delay departure for a brief while to see what might happen. Thus, instead of a weak and scattered second-line defence beyond Saint Aignan, the Poles ran into a quickly mounted ambush manned by the young fanatical elite of a proven fighting force under an astute and ruthless leader.

Nature and local knowledge also favoured the *Hitlerjugend*. The unfamiliar ground across which Jarzembowski and his comrades must advance was well known to the *Panzer* troops, whose corps headquarters had been located on this same terrain. What appeared to be a vast open field proved to be a kind of funnel which narrowed down until entering into a tight, deep ravine, an ideal place for an ambush. In the woods around the ravine, the *Hitlerjugend* had quickly brought up and hidden tanks and anti-tank guns. The Polish 2nd Armoured Regiment, with the 24th Hussars alongside them, were a fatally exposed target. Furthermore, the urgency and speed of battle had not permitted the synchronising of language translations, code names, radio frequencies and such. There was no way an English Yeomanry lieutenant could warn a Polish Hussars major of immediate peril.

Setting out with 54 Shermans and nine Stuart tanks, in just a few minutes the 2nd had lost 10 of their 75mm Shermans, five Firefly Shermans and two Stuarts on the open fields. At the end of the day, five officers and 47 other ranks were recorded as killed, wounded or missing. Among them was Lieutenant Ramon Sikora, the first Pole to lay down his life during this mission of revenge. In spite of these setbacks, the infantry of the division pressed forward, if much more slowly, on to its appointed objectives.

It was at such a moment that a man of Warrant Officer Aleksander Jarzembowski's experience and resolution was most needed, in an extreme emergency where younger raw recruits might have succumbed to horror and panic. Did he, as he sought to stiffen the resolve of the younger soldiers, remember that darkest of nights when, hopeless and surrounded, he had seen the vision of an angel in the sky and been inspired to fight on? Did he remember humiliating experiences, great and small, like sleeping in a coffin or taking part in the long retreat from the Ukraine to Warsaw, as he sought to reassure crews that tomorrow they could take a double revenge on the enemy? Did he feel, after internments, evacuations and retreats, that now was his moment for changing the fortunes of war? That he succeeded in maintaining morale is beyond doubt. Within a few days the regiment, and those alongside it, would prevail in one of the most ruthless contests of the entire Normandy campaign.

Almost inevitably, fate held more cruel surprises in store as the advance continued towards Falaise. The Polish division had been tasked to push straight forward the day after the Saint Aignan battle. But during the intervening night another armoured force, aiming to repeat the previous night's feat in a march over unknown country during darkness, mistook landmarks and went astray. At dawn it found itself off target, lost in strange terrain and surrounded by superior German forces. Polish units were diverted to try to find and possibly rescue their wayward allies. They were able only to discover the smoking remains of the lost force, which had been totally wiped out.

Yet another blow of fate was the result of one of the worst staff errors of the war in Normandy. Operation *Totalize,* which included the action around Saint Aignan, had been superseded by Operation *Tractable,* another set-piece battle planned to break forward past Falaise. Again a considerable air attack would be an important feature in destroying enemy defences. The Allied bombers needed to fly over the ground troops as the latter waited to advance. In such a case it was standing procedure, well documented in Normandy, for ground troops to set off yellow smoke signals to alert their airborne comrades as to where the front-line posts were located. Unfortunately the air planners had, for some reason, decided that the *Tractable* master bombers would themselves use yellow smoke to mark the enemy ground targets. Inevitably the mass of bomb aimers on arrival attacked both sets of yellow smoke, again inflicting serious material and psychological casualties on the frustrated and furious ground troops. Again, it was the veteran RSM, so experienced in frustration and reversals, who was at hand to maintain morale and discipline at the worst moments.

Remarkably, Maczek was able to rally his division and lead it in an extraordinary advance on 15 and 16 August. The fanatical young survivors of the *Hitlerjugend* were defending the area of Falaise and Trun literally to the death, with no surrender. Canadian historian R.J. Jarymowycz described Maczek's response as "a textbook example of an armoured division in action". With the division formed into three battle groups, the Poles probed forward, battle group fingers extended, finding gaps in the enemy lines, bypassing Trun and reaching the Chambois area to link up with the Americans. Thus, at 1900 hours on 19 August, the Allies closed the great trap on the German armies in Normandy.

In an urgent conference with Allied ground troops commander General Montgomery and Lieutenant General Guy Simonds (commanding II Canadian Corps), Maczek used his map-reading skills to identify two vital connecting hills ahead, marked as 262N and 262S and known as Mount Ormel. This feature dominated the land for miles around and sat on the sole remaining route of German retreat. Maczek noticed that the shape of the contour on the map resembled an ancient Polish weapon, the *maczuga* (or mace), by which name the Poles have remembered the following battle ever since.

There now followed an extraordinary combat in which the presence of an older, resilient soldier like Warrant Office Jarzembowski was essential. Enthusiastic though they were, some tank crews were still relatively inexperienced and would encounter dangers and exhaustion they could never have trained for or even imagined.

By daybreak on 20 August, most of the division's units were settled into defensive positions on the hills amid woods and the dense *bocage.* They were immediately assaulted from inside the trap by elite German units including the 2nd *SS Panzer Das Reich* and 9th *SS Panzer Hohenstaufen* under an experienced commander, Wilhelm Bittrich. Fresh German units from outside the trap mounted relieving attacks from the

Poles' rear. The steep *Maczuga* became a chaos of massed combat into which artillery from both sides poured more fury. Air strikes proved impossible because foes were so tightly interlocked. The 2nd Armoured Regiment's Colonel Koszutski himself fired machine gun and revolver as German infantry mounted his tank to attack him. Each Polish tank became a separate fortress assaulted by desperate enemies. Commanders fired their turret-mounted .5 calibre machine guns to the rear while turret gunners fired forward. At 1700 hours it was recorded that tanks were fighting gun barrel to gun barrel. A German Mark IV crashed into a Polish Sherman.

Koszutski later remembered:

> An incredible situation … All of the Regiment's machine guns firing at the same time … 44 tank cannons and around 90 machine guns … The nervous tension is incredible. One can feel it running like an electric current across all units. It cannot last. It is the culminating point of the battle, the war, life, of something fundamental. Something has to give. There is no leader in overall command, each one is fighting with weapon in hand.

Amid all this, the RSM of 2nd Armoured, Aleksander Jarzembowski, had to find a way through the *mêlée*, weapon in hand, to attend to other emergencies, braving the fighting, killing throng. The one available medical post was almost immediately swamped with casualties, both friend and foe. Another post had to be set up and organised. Hundreds of beaten enemy soldiers were now surrendering and had to be corralled in some way. The scarce resources of ammunition, water and food had to be doled out as each tank's own stores were exhausted. With no overall command possible, wilting men – weary, confused and bruised – had to be encouraged or driven on. This was not the time for sympathy or niceties, but for instant obedience to the familiar bark of the RSM.

At the battle's peak, A Squadron of the 10th Mounted Rifles had to be ordered out of the battle because it had exhausted every round of ammunition and there was no more available. One favourable factor was that Allied artillery units had managed to post five Forward Observation Officers on the heights and they were able to continue directing their guns – Polish. Canadian and American – on to specific targets.

By the morning of 21 August the Germans had lost most of their *Panzers*, but infantry attacks continued from front and rear. Then at midday Canadian troops broke through the retreating Germans to link up with the Poles on the *Maczuga*, thus sealing the last escape gap. At about the same time the Germans recorded that all ordered movement, in the attempt to break out or in, had now ceased.

A Canadian observer was appalled to see the condition of the Poles who still stood firm on the *Maczuga*:

> The picture at Hill 262 was the grimmest the regiment has so far come up against. The Poles had no supplies for three days; they had several hundred wounded who had not been able to be evacuated; about 700 prisoners of war lay loosely guarded in a field; the road was blocked with burned out vehicles.

Unburied dead and parts of them were scattered about by the score. The Poles cried with joy when we arrived.

The cost to the Poles had been high: 351 killed and more than 1,000 missing. The equipment could be renewed; there was always a supply of new tanks available overnight. The problem would be replacing the trained soldiers. But the defence of the *Maczuga* meant that countless German soldiers, who might have escaped, were eliminated from the war, their vehicles and equipment were destroyed, and the remnant which did get away could only flee in a disorganised state through the length of northern France and Belgium. In their sector alone the Americans counted 380 enemy tanks, 160 self-propelled guns and 5,000 trucks destroyed or captured within the trap.

In the confusion of this type of warfare, the strangest things could happen. At one point en route to Mount Ormel, Polish tanks were crossing the lines of retreating German vehicles. At a crossroads, an efficient German military policeman held up the lines of German vehicles to allow the unidentified Polish tanks to pass through quickly.

The use of ammunition had been profligate, but justified. One Polish artillery regiment on just one day alone fired about 7,000 shells, some of them over open sights at approaching ground troops. It may have been this wealth of supplies, compared to the sparse provision in the liberation wars, that inspired a post-war remark by Aleksander Jarzembowski. His son Edmund, a geologist, collected fossils, a hobby which the father never understood. He commented to Edmund: "I used to collect, too, when I was your age, but what I used to collect was machine-gun bullets, as the government was so poor."

Replacement tanks were available to the Poles from the Forward Delivery Squadron overnight. Reinforcements of trained crew were more difficult to arrange. The British conscript system still churned out numbers of reinforcements, but for the volunteer armies, Canadians and Poles, it was far more complicated. However, after a short period of reorganisation Maczek was able to command his division in the great advance from the River Seine to the Rivers Maas and Rhine, and eventually to the surrender of Germany. This was a period of considerable advances hindered by blown bridge and stubborn battles as the enemy also reorganised.

RSM Jarzembowski was wounded again. At a quiet moment in Holland there was a sudden commotion. Jarzembowski stepped out of his bivouac to investigate, looked sharply to the side and thus probably saved his own life. Instead of striking his upper head, a bullet penetrated his right cheek, ran right along the jaw line and smashed all his teeth. It was not enough to cause the veteran more than a brief period of first aid before continuing.

In Holland, during a fast advance, he saw at a distance some German soldiers harassing a number of civilians. In spite of the risk, but with long-acquired skill, he opened fire at the enemy with his turret-mounted machine gun, killing some of them and driving the others away, to the delight of the civilians, who maintained grateful contact with him after the war.

Now the long years of frustration gave way to a period of triumph and glory as the Poles rolled through tiny villages such as Posthauseñ, Stickhausen and Brinkum, and larger centres like Breda and Wilhelmshaven. Whereas contact with civilians in evacuated villages in Normandy had been rare, now French, Belgian and Dutch civilians lined the streets to welcome their liberators. Victory parades were hurriedly organised. WO1 Jarzembowski was the Regimental Standard Bearer for such occasions, relishing the unfamiliar glory of leading the parade as bands played, civilians cheered and the mayor paid glowing tributes.

Finally Jarzembowski proudly bore the standard for a ceremonial surrender of the great German naval base of Wilhelmshaven. The Poles were delighted by the long inventory of personnel and weaponry surrendered to them. How many other armoured units could claim prizes like the heavy cruiser *Prinz Eugen*, 18 U-boats, more than 200 smaller naval craft, two admirals, a general, more than 32,000 naval personnel and rations for 50,000 men for three months? For the Polish veteran, it was a long way from the anonymity of Sergeant Manka.

The war was at an end. Somewhere and sometime in the confusion of war, Jarzembowksi's wife had disappeared among the millions of slave labourers and other displaced persons. She was now legally certified as 'untraceable'. This meant that he was free to marry again. He met and married Halina Romaniuk from what is now the Ukraine, the sole survivor of a family which was subjected to reprisals after bodies of murdered German soldiers had been found locally. Forced to labour in munitions factories and then on a farm, at the war's end she began working as a nurse at a Displaced Persons' Camp in the Polish zone of occupation. There she met WO1 Jarzembowksi. They married upon his return to England, and eventually raised a family of four, Aleksander having joined the Polish resettlement corps.

Now, once again, fate turned traitor when politicians used the lives of disbanded heroes as pawns during international negotiations. The British Government under Churchill had announced a policy that "the British Government will give such assistance as is in its power to enable those who fought with us throughout the war to start a new life outside Poland with their families and dependents". But now Clement Atlee had been elected Prime Minister and had chosen as his Foreign Minister Ernest Bevin.

The new British Government decided to accede to a demand from Stalin, who insisted on the return of freedom fighters like the Poles to their countries of origin, now Communist-ruled. In a sad perpetuation of the 'perfidious Albion' legend, Bevin stated that he was satisfied with assurances from the new Communist puppet government in Warsaw of fair treatment for 'returnees'. He wrote to all Poles in Britain, saying: "Speaking on behalf of the British Government, I declare it is in the best interest of Poland that you should return to her now." Effectively, the expatriate Poles in Britain became stateless and unsupported overnight.

A minority returned to Poland, where numbers of them were charged and either executed, imprisoned for long periods, or denied full citizenship. There was history between the states: when the original Polish officer corps surrendered in 1939, Stalin had eventually, in one brutal act, had them all executed and buried in a mass grave.

Some Poles staying in Britain endured the hardship and eventually prospered. For others the task was beyond their ability to adapt. An extraordinary example of their travail was that of Maczek himself, peacetime Professor of Philosophy and wartime outstanding tactician. He was able to find work only as a bar tender in Glasgow. He managed to live on until after his 100th birthday when the new democratic government of Lech Walesa took power in December 1990. Walesa himself made the journey to Scotland to restore to the heroic general his rank, pension and reputation.

Meanwhile, with the Cold War hardening attitudes towards the USSR, Aleksander and Halina persevered in England, he qualifying and working until retirement with the Woolf engineering company in their electrical tools factory. He dedicated his spare time to organising and administering the Polish Combatants Association in London, ensuring continued Remembrance, later aided and succeeded in this venture by son Janusz. The youngest son of his first marriage, Tadeusz, founded 'Solidarity with Solidarity' in London in 1981, becoming the public figure in the UK of Walesa's Solidarity movement.

After so many years of war and disillusionment, Aleksander Jarzembowski had very firm ideas about life and warfare. He was specific about certain national characteristics in battle. He admired the Germans' technical prowess but not their individual fighting ability. He viewed the "Yanks" as poor fighters, "overloaded with so much kit as to make them soft", but considered the "Brits" to be "gritty and committed". On the whole he felt that soldiers were appreciated only in wartime. He was cynical about war films in general, terming them "*lipa*", or make-believe. He thought that politics and the army were generally separate entities, so he would blame politicians for wartime atrocities but not the soldiers who were forced to fight.

He did not blame the Nazis for everything, but pointed also to Russian crimes, including blaming them for the death of General Sikorski, (Prime Minister of the Polish Government in Exile from late September 1939) in an air crash in 1943. He considered that Communism would not prevail forever in Europe. Because of this, when an opportunity came to emigrate to Canada, he preferred to stay in London, saying that it would be a shorter route back home when the time came. His own time did not come, for he died too soon in 1988.

Herein lay the ultimate tragedy for many Poles who decided to fight on, for freedom and democracy, from a French or British base in 1939 and 1940. When the 10th Cavalry stood at the Tatarska Pass on the border of Poland and were ordered to evacuate and find their way to new battles, many must have thought it would be '*Daleko do domu*', a long way home. But for thousands, and not just those who fell by the wayside of battle, there never was a way back home.

14

Audie Murphy

First Lieutenant Audie Leon Murphy, Congressional Medal of Honor, DSC, Legion of Merit, American, 15th Infantry Regiment, US Army (Major, National Guard)

So many trials, so many battles, so many medals, so many fans, but neither fame nor the pistol under the pillow is defence against the ghosts that may lurk within the mind or behind the silver screen.

Rarely has the distinction between the hero and the man become so blurred. The calm assessment of his personal attributes, 'what he was', is so easily submerged in the saga of his extraordinary actions, 'what he did'. Was there a true man hidden under all those medals? Was he really what he appeared to be in this or that incarnation, Leon, Audie, Henry Fleming (his role in one film) or Joe Maybe (in another film)?

Some of the portrayals of Audie Murphy's outrageous courage might seem to suggest exaggeration. When blood counts are quoted stating precisely how many enemy soldiers were killed by one man, they can savour of simplification, if not enhancement. And, as any front-line soldier will witness, it is often impossible to know which bullet actually hit the enemy, whose gun fired that bullet, whether there was a multiple involvement or even if there was no bullet and simply a heart attack?

However, one aspect of Murphy's story, which might be termed a 'rags to riches' saga, carries an aura of authenticity. He was the very poor boy who made it rich in more than one respect. But what is not always queried is to what extent that humble boy continued and contrived to exist under the gaudy trappings of fame.

Audie Leon Murphy was born one of a family of 12 children, the son of Emmett Berry Murphy, a Texas sharecropper. A sharecropper farmed on a landlord's estate without rights of tenancy, and was prey to the erratic luck of the harvests. Murphy senior was an occasional apparition at the family home and eventually disappeared from their ken while Leon, as he was then known, was still at school. The boy had to abandon studies early, seek work and then take over as head of the household when his mother became ill and died. In order to eke out the meagre family income, Leon

Audie Murphy, the squalor of battle ended but
not forgotten. (United States Army photo)

went hunting regularly and kept the family cooking pot supplied. In this pursuit he became an expert marksman, skilled in field craft.

It was not surprising that he later had difficulty in adjusting socially. He spent much time alone, exhibited a quick temper and was subject to mood changes. If psychiatric services had been available at the time, he might have been diagnosed as suffering from depression, or even schizophrenia, and that possibly contributed to some of his post-war problems, if not to some acts in battle.

Having tried to maintain the large family by various poorly paid jobs, he then agreed with his eldest sister on a two-part plan. The three youngest siblings would be placed in care for their own safety and betterment, whilst his eldest sister would help him to falsify his age in order to join the armed forces. He could serve his country and also ensure a regular pay packet. Unfortunately, when he applied to the Navy, and then the Marine Corps, the recruitment officers surveyed his frail physique – a mere stripling, 5ft 5-in tall and 110lb – and declined to accept him. This left the infantry as an option, where his marksmanship would be most useful. Indeed, during initial training he quickly won a marksman's badge. At this time Murphy abandoned his childhood name of Leon and said "call me Audie or Murph". Was this a symbol of his new imperative?

Fighting initially in Sicily and Italy, Murphy soon began to gain respect, medals and promotion. Early awards were for mad, primitive charges. These seemed to spring not so much from sheer bravery or skill, but rather from a fervid impatience with the pace of the battle and the enemy's tardiness in surrendering. The high award of the Distinguished Service Cross related to a charge up a hill in southern France where several German machine guns were sited. One of the enemy made signs of surrender. Murphy's comrade stood up to accept the surrender and was promptly shot and killed. It was an understandable pure fury which sent Murphy on the quest to clear the entire hill of all living enemies.

The unusual number of valour awards, and the circumstances in which they were gained, tend to portray the man as almost robotic and not subject to the inhibitions of the average soldier. Murphy was quite frank about that:

> Ten seconds after the first shot was fired at me by an enemy soldier, combat was no longer glamorous. But it was important because all of a sudden I wanted very much to stay alive ... Sometimes it takes more courage to get up and run [away] than to stay. I got so scared the first day of combat I just decided to go along with it.

Having risen through the non-commissioned ranks very rapidly, Murphy was offered a promotion and commission. But he was dubious about his own mental abilities and refused the commission, fearing that his lack of formal schooling would render him unable to cope with the responsibilities required of an officer. Very soon, as he continued to display outstanding qualities, the offer was repeated. Already more worldly wise, as well as an inch taller and many pounds heavier, he decided to accept the challenge. It must be remembered that all this happened whilst he was still aged only 18 and 19.

This meant that by the time he and his battalion entered the climactic battle at Holtzwihr near Colmar, on the border of France and Germany, he was a lieutenant platoon commander. He was also wearing every gallantry medal available except the Congressional Medal of Honor, the American equivalent of the Victoria Cross. His earliest demonstrations of valour had been mainly the results of an almost instinctive reaction, employing a basic hunter's skills. Now, at Holtzwihr, he would be required to exhibit an extraordinary combination of tactical nous and physical prowess, almost the role of a patient poker player with a heavyweight boxer's ability to soak up physical punishment.

January 1945 saw the Germans clinging on to their last foothold on French soil in the so-called Colmar Pocket. In late August 1944, the Allies in Normandy had all but eliminated the German army there. The subsequent hectic advance from the Seine liberated much of northern France. It is sometimes forgotten that, at this juncture, vast areas of southern and eastern France had not yet been liberated. Free French and American forces, including Audie Murphy's 30th Division of infantry, landed in the south of France during Operation *Dragoon* and drove northwards.

By the turn of the year the Germans had been pushed back towards Alsace-Lorraine, territory that was constantly disputed between Germany and France over the decades. Hitler had a sentimental attachment to the region, ordering a 'fight to

the death' defence. His most powerful Nazi collaborator, Heinrich Himmler, head of
the *SS* and the *Gestapo*, took personal command of the Colmar Army Group.

In the strategic Holtzwihr area the Germans had introduced reinforcements from
the 2nd Mountain Division, which had been training in Norway, troops fresh, fit and
ideally suited to the weather and terrain. The infantry were supported by a *Panzer*
unit of tanks and tank destroyers. The battle would rage around the vital strategic
point of the Bois de Riedwihr, a large dense forest dominating the road to Holtzwihr
and a key element in closing the Colmar Pocket. The first two days of fierce fighting
caused massive casualties in the American units involved. Murphy found himself the
only officer left alive in B Company. Out of 120 other ranks only 18 remained fit for
battle, and in the bitter winter weather along ice-bound roads across a snow-covered
landscape there would be delays in bringing up reinforcements.

Overnight on 25 January, B Company was ordered to form a defence line along
the southern edge of the forest, dig in and await the inevitable counter-attack up the
rough road which led into the forest. The weather was described as 'Siberian', with
temperatures down to -20C and snow 3ft deep. It was certainly the coldest weather
some of the Americans had ever experienced as they endeavoured, with futile pick
and shovel, to make some impression on the solidly frozen earth. Texas lad Murphy
later reflected that at least the continuous digging saved them from being frozen to
death, a fate not unknown to soldiers that winter.

Dawn came, and sunrise, but as yet no attack. The company was reinforced by two
M10 tank destroyers. Known to the British as the Achilles, the M10 had an anti-tank
gun in an open turret, but was set on the tracks and hull of a normal M4 Sherman.
In addition to the big gun, there was also a .50 calibre Browning machine gun fixed
on the rear lip of the turret and originally intended for anti-aircraft work. It fired a
much larger round than the average machine gun, such as the .30 Browning or the
.303 Bren. This legendary heavy machine gun was to play a decisive role in the action
ahead.

About midday there was movement in the distance, and it was soon possible to
discern a mass of infantrymen with several tanks assembling for a counter-attack,
aiming to advance along the road and through the forest. The German mountain
troops were in their white winter smocks they began to advance towards the
forest. In front of them, a heavy German barrage crept towards the waiting men of B
Company and their two tank destroyer comrades. Murphy took the field telephone
and got connected directly to the artillery, giving them the location of the advancing
German troops. Within minutes the area was ablaze with two opposing barrages as
the white-clad mass of troops continued to press cautiously forward. *Panzers* just
ahead of them opened fire. One of the American tank destroyers was hit and caught
fire. The other fought back. Then the commander moved his vehicle, seeking a better
position. The tracks failed to grip on the frozen ground, the unwieldy vehicle sliding
off the road into a drainage ditch. It landed at such an angle that its gun would be
useless. The crew retreated.

Seeing the probability of his tiny unit being overwhelmed, Murphy sent them
back into the tree line. He remained lying on the ground, phoning to the artillery

commander the changes of range as the inexorable mass of enemy closed in, the *Panzers* adding their 75mm shells to the storm of fire, smoke and snow mist. In between talk with the artillery, Murphy was able to fire his carbine, but to little effect upon the general tide of advance. The range which he was calling in was now bringing friendly shells down on his own position as the enemy came within 20 yards or so. When a worried lieutenant from regimental headquarters came on the phone to enquire as to the present location of the enemy, Murphy, somewhere between humour and irritation, shouted back: "If you will hold the phone for a minute I will let you talk to one of the bastards."

This one diminutive man with a carbine and a field telephone was in a hopeless situation. Murphy was contemplating a fast retreat. Then the burning M10 caught his eye. With the poorly protected petrol and ammunition storage inside the basic Sherman hull, the 'Tommy Cooker', as it was known, would erupt in a cremation fire 30ft high. But this M10, whilst gushing smoke, was still apparently intact. And the big .50 Browning was there unharmed, conspicuous above the smoke.

Murphy ran across, climbed on to the vehicle and began to fire the gun, whose large bullets and violent clamour could strike fear into attacking infantry. At first the enemy seemed unable to account for the bursts of heavy machine-gun fire. Murphy became aware of enemy soldiers halted in the haze nearby, apparently discussing their next move. They never had the chance to make it.

The danger and difficulties of using the .50 can hardly be exaggerated. The gun and the gunner, perched high aloft above the battlefield, had no protection whatever. Effective though the gun was, the M10 carried only a limited supply of the large calibre bullets, which were stored in boxes of 50. Murphy had no loader to replenish his ammunition. He might have to push past two dead men in the turret to locate and load further rounds. He knew his supply was limited, so could only afford to fire short bursts. Above all, the fire within the vehicle must be approaching the high octane petrol supply, which would set off an explosion violent enough to consume a man before he could leap to safety.

The initiative was wrested from Murphy's hands. Two *Panzer* shots slammed into the M10 and Murphy was badly wounded. The .50 machine gun jammed; it was out of ammunition. However, with the American barrage continuing to devastate the entire area, the German attack began to falter and slowly move back. The *Panzers*, reluctant to be left without infantry support, were also retiring. Finally, the clouds opened and American fighter-bombers appeared, circling above. In one last phone conversation, Murphy guided the artillery as their guns put down coloured smoke to mark the enemy positions for the fighter-bombers to attack. At that precise moment the field telephone went dead.

Murphy limped back to his remaining men. In addition to his new injury, they saw that his trousers were soaked in blood from a previous wound which had reopened. As Murphy rejoined his comrades at the edge of the woods, the M10 exploded, blowing the turret completely off the tank. Although in pain, Murphy was still mobile enough to gather all available troops and surge back across the battlefield, ensuring that it was now totally clear of enemy troops. These latter, disillusioned and disorganised, were already in a backward movement which would leave the soil of France completely clear of Nazi troops before the end of the month.

One of those involved in this action, Charles Owen, commented: "He saved our lives. If he hadn't done what he did the Germans would have annihilated us. We were already beat down pretty bad and about out of ammunition." Private Brad Croeker said: "He was too darn daring for most of us. His middle name was 'Lucky'." Bill Weinberg added: "I think he was just willing to stick his neck out. But it was a matter of being careful too. He took more chances than others, but he did it in a calculated way."

The status of having won more awards for gallantry than anyone else was not achieved without physical suffering for Murphy. At Holtzwihr, as already recounted, an earlier wound reopened at the moment of suffering a further injury. In October 1944 he had been shot in the hip by a sniper, not the first of his wounds. The bullet had glanced off a tree and carried with it infecting shreds of bark. It was three days before he could be evacuated to a hospital, during which time the wound had become gangrenous. This cost him months in hospital and the partial loss of hip muscle. He also twice spent weeks in hospital for illness, including malaria. So much for physical injury; only time would tell the more complicated story of enduring psychological wounds.

For Murphy, the immediate aftermath of war was a continuing parade of welcome and celebration. His face appeared on the covers of publications. Away in Hollywood, leading actor James Cagney was impressed by the good-looking, youthful face and persuaded Murphy to try his luck in films. Murphy was soon cast as film star Alan Ladd's West Point roommate in 'Beyond Glory' (1948). A major role followed as Henry Fleming in 'The Red Badge of Courage' (1951). In that film, presenting the reverse of the real Private Murphy, Private Fleming is overcome by fear and deserts his regiment during his first battle in the American Civil War. The film was a success, as was Murphy's own portrayal of himself in 'To Hell and Back'. Another film saw him opposite Sir Michael Redgrave in 'The Quiet American' (1958). He was involved in a further 40 films, mainly of the cowboy genre, notably 'Ride a Crooked Trail' (1958). In that Western, playing opposite Walter Matthau, he was Joe Maybe, a bank robber-turned-sheriff. He later formed his own film company and also worked on television.

Critics have been particularly scathing about Murphy's abilities as an actor, but no more dismissive than the man himself. He observed: "Acting? Only one problem: no talent!" He also thought little of his chosen film genre, saying pithily: "I'm a two bag man! By the time I'm finished with shooting up all the villains, the audience has gone through two bags of popcorn each." Surprisingly, a viewer who trawls the backwaters of television channels 70 years later, in the second decade of the twenty-first century, is likely to discover a film featuring Audie Murphy as often as any other name from that period.

Hollywood had welcomed home established film stars who were also war veterans, such as Clark Gable and David Niven. It is a strange sidelight on Audie Murphy's attitude that, when invited to social gatherings of top stars, he often went missing. His friends remembered that he was more likely to be chatting not to the stars but to film technicians, camera crews and stunt men. When a gala event was organised to salute him in Dallas, Texas, he escaped to the kitchen, enjoying the company of the staff. Similarly, when all society went to the races he might be found not in the cocktail bars but sitting behind the stands playing his guitar and singing. Two different Audie Murphys were rapidly developing.

The public Audie had a brief, disastrous marriage to actress Wanda Hendrix, earned millions of dollars, bred thoroughbred horses, established a large ranch, gambled most of his riches away, became separated from an adoring second wife and had eventually to declare himself bankrupt. He had become addicted to gambling and it was said that he would even bet on which trickle of rain would be the first to run down the windscreen of a car.

The other Audie Murphy was writing songs of some merit, performed by singers like Dean Martin. Some of the songs were unrestrained cries emanating from a mental affliction, still not understood at the time, with lamentations like 'Is there a short cut to nowhere?', 'My lonesome room' and 'Leave the weeping to the willow tree'. One song requests 'Mister Music Man' to play "a tune to mend a broken heart, so play it tenderly". Perhaps the most striking is the poem 'The Crosses grow on Anzio', where "Hell is six feet deep".

It was not until 1980 that the American Medical Association and the Veterans Administration recognised the diagnosis and terminology of PTSD, Post Traumatic Stress Disorder. Murphy, potentially the most interesting case study for the illness, had been killed in a plane crash in 1971. Although there was in his lifetime no authorised definition of his condition other than 'battle fatigue', Murphy was well aware of it and decided to speak out when he saw how contemporary veterans were being treated by the armed forces. He had for a long time been sleeping with a pistol, a Colt or a Walther, under his pillow, enduring sleepless nights and, when he could sleep, waking up screaming. He became addicted to strong anti-depressants, including the habit-forming Placidyl. In his misery he locked himself inside a hotel room for a week to break the drug habit.

Second World War veteran and eminent politician Bob Dole later referred to Murphy as "a true pioneer in PTSD awareness" who had "helped to turn the tables on the stigma often associated with PTSD" and was an advocate for returning veterans of overseas wars. Using his gift of the appropriate metaphor, Murphy had condemned the military authorities, stating: "After the war they took the [army] dogs and rehabilitated them. But they turned soldiers into civilians and left them to sink or swim."

When Murphy was killed at such an early age in 1971, his message on PTSD was not silenced. His second wife, Pamela Archer, although separated from Audie in his last years, continued his mission. She worked for the Veterans Administration, at first employed and later voluntarily, as a veterans liaison worker. She encouraged mentally stricken veterans to seek professional aid. She ensured that the military and medical staffs made adequate provision, both for the individual and for the increasing multitude of men suffering after exposure to new types of warfare. Included were air force crews who had been required to slaughter civilians using weapons such as napalm bombs. Pamela carried on her campaign for nearly 40 years after Audie's demise.

One of her patients declared: "Nobody could cut through the VA red tape faster than Mrs Murphy. She was our angel." Her message would have been reinforced by her own awareness of the ways in which Audie has been afflicted and emerged as a dual personality.

Specific incidents illustrated the two sides of Murphy's behaviour. At the extreme of anger and provocation, he once drew a gun on his first wife. Later he physically assaulted a man in an argument and then shot at him. Being a remarkable marksman, had Murphy intended that shot to hit the target it would certainly have done so. However, he stood trial and was acquitted, but with consequent damage to his reputation at the time.

In contrast, it was reported that when a well-known Hollywood brawler named Lawrence Tierney began to insult a woman in Murphy's presence, the war veteran, without raising his voice or making any physical motion, caused the brawler to desist and leave the room. Murphy clearly had the power of *coup d'oeil* which compelled obedience. There were reports that some film crew were afraid of his cold stare. On the other hand, after their divorce, first wife Wanda could still comment: "Audie had a beautiful smile. Unfortunately he didn't smile much." Another friend described him as having "a fragile-looking physique, boyish looks and his speech was a gentle, unhurried Texas drawl".

In mid-life, Murphy had increasing problems with gambling, womanising, financial misjudgements and marital estrangement, yet he clung to certain high standards. He was offered a lucrative contract to advertise beer. His response was: "How would it look 'War Hero drinks booze'? I couldn't do that to the kids." Equally he turned down advertising opportunities for cigarettes.

So much about Audie Murphy's life, including his death by air crash, was extraordinary that it is difficult to identify the ordinary man behind it all. Greater understanding of PTSD enables a better assessment of some of the violence, to himself and to others in later life. It does not explain the apparent sudden eruptions of extreme violence in battle. Was there a repressed mental overdrive, derived from youthful frustrations, building up to danger level and only awaiting a channel of opportunity, good or evil? As a very young lad his prospects were totally restricted by stature, poverty, lack of education, loyalty to his siblings and care for a dying mother. The eventual valiant soldier must have been struggling to emerge throughout those years of helplessness. When that stress was released in the chaos of battle, the explosion was remarkable. Was it an early-life episode of PTSD?

Audie Murphy's incomparable list of bravery awards was compressed into a very brief time period as follows (in order of official merit):

Congressional Medal of Honor (gained 26 January 1945)
Distinguished Service Cross (15 August 1944)
Silver Star with bronze oak leaf (2 October 1944)
Second award of Silver Star (5 October 1944)
Legion of Merit (22 January to 18 February 1945)
Bronze Star with oak cluster (2 March 1944)

Second award of Bronze Star (8 May 1944)

Purple Hearts (in recognition of wounds) (15 September 1944, 26 October 1944, 25 January 1945)

As an illustration of the relative value of these awards, one of the Bronze Stars was gained for the single-handed destruction of an enemy tank at close quarters using rifle grenades.

Murphy produced an autobiography as well as starring in the feature film of his war experiences, with interesting variations between the two versions (a battle in the film is out of order, film makers being a law unto themselves). There is virtually no record of him ever boasting of his actions in normal social intercourse. His approach was too realistic. He admitted that: "I never liked being called the most decorated soldier. Many other guys should have gotten medals but were killed and never got a medal." Going further with his discomfort on the issue, he gave away many of his medals, mostly to young people.

He declared: "I was scared before every battle. That old instinct of self-preservation is a pretty basic thing. But, while the action was going on, some part of my mind shut off and my training and discipline took over. I did what I had to do." He had his own concept of valour which had little of the glamour of the films: "Bravery is just determination to do a job that you know has to be done. I just fought to stay alive, like anyone else, I suppose."

In one respect he made a positive statement of modesty. He knew that, as a holder of the Congressional Medal of Honor, he was destined to be buried in the National Cemetery at Arlington alongside great leaders and warriors of the ages. The head-stones traditionally had golden inscriptions. Audie Murphy willed that his headstone should be sober, grey and without gilt. So it was willed, so it was done and so it remains.

15

Maurice Rose

Major-General Maurice Rose, DSC, DSM, Silver Star and Oak Leaf Cluster, American, 3rd Armored (*Spearhead*) Division, killed in action 30 March 1945

You'll know him by the pink jodhpurs, his polished riding boots, his general's insignia and just two motor cyclists for escort. And you may well find that he has arrived at the start line before you.

Maurice Rose was exceptional in at least two respects: he was the only Jewish general in the American Army in the Second World War; and he was the highest-ranked American serviceman to be killed in action by direct enemy fire in the front line, or indeed ahead of the front line, during the campaigns from D Day to VE Day. The higher-ranking General McNair was killed in the front line in Normandy, but by friendly fire in the shape of an errant USAAF bomb.

Maurice Rose's extraordinary zeal to be always at the front is perhaps best illustrated by the experience of an ordinary GI, Art Diamond of the 104th Infantry Division. Towards the end of February 1945, near Cologne, Art's detachment had been sent to clear a roadblock which had been intensively mined by the Germans. There had been casualties but the enemy had been driven back and the roadblock was now dismantled. The leading American tanks, which had been waiting a mile back, revved up and rolled forward. An open half-track overtook them and rattled up to the roadblock. Art was astonished to see, jumping out of the vulnerable vehicle, a tall man with two white stars on his helmet: a general!

The general came up to the roadblock, looking forward along the road, then talking to casualties and "giving consideration to the men he commanded". After about five minutes the tall man departed. Art, who had never seen a general close-up before, asked one of the men in the half-track: "Who is this wonderful guy?" The reply came: "That's our man, General Rose. He's always up front. He's always doing things like this." That roadblock may not have been under enemy fire at that moment, but it was well within range. On an earlier occasion Rose had led from the front in an even more hazardous situation.

Maurice Rose, ever in close command. (Courtesy of
3rd Armored Division, 'Spearhead', Association)

On 28 August 1944, following the great Operation *Cobra* breakout from Normandy, American armour was driving rapidly south. Then the lead tanks came to a halt because the main bridge ahead of them had been mined, a normal German tactic. The first infantry company arriving had been able to remove some mines but was unable to guarantee that there were no undiscovered mines or booby traps left. They were waiting for an engineer to appear and confirm that the bridge was now safe to cross. Instead of an engineer there arrived a single jeep containing the divisional commander, Maurice Rose.

Upon hearing what the problem was, Rose's reaction was immediate and simple. He ordered his driver to drive him across the bridge. So they drove across the bridge. There was no explosion. To be doubly certain, Rose ordered his driver to take him back over the bridge. So they crossed the bridge again. Again, no explosion. Problem solved, the advance thundered on. It had been an enormous risk which might have deprived the American Army of a divisional commander.

Such an action might indeed have been interpreted as reckless, bearing in mind Rose's rank and strategic responsibilities. It does, however, provide an insight into his attitude to command, as also his scant regard for his own welfare. In the end it contributed to the swelling saga of valour and initiative that inspired an entire division, the *Spearhead*, to the point where it could lay a claim to being the outstanding armoured unit in the field.

Every aspect of Rose's career suggests that this son of a Jewish rabbi had developed his own rabbinical approach to military service: deeply thoughtful, highly principled and fiercely dedicated. His constant appearance at the front of the front was not the result of a daredevil or cavalier search for fame. It sprang from a conviction that this forward view always enabled him more promptly and accurately to direct the affairs of his huge military formation from the tip of the spearhead. He would have known and calculated the risks. His gamble with his own life held true until the end of the war was in sight. By March 1945 some combatants were, perhaps understandably, taking steps to avoid undue risk at such a late stage. Then, just 39 days before the guns fell silent, Rose's nemesis struck in a manner which no fiction writer would have dared to invent.

American armoured divisions were dashing to encircle the Ruhr, the industrial heart of Germany. Rose's division was moving along a number of roads converging on the vital city of Paderborn. Remarkably, nearly 100 miles had been covered in a day. Another such advance could possibly open up the road to Berlin itself. However, in the vicinity of Paderborn and Sennelager were several training establishments from which the Germans were able to form a substantial force of elite troops with heavy armour. The latter included the formidable new 77-ton King Tiger. The Americans also now had available, to replace the Sherman, the heavier, more powerful Pershing tank of 46 tons. However, it was not yet available at the front in sufficient quantities to cancel out German armoured superiority, and only three Pershings at most were as yet at the disposal of Rose.

As the converging attacks started forward on 30 March towards Paderborn, Rose attached his small headquarters group to one column of Shermans, Task Force Welborn. His own forward party consisted of no more than three jeeps, two motor-cycles and an M20 armoured car. In his jeep were the driver, Sergeant Glenn H. Shaunce, and Major R.M. Bellinger. Colonel F.J. Brown was driving himself in the leading jeep.

At first all went well. Then, in the late afternoon, the King Tigers suddenly appeared and began to blast the tanks of the orderly Welborn column into a series of raging funeral pyres. Surviving crews dismounted and dived for shelter. Rose's small posse leapt into a ditch to survey the chaos and assess their own situation of utmost peril. Night closed in, the darkness pierced by the confusing glare of burning vehicles.

Mounting up again, Rose directed his tiny convoy up a small hill in an effort to avoid the huge German tanks, all too audible as they moved across the battlefield. Colonel Brown drove the first jeep into a lane and was immediately confronted by a tank, presuming it to be one of their own Shermans. However, as Brown swung the jeep past the tank in the small space available, he realised that he was looking at the exhaust system not of a Sherman but of a German tank. Brown was able to squeeze past and hasten on. Rose's driver, Shaunce, following closely, tried to swerve and slip past the tank in the way that the first jeep had done. Perversely, the great bulk, seeming so much mightier in the darkness, slewed around at the same time. Rose's jeep crashed into the tank and became jammed and then crushed between the vehicle and a tree. The puny jeep was locked tight to a King Tiger.

The next few moments were of total confusion. Rose jumped down from the jeep as the German tank commander, a shadowy silhouette, stood up in the turret. The tank man was yelling incomprehensibly and pointing a sub-machine gun. Rose appeared to reach for his revolver, possibly to drop it in surrender. As Shaunce and Bellinger took evasive action, the tank commander fired a burst, hitting Rose. Two bullets penetrated his helmet and others hit his body. Immediately the general fell dead.

It appears that the German tanks proceeded on their way in the darkness, totally unaware of the identity of the man who had been killed. On the American side, an immediate enquiry studied the possibility that Rose had been surrendering and therefore the shooting should be considered as a war crime. Rose had been heard to shout back to the screaming, gesticulating tank commander, but his last words appeared to have been simply "*no versteh*" (I don't understand).

Whilst Shaunce thought that Rose's hands were raised in surrender, and repeated that at the official enquiry, Bellinger could not confirm it. Given Rose's normal imperturbability and the imminent end of hostilities, it is unlikely that the general would, either hastily or with due forethought, consider firing a pistol at a heavily armoured tank, with a commander waving a sub-machine gun up above and a gunner inside watching through a night sight. On the other hand it was a chaotic situation. In the confusion, Shaunce ducked underneath the enemy tank and escaped unharmed. The enquiry failed to pursue the 'war crime' issue and closed the file. The King Tiger tank commander was never identified.

The future general was born on 26 November 1899, in Middletown, Connecticut, the son of Rabbi Sam Rose. Sam himself was the son of a Warsaw rabbi but later emigrated to the United States. This meant that Maurice, who was educated in Denver, was just of age to enlist in the US Army for the First World War.

He had already revealed a disposition for military adventure. When he was only 16, the United States Army had advanced into Mexico in a punitive expedition against the outlaw and revolutionary 'Pancho' Villa. Maurice Rose falsified his age in order to join the Colorado National Guard as part of the venture. However, his family discovered this escapade and advised the commanding officer as to Maurice's true age. He was speedily sent home.

When America entered the war in Europe in April 1917, Maurice enlisted and was commissioned in time to participate in the first great American offensive at Saint-Mihiel, where he was wounded. After treatment he was able to continue in the fighting line until the end of the war. In peacetime he continued military studies, was gradually promoted and became a trainer, latterly moving from infantry postings to specialising in armoured warfare.

By the time America again entered a European war, via the 1942 *Torch* landings in North Africa, Rose was holding a staff appointment with 1st Armored Division. After severe fighting, Rose was sent to negotiate the first surrender of a complete German command amounting to tens of thousands of men. This success led to the invasion of Sicily, where Rose was promoted to brigadier general in charge of a Combat Command.

The Americans had two types of armoured division. Most of their armoured divisions were more or less of the size of British armoured divisions. There were also 'heavy' armoured divisions which could field almost as many tanks as the total number which the three British armoured divisions used for Operation *Goodwood* in 1944. However, for some battle situations a full heavy division was too large and unwieldy. A division would more often operate as three combat commands (CCs), designated A, B and R for Reserve, or CCA, CCB and CCR

On D Day, Rose was commanding CCA of the 2nd Armored Division en route for Normandy. It was in the immediate aftermath of D Day that he demonstrated both his genius for personal leadership and his mastery of tactical command of a large fighting force. The two American landing beaches, Utah and Omaha, were not contiguous but were widely separated, as distinct from the British and Canadian beaches which were continuous, the latter affording a quickly linked defence line. A dangerous gap existed between Utah and Omaha. Generals on both sides were well aware of this factor.

Veteran German airborne troops (the *Fallschirmjäger*) were sent to confront their equivalents from America (101st Airborne) and prevent the link-up of the two beaches. For several days the two elite formations fought each other to a standstill in the area around Carentan. The Germans had already brought in *Panzers* to boost their tired airborne men. By 13 June the moment of decision had come.

Rose's CCA had been destined for another task and was heading in a direction away from the Carentan confrontation. Suddenly, because of secret intelligence sent via Ultra (the code name for signals intelligence obtained by breaking high-level encrypted German communications at Bletchley Park), the entire command was required to break formation, turn around upon itself in a very constricted space and race in the opposite direction. The airborne troops were ordered to resume the attack and finally establish a firm link between the beaches, forming an unbroken defence line.

Understandably, the American airborne men were desperately weary and had dug themselves in deep where they had managed to advance. They seemed in no condition to mount another attack. Then, to their astonishment, there appeared among them a very tall, grim officer wearing a one-star helmet, jodhpurs and riding boots. His escort had been two motorcyclists. Apparently unconcerned about personal safety, he walked down the middle of the exposed main road with his only armament, his pistol, still in the holster. Finding an airborne officer, he ordered, in a voice loud enough for all to hear, that the infantry should get out of their holes and advance again.

Men who had fought and suffered high casualties for days, in what they called 'the Bloody Gulch', might have been moved to derision, or even mutiny, by such an intrusion from an unknown cavalry officer. But allied to the cool determination of this strange general there was the swelling sound of the leading tanks of CCA hurrying to catch up with their walking commander. It was a moment which swung a vital battle.

Soon both infantrymen and tankers were experiencing a hazard which Allied intelligence and planners seem to have ignored. Areas of Normandy were covered by the *bocage*, a wooded jungle. Its main feature, as any French farmer could have advised Allied planners, was the vast hedgerows, 12ft or more high, correspondingly thick and set up on banks themselves at least 2ft high. These ramparts, efficient enough to exclude wild animals or marauders of earlier centuries, were also ideal locations for men armed with modern weapons like the tank-destroying hand-held *Panzerfaust* or the ultra-fast *Spandau* machine gun.

Rarely could an infantryman break through such a hedge. Tanks might break into the hedge but, in doing so, would have to climb the bank, exposing the poorly protected bottom of the hull to any enemy stalker waiting beyond the hedge. To make matters worse, many fields were so small that, the moment a tank broke through one hedge, it needed to be revving up to charge at the hedge on the opposite side of the field.

Although Major Gneral Percy Hobart's 79th Armoured Division had been equipped with all kinds of 'Funnies', nothing had been done to prepare for piercing the hedges of the *bocage*.

It fell to two tank sergeants, Roberts and Culin, men originating from America's farmlands, to devise a solution to the problem. It was simply to fix steel cutters like plough shares to the front of tanks so that the lead tank could pluck up and demolish both the hedge and the bank supporting it. Fortunately Roberts and Culin did not have to contend with any snobbish rejection by higher command of an idea which emanated from mere non-commissioned officers. Within days sufficient tanks were equipped with the *Rhino* cutting device that quick penetration through hedges became a tactical reality.

Once the front around Carentan had been established, the Germans withdrew to make the town of St Lo their next defensive bastion. With British and Canadian troops still locked in a battle of attrition around Caen, thus engaging a major part of the German forces, it was planned that American armour should break out beyond St Lo to the west. In Operation *Cobra* this advance would develop into a rapid encircle-ment of the German armies in Normandy, linking up with the British, Canadians and Polish around Falaise.

Rose's CCA would be required to leap ahead at full speed, often bypassing static enemy positions and always probing for an opening towards the open country to the south. One of Rose's men, Lieutenant Belton Cooper, afforded an unusual view of the size of the force under Rose's command:

> The entire Command concentrated in an extremely small area in the Bois du Hommet. We had tanks, half-tracks, artillery pieces and wheeled vehicles jammed bumper to bumper, some 4,400 vehicles in an area approximately one mile square. This was completely contrary to our training. The fact that the German *Luftwaffe* showed little strength during daylight, and the fact that we had to concentrate like this for the massed attack to come off rapidly enough, made the risk worthwhile. An amazing sight.

Rose might have been considered to be busy enough directing the manoeuvres of such a large and complex formation and justified in leaving platoon or company detail to juniors. In fact his front-line instincts led him, in discussion with junior commanders, to devise a novel tactic for the small formation of tanks at the very tip of the advance. Within the first few weeks after D Day, the Americans were alerted to the disparity in armament and power between the Sherman and the German Tiger and Panther tanks. Even their version of the British Firefly, carrying a 76mm gun, though lethal as a defensive weapon shooting from cover, was, like the Firefly, a burden in an open attack. It was easily identified and an obvious first target for enemy guns, and still suffered from the relatively frail Sherman hull with poorly armoured storage of petrol and ammunition.

For this novel tactic, Rose's leading men would operate in a troop of five vehicles. A light Stuart tank would proceed along the central road, aiming to entice fire from hidden German guns. A very fast mobile tank, the Stuart, if not hit by the enemy's first shot, could prove an elusive target in a speedy withdrawal. To the left and right of the Stuart, amid hedges and woods, two Shermans would sweep and fire at targets of opportunity. Behind the Shermans would be two tank destroyers, whose larger guns would engage any enemy vehicle or gun unmasked by the Stuart.

In liaison with General Elwood Quesada of the US Army Air Force, Rose also introduced another immediate response weapon. Immediately behind the front command tank travelled another tank, called *Cuthbert*, commanded by an Air Force officer and using a very high frequency radio. This communicated with a 'cab rank' of four fighter-bombers which covered the lead tanks. Quesada reckoned that the previous average delay between a tank request for support and the arrival of the first plane was 88 minutes. This time lag was now eliminated. The planes up above were as closely connected into the battle network as the lead tanks themselves and could instantly respond, aiming at targets marked, if necessary, in smoke. This lead 'bunch' of troops was completed by a company of infantry riding other tanks a short way behind. The Allies had also failed to provide adequate armoured carriers for the infantry, at least until a Canadian general, Guy Simonds, invented the Kangaroo by removing turrets and guns from tank destroyer M10s.

Time after time Rose himself would appear at the point where the chaos of battle was at its worst, able to change orders and press on without delay. His arrival was always with minimum ceremony and not in a manner to alert any enemy ahead. He would be riding in an ordinary jeep distinguished only by a small rank plate, escorted by one or two motorcyclists. His frequent dress of jodhpurs and riding boots marked him out to troops confused by the fog of battle. It also added a gloss of morale-boosting distinction in the thought that, "This is our man and he is special". Whilst Rose was sometimes described as aggressive and even overbearing, there are also many reports of him stopping to talk to men at the battle's epicentre and, as Art Diamond expressed it, "showing consideration for the men he commanded".

Rose took risks, pushing the attack continually. In spite of initial losses, some of them from erroneous 'friendly' bombing, *Cobra* struck swiftly and was unleashed into open country beyond all expectations. On 7 August, Rose was promoted to major general, moving from CCA of 2nd Armored Division to command of 3rd Armored Division (also 'heavy') which he himself labelled the '*Spearhead*'.

There followed a period of open, mobile warfare which suited armoured formations more than did the enclosures of the Normandy *bocage*. Under Rose's leadership the '*Spearhead*' took part in the race across France, won a vital battle around Mons, was caught up in the bitter fighting in the frozen Ardennes and then rolled on over the

Rhine on the record-breaking thrust towards Paderborn. Along the way he became the first Allied general to lead his troops over the frontier into Germany. Even in the larger formation, Rose quickly established his almost bipolar method of command. Whilst keeping up with and inspiring the fighting men at the scene of action, he contrived to exercise remote control over his huge organisation, often widely spread across unknown country. He was constantly demanding more urgency from staff and unit commanders.

A somewhat humorous illustration of his penchant for always being as near as possible to the action occurred when his superior officer, corps commander General J. Lawton Collins, visited him in a magnificent chateau. Rose had taken the chateau as his temporary headquarters and Collins may well have assumed that Rose had been attracted by its luxury and comfort. The dining hall was indeed impressive. However, it quickly became apparent that, if anyone dared go out on the balcony to smoke a cigar, he immediately came under sniper fire from just across the river. Rose had 'camped' there because of its proximity to the enemy.

Rose himself was often portrayed as rather humourless, although there are photographs enough of a smiling Rose handing out awards to lesser ranks. He published very little, but one section of a serious article suggests a strain of humour. Rose was writing a report about a cavalry training exercise with horses in Panama in which he participated before the war: "The night of March 24th-25th was a perfect tropical night, especially designed for gay caballeros to whisper sweet nothings into the ears of coy *señoritas* to the accompaniment of the dulcet strains of strumming guitars, instead of the typical phrases so familiar to the cavalry picket line." This last metaphor referred to the atmosphere as orders, weapons and rations were handed out to his exhausted cavalry command, "which in appearance closely resembled the aggregation of a Pancho Villa, Sandino, or perhaps even Jesse James".

The essentially serious attitude of Rose's mind is perhaps better shown by the reputation of his mess table. When time permitted there was no encouragement for idle after-dinner gossip or banter. Rose always led into an in-depth discussion of a subject of some importance or profundity, in which all present were welcome to make sensible contributions. This attitude suggested a successful bloodline running from rabbi grandfather through rabbi father to analytical son. Rose had indeed been Professor of Military Science at Kansas State University. Yet he was no chair-borne intellectual. He played golf, polo and tennis at high levels, and could have been a professional at any of those games.

There is an interesting comparison between two lauded American generals, Rose and Patton. The latter, with his pearl-handled revolvers and strutting image, appeared to seek publicity and certainly was afforded the highest celebrity status, both by the media and by military commentators. The Allied ploy of pretending that on D Day Patton was commanding an army in the vicinity of the British east coast caused the German command to suspect that the main landings would be near the Channel ports rather than in Normandy. Rose did not enjoy the same media acclaim, although obviously operating at a lower level of what might be termed 'publicity interest'. But it might be said that the GI in the front-line foxhole appreciated the leader who could arrive unostentatiously, rather than one whose cavalcade might bring down enemy fire upon them.

Although born and raised in the Jewish faith, Rose had married a second Protestant woman, Virginia Barringer. There was some debate as to whether Rose himself had abandoned his family faith and become a Protestant. Arguments were offered each way, including that Rose had arranged for his son to be circumcised in the Jewish manner. However, this does not appear to have been a significant issue during Rose's lifetime.

Unfortunately, upon his death, the question arose as to whether his grave, in the Netherlands American Cemetery at Margraten near Maastricht, should be marked by the Jewish star or the Christian cross. This caused a certain animosity, setting the family against others who wished to claim Rose for the Protestant faith. The debate became heated when it was learned that a chaplain, Rabbi Benjamin Elefant, had written home to his father, Rabbi Gilbert Elefant, saying that he had "conducted service at the grave of the late Major General Maurice Rose and placed a Star of David on his grave". The argument raged for some time.

One reader wrote to the *National Jewish Monthly* saying: "I think we Jews are our own worst enemies. The whole world is acclaiming Maurice Rose as a great Jewish General … and down here is a little man with a big brush and a pot of black paint attempting to besmirch the name and character of a man who gave his life for our country."

The general view from within the US Army was that in practice Rose made no religious claims but was willing to attend any religious ceremony led by the various chaplains of his units. This attitude was confirmed by another rabbi who spent half an hour talking with Rose in January 1945. Rose's biographer, Ossad, discovered six references to Rose's religion on medical reports, ranging from 1918 to 1941. Four of these described him as "Protestant", another as "Methodist" and the last as "Episcopal". Be that as it may, there is no denying that this Jewish boy, from a distinguished rabbinical heritage and at a time of anti-Semitic attitudes, was commissioned as an American officer, rose through the ranks and became a major general, a progression unique at that time.

Two brief assessments of his character and status may sum up the impression made by Rose. A senior officer, General Ernest 'Old Gravel Voice' Harmon, stated that Rose was "a cool, able soldier, distant and removed in temperament, inclined to lead from the front … and in the end this would be his undoing". In contrast, a New York newspaper simply blazoned him as "the greatest Jewish warrior since Judas Maccabeus".

It is difficult to assess what Rose's future might have achieved had his jeep, like that of Colonel Brown, been able to shave past the German tank. He was a young general in an army which would have to maintain strength for the coming Cold War, already foreseen by some. He had academic connections and might have found the way open to various professorial opportunities. Looking back at his early attempts to enlist, and taking into account his extraordinary empathy with the GI in that front-line foxhole, he can certainly be described as 'a soldier's soldier'.

In a strange way any outcome might have been an anti-climax. There was something of inevitability, as also completeness, in his actual apotheosis: in the midst of a disintegrating vanguard, at the very tip of the spear point, his fragile jeep jammed tight up against a monstrous enemy King Tiger.

16

René Rossey

Matelot René Rossey, Ld'H (Officier), French, 1 *Fusiliers Marins* (Kieffer), attached to No.4 Commando

Under-age expatriate French boy, had never seen France, but wanted to fight for France, so tailed British troops to Haifa, but on D Day found himself first-footing ashore ... in France at last.

The statue of a bagpiper strides resolutely along the promenade at Colleville-Montgomery in Normandy, although the shrill of the pipes is no longer audible. It is a tribute to Piper Bill Millin who, against all military regulations, played the pipes as he led Lord Lovat's Special Service Brigade ashore on D Day. It is also a striking memorial for all those who fought, suffered and died along that stretch of Sword Beach.

But look again at the piper: something is missing. Where is that chubby, under-age French boy with his machine gun, and his comrades of the French *Fusiliers Marins* as they advance to storm the fortified Casino just ahead?

In Lovat's brigade, and more specifically in 4 Commando, served two troops of Frenchmen seeking revenge against the occupiers of their country. Lieutenant Colonel Dawson, 4 Commando, had courteously offered the two French troops the opportunity of being the first to wade ashore on to French soil. The *Fusiliers Marins* had gladly accepted the challenge, although inevitably to their own cost. And so *Matelot* René Rossey was there up front with his machine gun at 0730 hours on 6 June 1944. For him it had been a particularly long and arduous journey. The sea crossing from Southampton to Normandy had been only a brief final sprint after an exhausting marathon among marathons.

Rossey was born on 30 August 1926 in Tunis. His father was French, his mother Sicilian, but he had never yet trodden on the soil of *La Patrie*. The family lived in relative poverty, working mainly with olives and dates. Rossey dreamed of visiting France, but there was no money to spare for idle travel. Then in 1940, when he was at the age at which a boy might begin to plan his own long-distance adventures, Germany invaded France. The dream of visiting the home country was becoming more remote than ever as France collapsed.

Tunisia itself was to suffer the ravages of war as the British Eighth Army from the east, and the British First Army and Americans from the west, converged on the Tunisian coast in hard fighting against elite German troops. By now René's dream of a leisurely trip to France had hardened into a desire to fight for his country and defeat the invaders. He managed to join up with friendly British soldiers who were engaged in the last battles of the Tunisian campaign. There was no formal place for a rather small 16-year-old French boy within the British ranks.

Renée Rossey, wearing his treasured green beret. (*Association des fusiliers marins*, 4 Commando)

However, the Free French Forces were now recruiting and René might falsify his age in order to join them. But the nearest recruiting point was in Beirut, 1,300 miles away.

As the Allied armies in North Africa assembled to invade Sicily, a contingent of British troops was destined for Palestine. René managed to stay with the group. In Haifa in Palestine he was only a short distance from the Lebanese border and Beirut. Lebanon, at the time, was still a French mandate and was under the control of Free French Forces.

In Beirut the young René was directed to the headquarters of General Georges Catroux and, without much regard to details such as age, he was enlisted in the French Army. Recruits were urgently needed for Free French units being formed in Britain, so René was sent to London by Catroux. Having already travelled 1,300 miles from west to east, he now found himself travelling nearly 3,000 miles from east to west, having never before travelled more than a donkey trot from the family smallholding in Tunisia. At the London headquarters of General Charles de Gaulle he was sworn in as a *Fusilier Marin* with the rank of *Matelot* (seaman) and posted to the so-called Kieffer Commando.

Like the humble Tunis boy, the much older Philippe Kieffer was an expatriate. He was born in 1899 at Port-au-Prince, Haiti, of Alsatian parents, educated in Jersey and later undertook business studies in Paris. He then followed a banking career in Haiti with Canadian and American banks, before rising to boardroom level with the National Bank of the Republic of Haiti. In 1939 he decided to move to Paris. He was in France long enough to fall in love with an English lady tourist, whom he would marry. Then France collapsed, overwhelmed by the German *blitzkrieg*. Although almost 40 years old, Kieffer had volunteered for service in the French Navy as soon as war broke out. He served on a battleship and in a staff post. On the night of 18 June 1940, with the country in chaos, he caught a boat from Cherbourg to Southampton and joined the Free French Forces in England.

In 1942, impressed by the British Commando system, he volunteered to set up a Commando recruited from among French exiles in Britain. This group was already trained and active in 1943, carrying out night raids on the German-occupied coasts of France and Holland across the English Channel. By early 1944 Kieffer's group had grown into two troops incorporated in the British No. 4 Commando and were undertaking intense training in Scotland. Alongside them were other expatriate troops from Belgium, Holland, Norway, Austria, Yugoslavia, Hungary, Greece and even anti-Hitler Germans. All, like René Rossey, had set out on their own particular odyssey in order to fight for their occupied countries, even though they themselves were now so far away.

When René Rossey and others arrived at the Cameron of Lochiel estate training area near Achnacarry in the Scottish highlands, they were amazed to see graves with tombstones which stated that the occupants had been killed by live fire. Announcements indicated that only by total obedience and instant reaction to orders would trainees survive the tests and practices of the toughest of field training. René tolerated the additional transition from the sun-bleached sands of Tunis to the bleak snowfields of the Scottish highlands and answered every call. At the end of the course this still under-age, under-size exile was delighted to be awarded the coveted green beret and Commando dagger. He was affectionately known to his older comrades as the 'Benjamin' (youngest brother) and also as 'le petit Rossey'.

As Lord Lovat's brigade assembled at Warsash in Hampshire to load into their landing craft for the D Day assault, the *Fusiliers Marins* consisted of two troops, numbered 1 and 8. They were under the direct command of Kieffer, who was now a *capitaine de corvette*, equivalent to lieutenant commander. He operated from a Centaur tank where appropriate. They had small headquarters, radio, medical and transport sections. Both 1 Troop (*Enseigne de Vaisseau* Guy Vourch Lion in charge) and 8 Troop (*E. de V.* Alex Lofi) consisted of 66 infantrymen, although with naval ranks.

There was also a K Gun Troop in which *Matelot* René Rossey was the most junior member. He carried the Vickers K, a gas-cooled, rapid fire, .303 calibre machine gun fitted with a bipod and weighing almost 30lb. He also wore, on first landing, a back pack weighing another 80lb. The K gun was not in normal distribution to infantry. Early raiding groups (later the SAS) in the desert had favoured the K because it fitted neatly into any type of vehicle they might use. Upon formation as Commandos they retained faith in the K.

On 5 June the *Fusiliers Marins* climbed into their two landing craft, LCI/C 523 and 527, and sailed to join the mass of ships heading for what was still an unknown destination somewhere in Europe. A vast blanket of secrecy had been thrown around the preparations for D Day to avoid even the slightest leak of information or any aid to the enemy in breaking of codes. The last night before departing, the Commandos, like any other unit, were confined behind barbed wire to prevent desertion or leakage of information. Maps and orders for the landing were not issued until the invaders were out at sea.

Maps were very detailed in terms of topography and German defence installations. However, all place names were still replaced by an impenetrable code. However, several of the *Fusiliers* hailed from Le Havre and when they studied their maps they were delighted. They recognised the patterns of streets and courses of rivers and shapes of beaches. "It's Normandy. It's Caen and Bayeux," they cheered. In a comic moment, the lowly ranked French fighters had learned the secret which few below the rank of colonel had been permitted to know, and which the authorities, with all due earnestness, were still trying to conceal from the ordinary soldier until the actual moment of landing on a beach.

The Commando approached the beaches supported by heavy fire from naval ships, whose bombardment had already been targeting German defences for four hours. Initial resistance to the landing infantry was later considered to be relatively light, but casualties occurred from the first. As Rossey waded through the shallows he had to push his way through bodies which were floating in the deeper water. Reaching the sand he saw a comrade lying flat on the beach when it was imperative to rush forward. Angered at the man's presumed cowardice, Rossey kicked him in an effort to get him moving again. He discovered that he was kicking a corpse. Beside that corpse was another corpse, beyond which was a fatally wounded man for whom nothing could be done. In any case the orders were "Stop for nobody! Keep pressing on! *Toujours en avant!*"

Rossey's comrade *Matelot 1ère classe* Yves Meudal remembered that on reaching the promenade they found it blocked off by barbed wire which had not been cut. The Germans were directing a storm of machine-gun fire along the line of the barbed wire. They were trapped. What happened next was as weird as it was unexpected. Rossey tried to explain:

> We were pinned down on the beach, many of our comrades killed or missing. But when Lovat's piper walked up and down the beach, piping his lungs out, the Germans seemed stunned, as if they had seen a ghost. They briefly stopped firing, perhaps even to laugh, and in that brief moment we made it through the barbed wire at the top of the beach.

In spite of the danger, the consuming thought in Rossey's head, even amid all the turmoil and peril of battle, was, "This is my France. This is real. We have arrived." There was no time even for a ceremonial kiss of the sacred earth of *La Patrie*. Yves Meudal agreed: "The soil of France! This was an emotion so deep that it cannot be described. But it was there, in every one of us the same, driving us on."

The Commando had two main objectives on the bullet-swept promenade. To the attackers' right at Riva Bella towered a defensive monstrosity, the largest that Rommel had prepared along this line of beach. Termed a *Stützpunktgruppe*, it was a five-storey high blockhouse boasting six huge 155mm guns and a number of others of large calibre. It was surrounded by more than 20 machine-gun and mortar pits. It was obviously impregnable to a charge from lightly armed foot soldiers, and also to normal tank guns when available. An infantry action could do no more than isolate the complex. Its reduction would be a task for a combined force using all the resources of the 79th Armoured Division's 'Funnies'.

Away to the left towards the River Orne (the south-east boundary of Allied D Day expansion) was an apparently more attractive prospect for attackers, the somewhat ramshackle Ouistreham Casino. It was a poor shadow of the halcyon days of peace when Parisians enjoyed its location and diversions, but Rommel had been overseeing the adaptation of the building and had effectively sealed it to any simple attack.

There was no time to spend in contemplation because, once the Commando had cleared the Casino, it would not simply dig in and wait while taking counter-attack measures. The unit was required immediately to jog on a further six miles to the vital bridge over the Orne at Benouville, the famous Pegasus Bridge, named after the shoulder emblem of the British airborne troops who captured it in the early hours of D Day. This would seal the huge gap between the main promenade landings and the sector which airborne troops had seized along the river. Powerful *Panzers* waited somewhere down that road to Caen, ready to overpower any weaker formation or exploit any break in the line of battle.

So with Kieffer in personal command, René and his compatriots moved eagerly forward towards the liberation of France. The German gunners' accuracy took a bloody toll in front of the Casino. Some *Fusiliers Marins* managed to break into houses beside the Casino, but to little avail. Others found a street with a back entrance but no admission. Men fell on all sides. A medic treating a wounded man collapsed and lay still beside his patient. Troop commander Vourch was down severely wounded. Then his second in command, *E. de V.* Jean Pinelli, fell wounded, as did the other 1 Troop officer, Jean Mazeas. Firing his K gun, Rossey was wounded, but not enough to withdraw from the fight; he had come too far. Kieffer himself was more severely wounded, but also stayed with the unit.

Now was the key moment of their operation. Kieffer had the option of awaiting reinforcements, but that would risk them running behind schedule within the tight plan for reaching Caen, a goal which was always wildly optimistic. Or he could, in Casino terms, take one more throw of the dice by launching a suicidal attack and hoping that a few of his command would survive. He had just concluded that he must resume the attack when a rumble of tracks down a street announced the arrival of a tank. They all prayed that it was an Allied one.

It proved to be an amphibious Sherman DD (Duplex Drive) of the 13th/18th Hussars, one of the armoured force now hurrying ashore to support the foot soldiers. Its 75mm gun, firing both armour-piercing and high-explosive shells, could break down the barricades and flush out the Casino with overwhelming fire. Within a very brief time René Rossey was wielding his K gun to cover his first German prisoners. Their task was accomplished, but it was only one task in a lengthy list that must be completed. Rossey described how he thought his comrades had endured such an experience: "We had been so long in training, and we knew so well what we had to do, that everyone was just concentrated on their tasks. But, throughout the worst, I remember feeling such great pride at standing on French soil."

The losses of the Lovat brigade have been described as "relatively light", but that term can only be justified if related to the planners' estimate which had assumed a loss of one in every two men. The actual outcome of one-in-four in the first hour or so of combat was by no means "light", and the distribution of casualties was even more significant.

Kieffer could continue for the moment, but would then need to go back to England for treatment. Rossey could also continue, however tired and sore. Rossey's own K gun troop commander, *E. de V.* Pierre Amaury, was out of action wounded, while their third officer, *E. de V.* Augustin Hubert, lay dead. The three original officers of 1 Troop had gone for the moment, and also one of 8 Troop's officers. As for the medical section of three men, Medical Officer *L. de V.* Robert Lion had been killed. His assistant, *Quartier Maitre 1ère classe* Ouassini Bouarfa, was wounded and being evacuated. The dozens of casualties were left for the moment to *Matelot* Gwenael Bollinger, a basic medical orderly. But still their march must continue.

In the confusion of the first pelt across the promenade, a small group of *Fusiliers Marins* had separated, including another K gun man, *Matelot* Francis Guézennec (who, as an 18-year-old, had escaped from Occupied France by appropriating and sailing a tiny pinnace across the sea). They had veered between houses and found themselves rapidly advancing down an empty street with no opposition. Encountering nobody to fight, they eventually rejoined the main group as the survivors were being reorganised for the mission to the bridge.

The survivors of Commando Keiffer now set out towards this further urgent objective, and suddenly the sense of tragedy gave way to a kind of unintended comedy. Beyond the ravaged Casino battle zone, large crowds of local civilians had gathered, arms full of flowers, wine and fruit for whoever the liberators might be. They wanted to cheer, embrace, kiss, talk, welcome and dance. When they saw the 'France' badge on the soldiers' sleeves and heard the French voices of the *Fusiliers Marins*, their enthusiasm soared into delirium. It was impossible to shout down the crowd. The soldiers had, in the end, to thrust past, vigorously and even discourteously, in order to keep the tempo of their march fast enough to make up for earlier delays. Only a tiny slice of French soil had yet been liberated.

If they had hoped for some kind of relief, passing beyond Rommel's coastal defences and hastening out on the open road to Caen, they were disappointed. Rossey recalled: "All the artillery from Amfreville [beyond the river] was firing down on top of us as we progressed towards Benouville." However, there was no time to duck and take cover, waiting for a salvo to end. Away in the distance, British fighting men in red berets were waiting impatiently at Pegasus Bridge. There was no enemy in sight along the road as yet, but the link with the beaches must be made firm, the light scattering of airborne troops needing to be reinforced.

At the bridge Lord Lovat apologised for being a few minutes late. But for his men the day was still not done. Rossey and his comrades found themselves trudging back all the way they had come, albeit along the far bank of the river.

At Amfreville, roughly level with the Casino, the weary *Matelots* would happily have dropped their packs, settled down where they were and slept the sleep of their lives. Wiser counsels prevailed, however. Rossey, with his constant respect for the British leaders, stated:

Once one had arrived at Amfreville it must have been about half past seven in the evening. I remember very well that the English had said to us that it was essential that immediately we must dig [individual] holes, about 50cm wide, drop our packs into them, jump in ourselves and totally disappear. [As for] me – who did not know France – this was to have been my first night sleeping on her soil. What the heck! I have come such a long way and just to dig myself in deep and hide? It is bizarre, but it is the sort of thing that happens in life.

As Special Service troops, Lovat's men expected their mission in Normandy to be a quick 'in and out' affair. After a few days they thought they might be shipped back to Scotland for reorganisation prior to further missions. Such had been the case with raids in 1943, and further attacks might be made against other targets in Holland or Norway. It was this expectation, of a stay of only a few days in his beloved France, that may have impelled the young René Rossey to concentrate his attention on the beautiful church at Amfreville. He focussed on every detail of the building, so unlike anything in Tunis, trying to impress it upon his mind's eye so that, if the future again barred his way to France, there would be one indissoluble memory that he could carry with him forever.

Until the 51st Highland Division could be moved in, the area beyond the Orne was only sparsely held by the Allies, consisting at first of a narrow strip, about six miles long, that had to be defended. The Germans were expert at using such thinly defended spaces, and Rossey learned that there was as much peril in apparently quiet fields as in the deafening tumult of the Casino battle:

> I was lightly wounded at the Casino, but that had gone well. Now I was saying to myself that a sniper was going to close my account. Those first days one was afraid. The snipers were coming from everywhere here in the hedges around Amfreville. One never knew which way to hide. Are they going to get us from the left? From the right? From behind? But I believe we were well trained. We knew what to do. We knew it well.

The failure to capture Caen on D Day threw Allied plans into disarray. Far from being an unimportant corner of the front, the area beyond the Orne now provided great opportunities for German infiltrators and later required bitter battles to hold and extend. Instead of their few days of Special Service, Lovat's men were tied down to ordinary infantry duties. The days passed and turned into weeks, with casualties mounting.

It was well into August before the Special Service men were pulled out of the line and sent back to base for further operations. One of them, *Quartier Maitre 2ème classe* Leon Gautier of 8 Troop, said that they had been in action in the front line for 78 consecutive days. Out of the 177 *Fusiliers Marin* originals who had landed on D Day, only 24 survived the Normandy fighting unwounded.

After their withdrawal from Normandy, Rossey discovered that the next destination for his K gun section was indeed on another coast, this time the border between

Belgium and Holland. At the time of Arnhem and Operation *Market Garden*, the failure of the Allies to occupy the Antwerp seaway led to costly infantry battles in abysmal conditions in order to permit the entry of ships to the great port. With this aim Lovat's men were to land on Walcheren island as a part of Operation *Infatuate*. The French *Fusiliers Marin* now formed 5 Troop and 6 Troop, whilst a Dutch 2 Troop of 10 (Inter-Allied) Commando also participated in the action.

Going ashore from landing craft, 4 Commando was to attack the town of Flushing at dawn on 1 November. The landing craft containing the heavy weapons and equipment was sunk, but the foot soldiers pushed on. 1 Troop and 5 Troop advanced street by street against defenders who outnumbered them by three to one. 6 Troop then assaulted along the main street, capturing the central Post Office and taking more than 50 prisoners. Most of the town was occupied by nightfall.

The advance next morning was perhaps even more spectacular, later being described as "one of the bravest and most audacious feats of arms of the war". With the still numerous and well-organised German defenders dominating the last streets ahead, 5 Troop resorted to 'mouse-holing'. Employing ready-to-use charges, carried by every man including machine gunners like Rossey, they avoided the open streets. Clearing downstairs rooms and cellars, and immune from *Nebelwerfers*, they blew their way through house wall after house wall, thus always outflanking and wrong-footing the defenders out in the streets. Late afternoon saw 4 Commando in total control and a fresh strong Scottish brigade passing through.

In 1945 the Special Service troops were used to raid or occupy small Dutch islands as the war drew towards its close. Come the peace, some of the exiles commanded by Lovat, such as Czechs and Poles, could not be repatriated. But for Rossey and his compatriots, who were geographically close to home, there was a different problem. France was in a state of flux, with wartime animosities still affecting the transition to peace. There was no established and orderly demobilisation scheme such as the British one, which was regulated by seniority of age and service. Some soldiers were simply released, among them Rossey, who found himself in Paris, a long-time cherished goal but now an unwelcoming prospect.

He was now just a *pied-noir* (black foot), a mere colonial, and was classified *SDF* (*sans domicile fixé*, homeless). With no trade or educational qualifications, he described himself as "battering the pavements of Paris" in desperation, looking for odd jobs, unloading vegetables at Les Halles, begging, resorting to any means of obtaining something to eat. Through various twists of fate he managed at last to return to the home he left in Tunis, such a relatively short time ago but so many hard miles endured. He was still not old enough to vote.

To add insult to injury, at this point General de Gaulle himself intervened. Rossey and his friends were always most verbal about their admiration for the way the British had accepted and supported them. "The English," he said, "did it all. They welcomed us, they fed us, they equipped us, they formed us as soldiers." They had also received abundant Scottish hospitality. However, de Gaulle, who had risen to national pre-eminence largely because of the command structure provided for him in Britain, seemed to have borne some kind of resentment at having had to depend on a foreign country. This attitude, virtually a paranoia, was later to affect the larger arena of European politics.

De Gaulle unilaterally decided that any French units which had fought under British command could not be counted as French troops. He struck off the list of French units Kieffer's troops of French exiles. They would receive no recognition, recompense, awards or even mention. While the majority of Lovat's British veterans were properly demobilised and went home wearing medals, to be welcomed as heroes, their French comrades were denied any such reward.

Back in Tunisia, Rossey married and hoped for little. Then he learned that Philippe Kieffer (now MC, MBE) had survived his wounds and was in Paris. When Rossey once again reached the capital, Kieffer was delighted to help his old K gunner take up what proved to be a life-long career with Total Oil. The green shoots of fame also belatedly began to appear. As de Gaulle's influence declined, the appropriate French honours were restored for the veteran exiles. Medals could be worn. A new generation, free of wartime animosities, wanted to know what their own grandfathers had done in the war.

Veterans were reunited. Men of the old Kieffer Commando were flown back to the old training grounds near Achnacarry in Scotland to revive memories and make TV documentaries. Then in 1962 came the Hollywood war film *The Longest Day*. There on the big screen around the world were actors graphically depicting Rossey, Meudal, Gautier, Kieffer, piper Millin and all the rest as they splashed ashore on D Day.

Even though, at first sight, it may not have quite the same novel impact as the piper statue, there is also nearby, on that Normandy promenade, an eternal flame which remembers the expatriates who travelled thousands of miles from all over the world to be the first to land on French soil on D Day.

Then there were the great latter-day Remembrance events on the D Day beaches, attracting international leaders and royalty, producing brilliant pageantry and attracting many tourists paying their respects. And there, filmed for the television news and photographed for the newspapers of the world, sitting like a permanent fixture in the honoured row of international D Day veterans, is the amiable, rotund little man in the green beret, one of the first ashore with his K gun on that June day in 1944.

René Rossey died, widely recognised, on a June day in 2016. A friend said of him: "He was the incarnation of *le joie de vie*."

In his last halcyon days, Rossey was always sensitive to the thought that here he was, the most junior *matelot* in his troop, and only a *pied-noir*, but receiving such adulation for nothing more than, as he saw it, a fervent desire to tread and free the soil of France by any means. One of his last statements was typical of this sincere and humble attitude:

> I regret nothing. Everybody said to me 'why did you go off, to get yourself killed when you were not even 18 years of age?' The challenge of the time was to liberate France. I loved France. I could not say 'let all the others take the bullet'. That is why I went. Otherwise I would just have stopped at home, guzzling olives, raisins and grapes. That is why I went. But not to crow about it, no! no!

17

Fred Tilston

Major (later Colonel) Frederick Albert Tilston, VC, CD, Canadian, The Essex Scottish Regiment

He need not have been there. He could have cited age, pleaded wounds, even claimed glory at the first trench. But there was a second trench still, and a third trench beyond.

In an infantry battalion with a full establishment of fit officers, Fred Tilston, at age 38, might not have been the first choice, indeed might not have been the 10th choice, to be leading a company into action for the first time in a battle of such epic consequences. He might so easily have been safely selling aspirins in Canada, or sitting comfortably in a staff job filling out requisition forms for pharmaceutical supplies. But that was not Fred's way. And the regiment had no more reserves.

Fred Tilston was born in Toronto as long ago as 1906; by 1929 he had passed out at the University of Toronto with a pharmacy degree, and by 1936 was a sales manager for Bayer. When war broke out, Canada had no conscription system. All who served were volunteers. In Britain there was conscription, but Fred Tilston would already have been too old to be called up under the British system. Nevertheless, he felt compelled to go and fight for his country, but not in a nice cushy posting. With a little manipulation as to his age and his specialist qualifications, he managed to slip into the Canadian Army as a private. He was old enough to have served as a regular soldier and then retired. Inevitably, with his education and experience, he was soon commissioned.

His chosen regiment, the Essex Scottish, were destined to be tasked with more than one version of *'Mission Impossible'*. They were part of the catastrophic Dieppe raid in 1942, where high commanders were culpable and front-line troops helplessly heroic. Fred had been 'LOB', left out of battle, and thus was part of the cadre from which the regiment was reformed. Only three officers and 49 other ranks had returned from Dieppe out of 32 officers and 520 other ranks who had disembarked; 121 had been killed in action.

The Essex Scottish then went into training for the D Day landings. One day on the firing range a misunderstanding of signals exposed Fred to live bullets. One of them

Fred Tilston, ever cheerful, welcomed home by his sisters.
(Courtesy of the Essex and Kent Scottish Regiment archives)

smashed into his lung and tore the membrane covering his heart. It took four months of intricate surgery and careful rehabilitation before he was fit for duty again. It could have been a safe rear echelon staff job, but Fred insisted on returning to his line regiment. He was appointed adjutant, an administrative job which should have kept him out of the front line of fire in the Normandy campaign.

Fate again saw the Essex Scottish, with the South Saskatchewans, involved in one of the cruellest days of combat on 20 July 1944. Without adequate support, the two battalions were hit by a massive *Panzer* counter-attack. The hapless infantry advancing through cornfields were mowed down by the *Panzers'* guns and many were literally crushed to death under the milling tracks of the rampaging tanks.

Nine days later the battalion was sent as part of a succession of virtually suicidal attacks on the fortified ridge village of Tilly-la-Campagne. Again advancing over open exposed ground, the casualties were high. At one point the Germans sent in robot tanks to reinforce their defence. As the lines of the Essex Scottish wavered and formations became confused, Fred, as adjutant, came forward, racing across country in his jeep to try to sort order out of the chaos of battle. His jeep hit a mine and he was thrown out. The explosion burst both his ear drums and he was hit in the eye by shrapnel, causing damage to his sight which, as a result, deteriorated after the war. Undaunted, he remarked: "The jeep went one way and I went the other. Fortunately the floor was sandbagged for protection [against mines blowing underneath the vehicle]." Again hospital treatment was necessary, and again Fred returned to active duty.

Further horrors awaited the Essex Scottish. In February 1945 they were involved in what was the still costly task of working out from the original single 'Arnhem Road' into the area around Goch and Calcar. The German Army was again an efficient and highly disciplined organisation capable of exacting substantial casualties for every mile of ground conceded. Once again the regiment was thrown into murderous fighting, gained a modest stretch of ground, bled casualties and had to be further reorganised.

Beyond Goch and Calcar, German forces were still holding out to the west of the River Rhine. Now Allied progress was challenged by the obstacle of the dense Hochwald forest. It was necessary to push past this landmark, from Uden to Xanten, in order to capture the major Rhine crossing at Wesel. Only then could the Allies cross the great river into the heart of Germany and try to end the war.

The battle to clear the Hochwald area was planned as a massive armoured assault. Unfortunately, the relatively vulnerable, if more numerous, Sherman tanks of the Allies were unable to make progress against the German Panthers, *StuGs* and Tigers. The German troops fought desperately to retain their last major defences before German soil, whilst weather and terrain also conspired against the attackers. As so often happened, the infantry were left to slog it out at company level.

The defensive line occupied by the crack German 84th Division, and reinforced by elements of another nine divisions, has been aptly described by Colonel Rae Martin, a more recent commander of the Essex Scottish regiment:

> Hitler had given direct orders to his fanatical troops to fight to the death. Any commander who did not stand his ground until the end faced summary execution … The Hochwald was a black, murky thick forest. It was described as an evil place: it stank of danger … Anti-tank ditches, belts of trenches two or three lines deep and bands of barbed wire, all covered by enemy guns. Unbeknownst to the Canadians the Germans had brought up fifty 88mm guns sited in enfilade, 717 mortars and 1,054 artillery guns. Mixed into this bombardment from Hell were 54 *Nebelwerfers*, projectors firing banks of 15cm and 24cm rockets … accompanied by minefields and muddy ground it presented an ominous obstacle.

Having endured, on 19 February, a murderous artillery barrage which inflicted severe losses, including a company commander, the Essex Scottish advanced towards Louisendorf. Major Tom Stewart, although all too unwillingly, was ordered away on long overdue leave, so Fred Tilston was brought forward and promoted to acting major to command Charlie Company. The battalion reached Louisendorf village by

28 February. That evening, in chilling rain and with little opportunity for rest, they set out on a 10-mile march to their assembly line for the next attack. Tilston thus faced his first battle in command of a company. H Hour was scheduled for 0715 hours on 1 March.

Arriving at the start line, even in the half-light and with rain affecting long vision, it was clear that the infantry faced a formidable task. Ahead stretched 500 yards of open farmland, divided by a road which ran down the centre and led into the dense forest. It was planned that tanks should accompany the infantry and pour fire into the first lines of enemy defences in the fields and at the edges of the forest beyond. Fred's Charlie Company would advance on the left of the road, with Alpha Company under Major Paul Cropps on the right. The Germans could maintain constant 88mm and heavy machine-gun fire directly along the road, making it almost impossible to cross from one company to the other.

However, there was a delay at H Hour. A first test by tanks on the left revealed that, due to the saturated, swampy state of the fields, the earth was too soft for them to move across it. On the right, at a slightly higher elevation, the tanks supporting Alpha would be able to find some solid ground and move accordingly. Charlie Company would have to advance without the vital tank support. A further problem was the combination of rain and sand which clogged the barrels and triggers of Sten guns and rifles, demanding constant cleaning.

Then, after almost two hours of delay, the Canadian barrage thundered down immediately in front of the foot soldiers. As they began to walk, the barrage edged forward. An enemy barrage intermingled with friendly fire in one confused hurricane of blasts, flashes and belching smoke clouds. Tilston himself stepped forward into the skirts of the barrage, with two forward platoons close behind him. The enemy machine guns ahead promptly joined in with the shells of the heavy artillery and the rockets of the *Nebelwerfers*. Men began to stagger, to fall, to struggle or lie still. Urging his platoons forward, suddenly Tilston himself was down, hit in the head.

The walking lines faltered. Tilston staggered up and doggedly walked forward again. Other men still fell. A hundred had started together; there must have been 10, 20 or even more already out of action. But there was no time to count casualties. They had to grit their teeth and splash on, near enough to pull the triggers on their Sten guns, lob grenades and break into a run. Halfway across the open ground, a first line of concealed trenches was revealed as the barrage passed on. The high-speed rasp of *Spandau* machine guns at a few yards' range meant more men falling. It was kill or be killed.

The Essex Scottish on the extreme left were then grievously hit by a machine gun at point-blank range. Tilston turned that way and charged, throwing a grenade, firing his Sten and silencing the pestilential *Spandau*. One German desperately raised his hands: the first prisoner. The first line of hostile trenches was suddenly silent. Tilston called the reserve platoon to mop up any enemy still in the field, round up the prisoners, collect the wounded and watch the open left flank. Then it was "On again!"

For the Essex Scottish there was no relief from the enemy bombardment. But their own creeping barrage lashed the edges of the forest, killing and disabling, causing machine gunners to duck down. As rain washed away the smoke, the attackers could clearly see the next daunting barricade, a belt of barbed wire 10ft thick, rusty, tearing and tightly anchored. Tilston, always in the lead, explored the wire himself, firing to keep enemy heads down. He found a gap, and fighting the clinging, stabbing rusty wire, forced his body through, always firing. Charlie Company – or what is left of it – followed, filtering through fast.

Pushing through the trees and poised high above their tormentors, the Canadians fired Bren and Sten volleys and lobbed grenades down into the deep trenches which had been the Germans' safe shelter but had become death traps. Leading out of the front trenches were narrow tunnels to the rear, where the Canadians must go to drive the Germans out of every nook of shelter.

Someone found a stock of abandoned German stick grenades. In a mad flurry, the attackers tossed the unfamiliar grenades at the shocked Germans almost at arm's length. Lieutenant Charlie Gatton later recalled: "I can't remember how many boxes of grenades we used up. You wouldn't believe it. It was just like a snowball fight really." On a more serious note, he remarked on how cool Tilston remained: "He has no regard for enemy fire. He never gets down into the trench. He just stands on the parapet or squats beside it, just discussing our problems as if we are at a board meeting."

So far so good, but two dangerous problems loomed: the shortage of fit men and the congealed dirt in their guns, with triggers and barrels gummed up. Private Bob Fields, now wounded, knew that normally a wounded man was advised to lie still, stand his rifle upright in the earth and put his helmet on top, waiting for aid. In their dire situation, with a massive enemy counter-attack expected and two-thirds of Charlie Company lying dead or badly wounded, Tilston came by, his face and uniform bloody, pulled up the planted rifle and told Bob to keep on shooting where he lay for as long as he could.

It had been raining all day. The soil was sandy and constant explosions were filling the air with all matter of filth. Bren and Sten guns now clogged up and jammed. Tilston rallied several other wounded men and got them cleaning weapons, using shirts and underwear as necessary, in order to maintain the firing.

The Canadians then come under fire from a hidden 75mm anti-tank gun. Tilston threw a grenade, straight and true. The gun crew, brave against tanks but outclassed against infantry, fled, leaving the gun as a prize. As if in revenge, a missile smashed into Tilston's hip and he was thrown to the ground. He struggled up bleeding badly from this further wound.

Time was passing, and with the enemy massing, Charlie Company was down to little more than a third of its starting strength, was totally out of ammunition and had no working wireless set. On the other side of the road, it was possible to see that Alpha Company, with its attendant tanks, had reached its objective. Every one of Tilston's men was urgently employed, their Bren-gun carrier busily ferrying the seriously wounded back for treatment, so Tilston decided to cross the road himself and get supplies. However, the German 88s, mortars and heavy machine guns firing on fixed lines, were still enfilading the main road, making it a 'no go' area. Undeterred, Tilston went limping across the road, one leg now dragging.

Major Paul Cropps of Alpha Company saw him coming and stared, amazed: "There he is, as if no worries, just a smile on his face and in he saunters and says 'We are short of ammunition. What can we have?' So we supply him. He is bleeding from a number of wounds. So we patch him up and send him back." Charlie Company's now crippled major hiked back to his men, bringing ammunition and a working wireless set. Alpha Company turned back to the renewed German attacks on their side.

The German counter-attack then struck Charlie Company in all its brutal force. From hurriedly sought shelter amid the trees and undergrowth, the diminishing number of Canadians who could pull a trigger fought back. They were down, at this decisive moment, to just 26 men fit to fire. The enemy swarmed in by the hundreds, as witnessed by the fact that Charlie Company would take over 100 prisoners in addition to accounting for at least as many enemy killed or wounded. Tilston had to cross the road a second time to borrow boxes of bullets and hand grenades from Alpha Company, then a third time and a fourth, strolling among his men, inspiring them, lobbing grenades, displaying disdain. Charlie Gratton thought at the time: "He must be beyond caring. He never gets down into a trench. He is absolutely cool."

The weight of the counter-attack begins to ease slightly, but there was still more fighting ahead. Once again a load of ammunition was required from Alpha Company, who were fighting their own continuing bitter battle against a skilful enemy. Tilston had been hit in one leg, virtually disabling it, and was having difficulty in walking. But there were no men yet to spare as runners, and as he tried to cross the road yet another time, an explosion engulfed his usable leg and amputated it below the knee. His balance disintegrated totally, the mind no longer able to fight the body. He collapsed unconscious into a shell crater beside the road. Around him all the company's survivors were totally engaged in the fierce last exchanges of the battle, all eyes riveted on the enemy.

Tilston lay there, rousing, fainting away and then rousing again. He woke enough to think "Morphine", managed to fumble around, reach the emergency pack in his front trouser pocket and give himself a dose. Once again unconsciousness blackened out the world. Then a Canadian voice shouted: "There's another one over here." Stretcher-bearers hurried to feel for life signs, lift him from the hole and begin to move him away from the firing. Suddenly aware again, he halts them and calls for the last remaining Charlie Company officer: "Who is left?" He felt he must ensure that the lieutenant knew precisely what had to be done, how to maximise defences, even as the noise of guns was becoming sporadic and the anger of battle gave way to the cries of the wounded, distant German voices pleading "*Kamerad bitte*, Tommy! *Kamerad!*"

Dr Donald R. Clark was the field surgeon to whom all serious cases were referred. His operating theatre had stood almost empty through the morning. He said: "Unexpectedly in the afternoon we were flooded with approximately 80 to 90 wounded, many severe. They were mostly from the Essex Regiment." Among the worst casualties was Major Tilston, but he obstinately refused to be touched until every other wounded man had been attended to. At that moment the Roman Catholic padre, Captain Murphy, appeared. The two ministering men were both impressed by the major's concern for his men, but he simply would not allow them to give him priority.

The padre suggested: "This man is one of ours. Let me take over the task of comforting him until you can attend to his wounds." As other ranks were treated, Father Murphy consoled Tilston, who by now would have been highly fevered. The padre was able to talk as at the Confessional, as a religious counsellor, perhaps breathe a prayer, helping Fred fight back as the stupefying initial shock gave way to unimaginable agonies wracking the body. The surgeon was of the opinion that this gentle priestly intercession enabled the major to survive the radical operation that had to be carried out in the most primitive of conditions: the double amputation.

The skills of Dr Clarke were able to stabilise Fred's condition and prepare him for the rigours of hard travel. It was then aboard a reliable but basic and uncomfortable Dakota transport plane to reach the specialist hospital in England. There weeks of painful treatment would inevitably lengthen into months of persistent, gruelling rehabilitation.

Fred Tilston was awarded the Victoria Cross on 22 May 1945, the citation stating: "By his calm courage, gallant conduct and total disregard for his own safety, he fired his men with grim determination and their firm stand enabled the Regiment to accomplish its object which in turn enabled the entire advance of division and army to continue." Amazingly, although so badly wounded on 1 March, Tilston was able to be lifted into a wheelchair on 22 June to attend the investiture at Buckingham Palace. It would have been a great feat of physical achievement and mental strength for a much younger man; he had just passed his 39th birthday.

However, in addition to the uncomfortable and tedious process of ambulatory rehabilitation, Fred's physical ills were not yet over. Five years after the actual wounding, that piece of shrapnel cost him the loss of the sight of one eye. It might be thought that a person facing such physical challenges would be inclined to seek a less pressured civilian occupation than his pre-war high-powered sales responsibility. It might also have been thought that the board of an important international company, highly competitive and always under strict public and official scrutiny, might be reluctant to delegate too much responsibility to a badly disabled veteran who might have suffered untold and as yet unrevealed mental injuries.

In fact Fred not only returned to prove himself in his former capacity, but in due course ascended first to become president of the company and later chairman. One observer, G. Kingsley Ward, who accompanied Fred on a return visit to the battlefield, commented on his vigour: "Col. Fred Tilston V.C., who said little and missed nothing with the one eye the good Lord had left him, striding everywhere on two artificial legs while he visited 'his boys' in their war cemetery."

The same commentator noted both Fred's sensitivity and his ready sense of humour:

> Make even a small show of sympathy to Fred and he will quickly tell you how lucky he is: only has to wash his socks every two weeks and his feet never get cold in winter. He stated if ever you feel sorry for yourself, visit the burns units in the military hospitals. Then you know how fortunate you are.

It is that attitude to one's own impediments which may explain why there seems so little evidence of Post Traumatic Stress Disorder in Fred's record of post-war success. Clearly, if he had suffered some of the wild terrors of battle stress in his latter days he is unlikely to have made that known. But it could be that the immense effort necessary to conquer his disability, and the combination of a calm temperament and a humorous slant on life, could have diminished or banished the nightmares experienced by many veterans.

A fine example of Fred's persistence and indeed continued physical agility is related by Colonel Rae Martin:

> I never heard him complain about his disability and never witnessed it preventing him from doing whatever he pleased. His good friend and past commanding officer Ken Kersey, along with Ken's son-in-law, own a piece of rural property overlooking Red Deer Lake, north of Kenora, Ontario. It required a careful descent down the path to the lake below for boating or fishing. I have had the pleasure of invitations there many times. One of my main concerns for Fred was the trek down that path to the lake. I felt it was a challenge for a mountain goat let alone a man without legs. As I stepped in front of Fred to act as a guide should he stumble, his big hand fell on my shoulder and all he said was 'Give me your shoulder, Rae'. Arriving at the lake he lay down on the dock and simply rolled into the boat. Returning to the dock the procedure was repeated until we reached the top where the cabins were.

Another acquaintance, Jim Herder of St Andrew's College, Aurora, one of Fred's beneficiaries, concurred: "He was quite a man. I would describe him as an unassuming hero. He was an optimist, a man who always looked to the positive side of everything. With his extraordinary injuries he always kept a positive outlook on life. He never gave up. He would never submit."

Among various foundations and memorials where Fred's name is remembered and revered, a typical example is St Andrew's College, where an annual Colonel Fred Tilston, VC, award is made to a student from each grade. Typically, the award is granted to students "who have shown courage in the face of adversity".

One of the charming facets of Fred's character was a certain forgetfulness. Rae Martin cites a photograph taken at a ceremonial dinner at the Royal Canadian Military Institute where, in the centre, "with a big grin of his face Fred stands resplendent in a white dinner jacket when all the rest are in black Tux as announced. Friends would always be alert at such occasions in case Fred had forgotten something. Undaunted, Fred would simply say, 'I must have misread the invitation', with a guileless smile."

However, this winner of the Victoria Cross was not immune from displays of righteous anger when appropriate. Canada is formally bilingual and there are sensitivities in that regard. At a Dutch war cemetery, the ambassador and a padre had both spoken in French. Fred had noticed among some Canadian spectators an adverse reaction to the use of French. Douglas Fisher, who was present, recalled:

Fred was out of sorts, angry, fuming, disturbed. He called to a cluster of us 'Come along these rows of graves. Just note the names. Figure the proportion that is French.' He duly led the dissenters to one grave where the epitaph to Private C.E. Belzile of Les Fusiliers Mont-Royal read '*Pour Dieu et mon Canada*'. Fred commented '*Notez bien! Il dit mon Canada* [Please note! It says my Canada].' Fred followed this incident up by writing an open letter condemning people who sought to indulge in, or incite division and hatred.

Fred was never heard in any way to introduce himself as a VC, or enter into a conversation in such a way as to quickly lead to questions about his war experiences. Where some men might have seen the opportunity for a little gentle publicity on their letterhead with armorial bearings and awards such as his VC, CM, LlD, BPharm, on their letterhead, Fred's letterhead read simply 'F.A. Tilston, Rural Route 1, Kettlebury'.

His essential calmness and humour remained undiluted to the end in 1992. There was a move to rename the old University Armouries as the F.A. Tilston Armouries, the name which the building now carries. Fred was thrilled with the idea. However, the Canadian government ordained that Federal buildings could not be renamed until after the eponymous person had died; but the name change would be processed at that time. It fell to Rae Martin to visit Fred in hospital and tell him:

> I had good news and bad news. The good news was that the idea to rename the building was acceptable. But the bad news was he would have to depart this scene first. He looked at me for a second. Then the big grin came on his face and he said 'Oh, well, it looks like I am going to miss a good party'.

It might have been that slightly irreverent sense of humour which inspired Fred, when a newspaper reporter asked him what one quality was vital for winning the medal, to answer with one word: "Inexperience". However, in a more serious vein, when admirers ventured to commend him on his acts of extreme valour, his usual response was simply: "I was not in the Hochwald Forest on my own."

The same sentiment was developed further in conversations with Colonel Rae Martin and, no doubt, with others comrades. He stated that whenever he wore his Victoria Cross it was always on behalf of the many who performed equal acts to his or, indeed, far greater acts that had gone unreported, overlooked or unseen, for which no award had ever been presented.

At ceremonial events of what is now The Essex and Kent Scottish Regiment, the pipe major enters proudly playing 'The Colonel Tilston March'. The irony would not be lost on Fred when contrasted to his own crippled progress through the Hochwald, where 'fame' or 'glory' were remote phantoms, alien to all that was happening there.

18

Michael Wittmann

**Haupsturmführer (Captain) Michael
Wittmann, Knight's Cross with Swords,
German, 101st Heavy *Panzer* Battalion, killed
in action 8 August 1944**

*Flags waving, trumpets blaring, newspaper headlines screaming for the greatest ace,
the incarnation of Siegfried, all along the long, long road, but a roadt which led
only to the gates of Valhalla.*

"Villers-Bocage! You will remember that name," said the colonel portentously, his
pointer tapping the large map as he addressed the tank crews. "At Villers-Bocage we
can outflank the enemy, drive into empty country beyond, and the road to Paris will
be open. You will be in reserve, ready to storm through the gap."

He did not mention Michael Wittmann. He had never heard of Michael Wittmann.
None of us had heard of Michael Wittmann.

None of us would for another 40 years, until his revolver and belt buckle rose again
from a temporary grave. Then the surviving veterans would learn about Michael
Wittmann, both those who suffered the ignominy of Villers-Bocage and those who
were privileged to exact the revenge. For Michael Wittmann did not introduce
himself by name on arrival. His calling card was an 88mm shot, delivered white hot
at 2,700ft per second.

The German public had heard of Michael Wittmann. Nazi 'spin' wizard Joseph
Goebbels' propaganda machine was only too glad to be able to laud a new hero.
In Britain in the 1940s, even RAF aces were not accorded quite the same celebrity
status as those of the First World War. Tank aces were rarely, if ever, featured on
the BBC News. But in Germany the aces still rated high: air aces, submarine aces
and tank aces. The young tank commander Wittmann – slim, erect and immaculate
when photographed in his black uniform – claimed the headlines because, during
the greatest tank battle of all time at Kursk, his Tiger tank was recorded as having
knocked out no less than 30 Russian tanks. The proclaimed number of his victims
subsequently ascended into the hundreds.

Michael Wittmann, signed photograph a month before his
demise. (Kind permission of the Peter Mooney archive)

When the Allies landed in Normandy, a number of elite German units had been
recalled from Russia to combat them as they pressed inland from the beaches. D Day
found the 101st *SS schwere* (heavy) *Panzer* Battalion, equipped with Tiger tanks,
awaiting orders north of the Seine at Beauvais. It included 2 Company commanded
by 30-year-old *Obersturmführer* (equivalent to 1st Lieutenant) Wittmann. Ordered to
the Caen area on 7 June, they had to endure nights of slow progress along thronged
roads because Allied command of the air made it impossible for even the mighty
54-ton Tigers to risk moving in daylight. French Resistance fighters added to the
delays. Imperious in battle, the Tiger's Achilles heel was its tendency to break down
mechanically, and the battalion shed numbers of its tanks en route. Wittmann's 2
Company arrived at its assembly point around Caen with just five fit tanks. He was
summoned to an urgent meeting with senior officers.

A wide gap was opening between the German units facing the British and
Canadians around Caen and those defending Utah and Omaha beaches where the
American had landed. The German defenders had been forced into battle according
to the concentration of the attackers at certain points. The German line in the Caen
area petered out near Villers-Bocage, a small town with a population of less than
2,000 but a vital crossroads. 1st *SS Panzer* Corps Commander Sepp Dietrich and
others feared that the British might try to overlap the truncated defence line. The
two companies of Tigers, who were just arriving, could be sent to cover the gap.
Wittmann's specific task was to "go and look" at Villers-Bocage and report back, but
with discretion to take action if an absolute emergency arose.

Late on 12 June, 2 Company had arrived in the vicinity of Villers-Bocage and the nearby Point 213 which dominated the landscape. The company had taken up a sheltered position in woods ready to observe and report. Next morning an infantry sergeant on outpost duty alerted Wittmann to a group of strange vehicles down on the main road, within sight but obscured by trees. Wittmann himself was surprised to see that the road, which ran through the town, was already thronged with British vehicles of all kinds, obviously the vanguard of a brigade or perhaps a division aiming for the vital gap, whilst also occupying the pivotal town. Wittmann could see tanks in the column, but also half-tracks and other vehicles, indicating a considerable body of supporting infantry. This was a far bigger show than he had been led to expect. This was indeed an emergency.

There was now a need for two urgent decisions: one tactical, the other personal. Tactically, should he comply strictly with orders, returning to headquarters with his company to report in detail and be part of a larger riposte towards the town? Or, in view of the mass penetration already made by the enemy, should he risk attacking a considerably greater force and try to stall the enemy's momentum for the time being?

There must also have been some personal query, however brief. Whilst he was commanding the great beast of the 1944 battlefield, the Tiger, with four other such tanks in support, a Tiger could be killed. If hit by a shell, the ammunition in a Tiger could blow off the entire turret with the crew still inside. Survival through the Balkans and Russia did not invest him with immortality, whatever Goebbels' media trumpeted. He had seen good comrades obliterated in other battles. The safer way would be to return and report as ordered. Even aces can be discarded in the ruthless poker game of war.

However, the ingrained reaction of any German commander was to counter-attack immediately. Even an hour's delay might allow the British to consolidate their hold on the critical crossroads and dig in solidly on Point 213. Wittmann therefore decided to strike. Ordering two other Tigers to advance directly on Point 213, he directed his driver down the hill towards the halted column on the road. But it was not an auspicious beginning. After the gruelling rush from Beauvais, his own Tiger was not yet fully ready for action so he jumped into another tank, together with his long-term gunner, Bobby Woll. The Tiger started up and moved off. It rolled forward 20 yards, but there was something not right about the sound of the engine. Wittmann jumped down, again with Woll following, and ran to yet another Tiger. This one roared out from cover and quickly covered the 200 yards to the column of assorted British vehicles, hitherto obscured by the mask of trees.

With its crew still unsure of the detailed make-up of the Allied force, the Tiger came upon the tail of the column to be confronted by a Cromwell tank. A glance showed that the column was at rest, crews taking a brief break and not ready for action. Only an infantry sergeant had spotted the Tiger and was fruitlessly trying to raise the alarm. Woll's first shot wrecked the Cromwell. Beyond it stood a Sherman with a much longer gun than normal. The German crew had never seen a Sherman Firefly, but there was no time to wonder if this longer gun meant a more powerful muzzle velocity and an unexpected challenge to the Tiger's superiority.

Woll's next shot crashed into the Firefly, rendering it impotent. As loader Gunther Boldt fought to keep the huge 88mm gun firing, it was obvious that there were no more large tanks in the column. But here and there an anti-tank gun lurked, and infantry vehicles which could be carrying PIAT projectors, all capable of damaging the German tank.

The hull and turret machine guns were sending out a storm of bullets to warn off any heroic individuals and smash smaller vehicles as the Tiger motored steadily down the line. More than 20 wreckages now blocked the road and the Tiger still lumbered on. Three Stuart light tanks had been placed at the far end of the column, their combined weight of 46 tons still less than that of the one Tiger and their 37mm guns mere peashooters compared to the 88mm. Yet a suicidal British troop leader deliberately drew his Stuart across the road, endeavouring to block the progress of Wittmann's tank. Inevitably and imperiously, the Tiger, with milling tracks and blasting gun, reduced the three tiny combatants to just more wreckage. The road now cleared, Wittmann turned into the town itself and chaos replaced the leisurely duck shoot along the infantry column.

Immediately ahead was a headquarters troop of Cromwell tanks, fast when moving forward but slow when reversing. Only half the weight of the Tiger, the Cromwell had the less powerful 75mm gun. At normal tank fighting ranges over hundreds of yards, the 75mm would have been useless, but at 20 yards, who knows? A lucky strike might impede, if not disable, the Tiger.

Woll instantly fired into the clutch of tanks and the street became a thundercloud of black smoke with its own repeated explosions. One Cromwell backed between two houses as the Tiger ploughed through the murk and ruins. Further along the street stood a Sherman and another Cromwell. The Tiger's gun spoke again and again. Wittmann could not understand why the Sherman did not reply, not realising yet that it was an artillery observation tank with a wooden gun barrel.

At this point the invincible Tiger came face to face, at point-blank range, with an untested usurper, the Firefly. The colossal belch of flame and tremendous blast from the Firefly's long barrel heralded a snap shot which clipped the Tiger driver's visor, distorting vision. The Tiger, swerving, crashed into a high wall, collapsing it on top of the Firefly, leaving the British commander struggling to extricate his tank from the mountain of debris so as to continue the action.

Meanwhile the surviving Cromwell, which had reversed out of the street, had issued forth and was now following a few yards behind the Tiger, sending 75mm armour-piercing shots into the supposedly more vulnerable back plates of the Tiger. Nothing happened, except that the great 88mm gun, constricted in the narrow street, swung carefully round and, now reversed, blasted a killer shot into the pestering Cromwell, blowing the commander right out of the turret to land at the side of the street, shocked but miraculously still alive.

Rolling on, the Tiger entered the sights of a static 6-pdr anti-tank gun set up along an alley. The first shot of the gun hit the Tiger's track, severing a link so that, under extreme tension, the track, like a tensed spring, broke and unravelled, rendering the tank immobile and vulnerable to infantry action. There was no way that Wittmann and his crew could get their tank into working order in that perilous bedlam. Hoping to salvage the vehicle later on, the crew grabbed personal weapons and bailed out. The two gunners had been using their *Spandaus* to drive away any enemy infantry who might wish to make an heroic stand. Thus, at the epicentre of battle, Wittmann, Woll, Boldt and the others were able to walk out of the streets, across the wooded slopes and eventually report to Major General Fritz Bayerlein at the *Panzer Lehr* divisional headquarters five miles away.

The action at Villers-Bocage occurred immediately after the German media had finally to confirm the desperate fact that the Allies had succeeded in landings on Normandy beaches, breaching Hitler's vaunted Atlantic Wall. The relatively minor victory at Villers-Bocage, although virtually nullified next day by British resistance, was a gift to the Nazi propaganda purveyors. Wittmann received an immediate award of swords to his Iron Cross and promotion to *Hauptsturmführer*, equivalent of captain. However, not all German commentators were, or have since been, totally complimentary. Some have considered that Wittmann was reckless and lacking in tactical skills when risking his tank and the element of surprise in his solo action. His own comment on the action was restrained: "I had no time to assemble my company. Instead I had to act quickly as I had to assume that the enemy had already spotted me and would destroy me where I stood."

On that afternoon of 13 June, and the following morning, Allied tanks fought back, trying to hold Point 213 and knocking out a number of irreplaceable Tiger tanks. German industry could not produce these huge tanks fast enough to reinforce Normandy and also supply the Russian Front. In a strict military and industrial sense, one Tiger destroyed was worth maybe five Sherman or Cromwell tanks lost.

The British armoured regiment involved at Villers-Bocage was the 4th County of London Yeomanry. The valiant Stuart troop leader was Lieutenant Rex Ingram. The commander blown out of the frustrated Cromwell was the adjutant, Captain Pat Byas, who later described how he saw his solid shots "bouncing off the Tiger's armour like tennis balls".

Remarkably, with the front line relatively stabilised, on 14 June it was decided to withdraw the British force from Villers-Bocage. The vital road axis then languished under German control for another two months. The British commanders at corps, division and brigade level were all relieved of their commands. The reserve tank commanders briefed as in the opening paragraph above, were never called forward to reinforce the breakthrough. Wittmann's immediate intervention, even if tactically unsound, may have been the red light which caused British high commanders to abandon their more aggressive intentions.

It had been a long journey from life as a farm boy in Bavaria to command of a company of Tigers for Michael Wittmann. Whilst the Wittmann family enjoyed a reasonable level of existence, it was still necessary to go hunting in order to keep the family table well supplied. Surprisingly, the young Michael experienced problems in killing wild boar, due to a boyhood love of animals and nature in general. In time he became a successful hunter and acquired skills which would prepare him for a soldier's duties.

Hunting, dangerous enough where wild boars were concerned, required an ability to discern movement and objects at a distance, and then the stealth to make a successful approach. The physical act of firing a gun taught correct habits such as the pause before firing and the light finger on the trigger. At the beginning of his military career in the lowest rank of infantryman, this gave the new recruit considerable advantages. Eventually his skills enabled him to transfer to an elite unit and go into action in an assault gun battery.

Unlike a tank, which has a turret traverse of 360 degrees, that of the *Sturmgeschütz*, or *StuG*, used by Wittmann's first crew was limited and required the entire vehicle to be turned on its tracks for sighting a target only a few degrees to either side. In some ways the number of enemy tanks knocked out by Wittmann and his crew from a *StuG* was as remarkable as any higher sum of 'kills' recorded from the fearsome Tiger. During this first period of service it took Michael Wittmann three years of steady progress to achieve officer rank, by no means a meteoric rise.

The greatest tank battle in history took place in Russia around Kursk in July 1943. Although launched as a German offensive, Operation *Citadel* became remarkable for the massed counter-attacks by overwhelming numbers of Russian tanks. The Soviets were willing to accept up to a six-to-one ratio of tanks destroyed in order to halt what would prove to be the last major German offensive on the Eastern Front. Over that month alone, Wittmann's crew, with Balthazar 'Bobby' Woll as gunner, claimed 30 tanks and 28 guns destroyed. Other commanders scored similarly. On one day, 20-year-old Tiger commander Franz Staudegger claimed 22 Russian tanks destroyed by his Tiger in a single protracted action.

These claims may make it sound as though the Russian tanks were easy prey for the bullying Tigers and Panthers. But it must be remembered that this was, in the end, a great German defeat, with losses of over 50,000 men. During July 50 Tigers were destroyed and 240 damaged. Out of 184 Panthers available originally, only 40 were left active by the end of the second day. Many Tiger and Panther crews died or suffered hideous injuries. Wittmann escaped unharmed from Kursk, although he had earlier been wounded in the face, necessitating some dental reconstruction which proved vital to his identification 40 years later.

Little record remains of mundane details of Wittmann's experiences in Russia, where the war has been described as particularly cruel and inhuman. However, it appears that on one occasion in a very close encounter Wittmann's crew destroyed a Russian T34, from which the crew bailed out on fire. On that occasion Wittmann's crew is credited with having put out the flames by wrapping the wounded men in blankets before handing them over to the battalion's medics. This story is not likely to have been concocted by Goebbels' 'spin doctors', as it could have suggested sympathy for men who, according to strict Nazi doctrine, came from a despised and inferior race. It would have revealed a human weakness not expected in the fanatical Nazi fighter as usually portrayed.

In March 1944 Michael Wittmann married Hildegard Burmester at a small Catholic church in Bavaria, with Bobby Woll as witness. There were stories that Hitler had attended the wedding, although at that time Hitler was living and working in a remote bunker on the Eastern Front. Also during this period, and not for the first time, Wittmann rejected an opportunity to transfer to a safe staff or training post, preferring to continue in command of his Tiger company. So his road led on, via Villers-Bocage to taking part in another slaughter of British armour during Operation *Goodwood*. By this time Wittmann and his crew were credited with having knocked out 141 tanks and 132 assault guns during their war career.

On 7 August formations of Allied tanks stormed the vital Bourguébus Ridge and stood at the crest around Saint-Aignan-de-Cramesnil and Cintheaux. Two defending infantry divisions had been decimated, but behind their fleeing remnants lingered the formidable 12th *SS Panzer* Division *Hitlerjugend* (Hitler Youth), supported by Wittmann's 2 Company. The *Hitlerjugend* were under orders to move towards the great American *Cobra* breakthrough to the west, but their commander, Kurt Meyer, was using his discretion to wait a while longer because of ominous signs of Allied activity down the ridge towards Caen. Meyer had left observers in strategic villages like Saint-Aignan and Rocquancourt to sound immediate alarms if the Allies attacked.

By clear daylight on 8 August it was obvious that the crest had been occupied by Allied tanks in force If those tanks could swarm yet further forward and overwhelm the depleted but still formidable *Hitlerjugend*, the main road would be open for the Allies to encircle and trap most of the German army in Normandy around Falaise. Meyer, known to his men as *Panzermeyer*, could stand on the main road and see with his own eyes the dust and movement of large numbers of the enemy massing for a further advance. But he still had Wittmann's company, or what was left of it, ready to march.

From the area of Cintheaux, Meyer and Wittmann looked along the main road, across a wide stretch of open cornfields to the church, houses and farms along the ridge crest. On both flanks those exposed cornfields were bounded by thick woods, dense orchards or high hedges. Could the Allies have penetrated that far? Wherever they were, Meyer's orders were clear: "Recapture Saint-Aignan". The group of staff officers remembered Meyer shaking hands with Wittmann and sending him into a typical Tiger counter-attack to hit the enemy hard before he could settle. More than one officer also remembered Wittmann evidencing a certain disquiet about such an attack made without due reconnaissance; they all now knew about the Firefly's hitting power. Allied tank regiments were appearing with one Firefly to every troop of four tanks. What *Panzermeyer* could see in the near distance would be far greater than a troop: maybe a division, or even several divisions, so how many Firefly tanks?

Meyer had ordered Major Waldmuller to send his *Hitlerjugend* Mark IV tanks and infantry through the woods to their right. Wittmann was to attack straight ahead across the cornfields. He lined up his four fully fit tanks, survivors from four various companies. A fifth tank was also available but would not be able to keep pace. This composite troop of four tanks should have been commanded by *Hauptsturmführer* (Captain) Franz Heurich, but this was his first time in action. Wittmann therefore decided to relieve Heurich of the responsibility; he himself would take direct command of the sortie.

The first three tanks – commanded by Dollinger, Iriohn and Kisters – lined up behind cover. They could hear, over to their left beyond a high chateau wall, enemy guns of tank calibre firing. But on their right there was no sound or movement as yet. The first three Tigers emerged into the open ground line ahead. To the right lay perhaps 500-800 metres of open ground bounded by woods and apple orchards. Normally, on crossing such exposed terrain, one of the three tanks would have had its gun traversed to cover the right flank. But, as the unseen guns on the left continued to fire, all the Tigers traversed that way, ready for immediate action from that quarter. Deep in the ripening corn, the great 54-ton tanks rumbled forward.

But then, catastrophe struck, with an almost simultaneous double 'crash' as a massive flash flared from the woods on the right. The flash was barely perceived before a ball of fire erupted from the side of the third Tiger in line. Smoke gushed up and the crew bailed out. The second Tiger in line, furiously traversing, fired without clear view of a target, but too late: the inevitable flash, crash, smoke, flame, and then figures leaping and falling from a second slain Tiger.

The foremost Tiger, suddenly isolated, had seen and sighted on the gun flashes at the gap in the trees in the woods. It fired, sighted and fired again, but there was no responding explosion. The enemy gun must have moved into another hide. It was difficult to discern. Other enemy tanks in the woods were firing machine guns and lighter shells, 'brassing up' the surviving Tiger, keeping the leading tank commander's head down and blurring vision for the driver.

Now, as Wittmann's Tiger roared towards the fray, there was another fatal flash, explosion and smoke, and the remaining Tiger ahead had stalled, burning and then exploding. Woll traversed to the right, towards a dense wood, seeking the lurking enemy at about 800 metres' range.

Unexpectedly, where the invisible guns had been firing on the other side of the road, an enemy Sherman smashed its way through the chateau wall bordering the road, a mere 150 yards away. Before Wittmann or his gunner could react, a shot smashed into the Tiger's turret ring, penetrating and ricocheting amid stacked 88mm ammunition, sparking it into a volcano of flame. Its force lifted the very turret – two tons of armour-plated steel – off the tank, sending it crashing down yards behind the vehicle. Nobody climbed out.

Waldmuller's infantry and Mk IV tanks were pressing forward on their right but had run into intense, accurate fire from the British troops around Saint-Aignan. Some of the *Hitlerjugend* were killed and others went to ground, but on that exceptionally hot August day the ripe cornfields were catching fire. Wreathed in choking, poisonous smoke, the young, fanatical foot soldiers and their Mk IV tanks had no alternative but to retire, leaving the four destroyed Tigers on the fatal stretch of exposed ground.

From Cintheaux, staff officers, including adjutant George Isecke and medical officer Dr Wolfgang Rabe, had watched the destruction of the Tigers. Few crewmen were seen emerging from the burning tanks. Somewhere amid the shimmering spectacle of dense smoke and leaping fire was Michael Wittmann. Dr Rabe was determined to try to cross the open plain, discover if anyone remained alive and render aid if possible. But he found that Allied guns from three sides were pouring an impenetrable curtain of fire around the stricken Tigers and behind the retreating *Hitlerjugend*. Asphyxiating fumes poured from the burning corn. It was impossible for human flesh and blood to survive there. Dr Rabe withdrew, and in doing so generated the haunting mystery of 'What happened to Michael Wittmann?'. The official response was 'Missing'.

Almost four decades later, in 1983, roadworks led to an archaeological search of the area where stunted crops revealed the site of tanks 'brewing up' long ago. A German team found and identified the pitiful remains of the Wittmann crew. Dismembered skeletons, they were confirmed mainly by discovery of driver Heinrich Reimers' identity disc. Experts also examined teeth from the grave and found some which corresponded to records of the facial repairs carried out on Wittmann's earlier Russian wound. This became a story of world-wide interest.

Back in 1944, as Canadian and Polish tanks rolled south towards Falaise, Allied Intelligence Officers wrote up regimental diaries. Captain Crosby of the 1st Northamptonshire Yeomanry recorded that Captain Tom Boardman's group of tanks had confronted the Tigers and Trooper Joe Ekins had knocked out three in only seven minutes. The Canadian Sherbrook Fusiliers noted how one of Major Sydney Radley-Walters' tanks had broken down the chateau wall and entered the fight. But neither diary mentioned Wittmann. Neither Tom Boardman nor 'Rad' Walters had yet heard the name Wittmann; they did not know what he had achieved in combat, so it did not matter to them whether Wittmann was amongst the dead or not.

One German report said that "the loss of their beloved Michael would send shock waves through all the ranks of the *Waffen SS*". His friends said that he was "a quiet man, even during combat", and that he had a sixth sense to know how and where to engage the enemy. One said: "Highly admired by his comrades and very highly thought of by his superiors."

Comments by observers from other nationalities tend to see him as a typical servant of the Nazi regime, something of a 'heel clicker' and a publicity tool of Goebbels' media machine. A great-nephew described him as a man "of humble origin who got caught up in the fervour of the time as his friends wanted to participate in the renewal of Germany. As with many young men in American service, he wanted to be in the elite of the elite." Had Wittmann survived only a few months longer, his post-war actions might have thrown more light upon these hotly disputed assessments.

Wittmann's story raises two profound questions: one moral, the other tactical. Firstly, morally, "can the righteousness or evil of a regime serve as a lodestone in the assessment of the bravery in battle of an individual soldier of that regime?" Or, perhaps to frame the question more pertinently, "could a highly indoctrinated devoted Nazi, trained to shun normal emotions, be said to be brave?" Secondly, tactically, "if a soldier is equipped with, and sheltered within a weapon of such superiority that he can demolish weaker units with almost total immunity, can he ever be considered to exemplify the same level of bravery as his victims?"

Taking the second question first, any warrior who steps into the front line of battle is immediately at risk, no matter how the odds against his survival compare with those of his enemies. There is no totally safe billet in battle. Wittmann himself is proof of the eventual vulnerability of all who join in combat. In 1944 the fate of some Sherman crews was particularly horrifying. That tank, nicknamed by the Germans 'the Tommy Cooker', was capable of bursting into an inferno of fire which could cremate crew members within a few seconds. The Tiger did not have so horrific a reputation. But what could be worse than an internal ammunition explosion which, as it burned the crew alive, blasted the entire turret out of the hull with crew members still inside? That this did happen on 8 August 1944 proves the danger that even a Tiger crew had to face.

When it comes to the moral question of fighting under a good or bad flag, it might be relevant to mention an experience peculiar to the front-line soldier. In Normandy, and subsequently, when taking and talking to prisoners, there could be a curious sense of empathy, of having shared a profound experience vouchsafed to very few, a kind of freemasonry of the front line. Rarely, if ever, did one meet an enemy who appeared to be driven by an automaton mind that permitted no sense of fellow feeling, although such individuals must have existed (and Stan Hollis, VC, had needed to shoot one).

Certainly those who stood at Wittmann's last start line on 8 August noticed something tremulous, some hesitation which was not typical of his usual bold response to a challenge. Much of Wittmann's persona was the creation of a publicity machine. The real man within the black uniform remains an enigma.

In 1983, all that was left of Wittmann, apart from those vital teeth, was a revolver and a belt buckle. On the buckle was inscribed *'Meine Ehre heisst Treue'* (My Honour is called Loyalty). It has the ring of a noble commitment. But to the members of the *Shützstaffel* (SS), 'loyalty' was solely, specifically and irrevocably to the person of Adolf Hitler.

Those of us who saw the smoke of Wittmann's burning had taken up arms, accepting and motivated by the information dispensed to us by our parents, our preachers and our politicians. We were ready to obey the orders of those set over us. In what way were we standing on higher moral ground than a country boy similarly, but so differently indoctrinated, and disciplined to obey the orders of those set over him?

History and hindsight appear to support our claim to higher moral ground when winning 'the one good war'. But, on 8 August 1944, were we individually more virtuous and less culpable than the 18-year-old youths asphyxiated in the burning corn or the 30-year-old veteran blasted out of his tank? He was then our present prey but provided our future fame.

19

The Resistance

Jeanne Lotton (French)
Guy Merle (French)
'Harry', Eugène Colson (Belgian)
Piet van den Hoek (Dutch)

While we blunder over the land, crunching ruins under our tracks, vaunting our fearsome weapons, they for long years wait quietly, subject to betrayal and indescribable torture, yet gnawing away like termites at the enemy's power and morale.

Encounter

The tank halts in a street on the outskirts of Eindhoven near the Philips Electrical Factory. Men wearing the orange armband of the local Resistance mount the tank, greet the liberators and explore the vehicle. They introduce a 17-year-old boy, frail and looking young for his age. "This is our radio operator, our BBC man," they say. They produce a large book. A section inside the book has been removed and a small flat cigarette tin nestles there. The lad opens it up, touches wires, tickles tiny points. From London, a BBC voice speaks clearly and precisely with true news of the battle's progress. "It is all his own work," say the older men.

Later, the tank crew discuss and wonder, "what if?" It would only need a word from a traitor, a swift Gestapo raid, and that youngster would pay a horrific price. The crew agree: these are the true heroes. Us, with our hulking great war machines, are not in the same class of valour and endurance compared to this vulnerable young 'BBC man' and his ilk of the Resistance.

Jeanne Lotton, *L d'H.*

When it all began she was just a pretty, petite 16-year-old girl cycling contentedly along country roads near her home farm, La Bajolière, outside the small village of

Jeanne Lotton, the petite heroine, 70 years on, with Jai and
Ken Tout. (Courtesy of Myriam Lotton)

Bellavilliers, to the east of Alençon. A picture of healthy innocence, nobody would
have guessed that her bicycle saddle might be hiding vital messages from the French
Resistance. Or that if she was challenged, it could mean arrest, the *Gestapo* cellars,
torture, a concentration camp and shot at dawn, or worse.

In June 1942 a friend, Suzie, had introduced Jeanne Boulay, as she then was, to a
local Resistance *reseau* (network), code-named 'Squirrel'. It was composed entirely of
local French patriots. One of Jeanne's duties was to deliver to local lads forged documents indicating that they were younger than their actual age, in order to protect
them from any kind of German conscription. For security reasons the person who
delivered the cards did not meet the recipient face to face, but often would slip into
a house and leave a card tucked into the bed blankets. Superficially it did not seem
to be particularly dangerous work. The *reseau* met in secret at the local youth hostel.
Members were known by code names, and Jeanne was variously 'Bettie', 'Solange' or
'Genevieve'.

Unfortunately, one man, 'C', became jealous of Bertin, another Resistance youth
whom 'C' thought ws attracting the attention of Jeanne. Deviously, 'C' informed the
local German *feldcommandantur* that Jeanne had delivered a false identity card to
Bertin. On 3 March 1944, as Jeanne and Suzie were walking near the Boulay house,

four German soldiers drove up, stopped the girls and asked Jeanne, "Are you the Boulay girl?" She was arrested and conveyed to the local headquarters at Mamers. Suzie later disappeared into a concentration camp and was never heard of again.

The headquarters was shared by a few German soldiers and the French *milice*, the paramilitary collaboration unit, who took charge of interrogation until a *Gestapo* agent should arrive. The German major in charge was correct and respectful, but left civilian affairs entirely to the *milice*. For 10 days Jeanne was interrogated and beaten. She was even paraded outside the headquarters in the hope that witnesses might come forward against her. The *milice* were crude and cruel, but perhaps partly restrained by the strict discipline of the German soldiers. Through it all there was the faint hope that the *Gestapo* might not take an interest in such a young girl. Jeanne felt that this was a false prospect.

It was at night that the German major came into Jeanne's cell. He appeared despondent. He informed Jeanne that he was being posted to the Eastern Front and described the horrors he expected to encounter there. Then he said: "Ah, the youth! I have a daughter who is your own age ... Goodbye, *Madamoiselle*." As he left he added in a low voice: "Tonight a door might be open."

After the major had departed, Jeanne waited a little while. Then, still suspicious, she went to the door. It was unlocked. She crept into the passage outside, where another door was also unlocked. A rear exit from the headquarters was unlocked too. Then Jeanne was out in the lane, seeking the darkest shadows, running fast towards the woods. She ran to the Leveau mill, where the miller hid her for a while. Another Resistance man, M. Kerval, then took her to a small church, which she did not recognise, but where she was to be kept in hiding for another month. At that point it was considered safe for her to emerge. Teaming up with a 'Suzanne', she was sent to Paris, again delivering counterfeit identity cards. A further shift took her to Brittany just before D Day, where, among other tasks, she was engaged in lighting flares for clandestine aeroplane landings. As a final act, with the fighting close at hand, she led a group of over 20 denounced Resisters and hid them in the dense Forêt de Bellême, a few yards from her home farm, La Bajolière.

As Allied troops advanced she could emerge in her own area and marry Henri Lotton, a member of another *reseau*, whose leader was M. Kerval. The next day Allied troops entered Alençon.

When the Allies advanced into Germany, Henri Lotton volunteered to serve in the Army of Occupation. Whilst he was away, Jeanne, now pregnant, continued running the family farm with the help of three German prisoners of war. On Henri's eventual return they moved to La Perrière, where Henri took charge of the sawmill and became mayor of the town. Jeanne was content to settle down to a quiet country life, raising their four children.

Ever modest, she was amazed when, after the war, a dramatic film based on her adventures was made to widespread public acclaim and she became famous nationally. Seventy years later she was happier when her granddaughter, Myriam, made a more accurate documentary of the same story, entitled '*Murmures*' (Whispers). During an anniversary return visit by veterans of a liberating tank regiment in August 2014, she was astonished to be called forward to stand with the liberators; she considered that her own adventures paled before the experience of those who fought great battles. On the contrary, the veterans considered that her covert unarmed actions, especially when repeated after imprisonment, were far braver than any heroics they might have committed on the open battlefield.

Guy Merle, *L d'H, O du M.*

"He was a very fearless young boy," said Lieutenant Buzz Keating of the Canadian Regina Rifles. In the early hours of D Day, Buzz Keating already knew precisely the time and place of his stepping ashore on the Normandy beaches; 19-year-old Guy Merle had, as yet, only a vague idea about his immediate destiny.

Guy was one of a group of French Resistance youths, under Resistance leader Leonard Gille, selected to be guides to Allied troops after their landing on the beaches. They had been listening to the BBC news bulletins. The wireless was alive with messages, but nothing that affected them yet. In the end they were galvanised into action, not by a mysterious code word over the air but by an explosion; one brief explosion which swelled into a tornado of noise from the sea. Then shells were landing inland. The pre-dawn sky was aflame with a dazzling unnatural light. The lads shouted: "This is it. They are here. *C'est le Débarquement* (It's D Day)."

For the next six weeks Guy Merle was at Buzz Keating's side, supplying those vital, tiny nuggets of information at each step of the perilous advance: a way down a back alley, a gap in a hedgerow, the entrances to a warehouse, the best place to dig a grave, the stability of a river bank, the vagaries of a river current, or "Wissht! – was that a genuine Normandy bird call or a more sinister signal?" When the Reginas and Buzz were in the thick of the fighting around Caen, Guy was there too.

South of Caen curved the River Orne, beyond it the railway station, industrial suburbs and then the wide open plain across which the Allies hoped to send their masses of tanks in a decisive breakthrough. But the Germans had blown the bridges, and when the Allied infantry launched kapok boats into the river, enemy machine guns riddled them full of holes. Twisted rails still lay across the railway bridge, but no footway. Buzz Keating called Guy to help find planks to lay across the railway rails so that the heavily loaded infantry, some of them with bicycles strapped on their backs, could crawl across. "A little trapeze exercise," thought Merle. Then it was on to the railway station.

As Merle indicated the way to the freight section, the fighting was intense, he recalled:

A German mg opens fire. Our mgs fire, sweeping underneath the abandoned goods wagons … slowly we progress. An order: 'four men to the right with smoke bombs!' They detach, throwing bomb after bomb into the immense warehouse. A moment, and then like ants from an anthill, *Fritzes* flood out. We profit and make a leap towards the waiting room. After a serious cleansing of the cellars we round up 69 prisoners. The station is fully occupied.

Guy Merle, as a boy, went scouting for the Canadians.
(Courtesy of the photographer, Daniel Borzeix)

Towards the end of July the Reginas were moved back to rest and refit for a while. Guy Merle was ordered to join the North Nova Scotia Highlanders, reporting to the major of Charlie Company, whose name he was not told. At midnight on 24 July, North Novas' Lieutenant Ward was ordered to take six other ranks and two Free French guides to patrol the D250 from Bourguébus to Tilly-la-Campagne, the latter village still something of an unknown quantity. Guy described the episode:

> We were to avoid anything that would give away our presence. We made ready by smearing our faces and hands with charcoal. We left Bourguébus, crossing gardens, climbing over walls, or going through holes made by the bombardment. We reached the hedge [on the outskirts of Tilly]. A deep ditch ran parallel with the hedge. We all settled down. Our eyes sought to see through the thick branches. Our ears finally gave us satisfaction.
>
> Two fellows walked by in a ditch parallel to ours on the other side of the hedge. They had no idea we were there. We counted four voices. The others were occupying a fixed position, without doubt a machine gun nest. A slight tickle in my throat gave me a chilly feeling. I wanted to cough. I swallowed saliva desperately. Four times the walkers came and went. At last they moved away. One by one we left the ditch and crawled the first two hundred metres. 'Halt!' It

was our own sentry. 'Daisy' [the code word] I whispered. 'OK. Come in!' And people were slapping our backs. But we knew we had to go out there again soon.

When the battalion attacked they suffered from a freak occurrence for which no human mind was responsible. In the darkness searchlights were being used to reflect light from the clouds. This tactic had already been used with some success. However, as the North Novas rose to attack, a mist formed behind them and rolled up into a kind of photographer's screen, reflecting the searchlight glare so that the advancing infantry were silhouetted clearly as targets when the German machine guns began to fire. Merle was walking beside the major commanding Charlie Company:

> The major was soon to give the word to rush forward but where were the enemy posts? Why was there no reaction? Had we made a mistake? NO! As I was asking myself these questions, enemy automatic weapons opened up on all sides. At the first bursts shouts rang out all over. The major was hit in both legs. Two Canadians and I tried to stop the blood which gushed out in red spurts. He turned over on his back and, as though nothing had happened, shouted as loud as he could, 'Come on, boys!' But all around us men fell with abominable screams which mingled with the groans of those already wounded. The major's voice kept weakening.

Three company commanders and other officers were already down, dead or wounded. Merle continued:

> Advance turned into retreat. The enemy redoubled his volume of fire. We soon had nothing but dead bodies around us. A remaining Canadian and I dragged the major. Bullets whizzed by our ears. The major no longer seemed to hear us. Finally we reached the bank and the rail tracks. The major was saved. Each of us in turn carried him on our backs. His bloody legs dangled, which must have aggravated his wounds, but what else could we do?

Nineteen-year-old Guy was not to know that the elite enemy facing them, or treading along a trench just a breath away, were already describing these very battles as the worst fighting they had encountered anywhere. But he was to learn that even the worst battles may incorporate moments of hysterical black humour that seemed not so funny at the time. Again his own words are graphic:

> When my wounded major was taken away I stood there dazed, utterly drained and morally devastated. I was told that almost two hundred fellows had been left on the field dead. My battledress was covered with blood. Blood had mixed with charcoal and had turned into a gooey paste on my hands. Around me all was bedlam … All of a sudden about a dozen wild men rushed at me, shook me up roughly, shouting 'You're a spy, a German spy'. Nobody knew me except the major and, in the rush of my assignment, I had never had chance to learn

his name. The frenzied survivors were shaking me while I shouted 'I am a Free French'. They backed me up against a wall.

But my blurred vision noticed another soldier running towards me. His battledress like mine was covered with blood, the same blood since it was the major's: it was my Canadian night companion! He shouted 'You are crazy. He is the one who saved the major.' The weapons were lowered. The wild men's faces decontracted. They rushed towards me again ... But they picked me up off the ground and carried me around triumphantly. Such was the madness of battle.

When the Allies burst out of Normandy, Leonard Gille's guides were no longer needed. The Free French army was recruiting. Guy Merle enlisted, already an experienced soldier. He would rise to become Lieutenant Colonel of Reserve Merle, a Commander of both the Legion of Honour and the Order of Merit, Mayor of Treignat (in Limousin) and Vice-President of 2nd Armoured Division's veterans' association. A man of incredible activity and durability, in February 2015 he was delighted to be able to return to Strasbourg and join in the celebrations of the 70th anniversary of the liberation of that city by his armoured division. Sadly, Guy passed away on 24 January 2018 during revision of the above section.

'Harry' *alias* Colonel Eugène Colson, MSM

The exploits of 'Harry' represent the Resistance, in this case Belgian, at its most powerful stage of mobilisation and tactical relevance, and also supreme secrecy. He looked and behaved like any workaday Antwerp docker who might be called Harry.

In just a few days Allied troops had dashed from the Caen/Falaise area to the environs of Antwerp, an extraordinary advance greeted with ecstatic jubilation by the liberated peoples. But the leap across countries produced a major problem. With most of the Channel ports still in German hands, the supplies for several Allied armies still had to be transported by road from the Mulberry dock in Normandy to northern Belgium. At the beginning of September 1944, in what became known as the Red Ball Express, fleets of lorries were rushing supplies over those 400 miles of thronged roads. The capture intact of the great port of Antwerp would reduce such journeys to just dozens of miles.

The Germans were well aware of this, as were also the dock workers themselves. The Germans prepared to destroy all the apparatus of the port before retreating. The Belgian underground movement, however, planned to prevent such action by the enemy. The leader of the Belgian Secret Army, Lieutenant Urbain Renniers, had appointed a sea captain, Eugène Colson, to organise the dock workers. Code-named 'Harry', he would be the invisible man charged with welding the disparate mass of workers into an equally invisible 'battalion' about 600-strong, ready and briefed for the day of liberation.

This had to be accomplished without the use of mass propaganda and recruiting, without rabble-raising public speeches, uniforms or visible identification, without

'Harry', Antwerp man of the shades. (Centre), with mayor and army chief. (Courtesy of *Felix Archief/Stadsarchief, Antwerpen*)

compromising the existing dock authorities and without any public exercising of groups at section, platoon or company strength. Individual word of mouth, and circumspectly at that, would have to suffice. In addition, considerable amounts of guns and ammunition had to be smuggled in, allocated and hidden. Use of weapons was taught without access to the normal range practice. Amazingly, when the day eventually came, the dockers were equipped and ready to move to their appointed posts and defend the docks, canal bridges, vital machinery and communications. Others, acting as liaison agents, were waiting at strategic points to guide the Allied troops quickly on to their objectives.

News filtered through from the BBC. The Allied armies were rushing through France into Belgium and towards Antwerp. There was ony a matter of days to wait. Then, at the end of a BBC news bulletin, the vital words were spoken: *"Pour François la lune est Claire'* (For Francis the moon is clear). It was the message saying to Harry, "Go! Go! Go!"

One of the leading tank commanders arriving in Antwerp was Major Bill Close. He was surprised by a dishevelled Resistance worker "in a rather dirty old mac, but with a Sten gun slung over his shoulder, who fought his way through celebrating civilians" in order to guide Bill to his first objective in the city. Another squadron leader, John Dunlop, finding a canal bridge blown, was greeted by an engineer named Vekemans who guided him to another smaller but still navigable bridge. It later emerged that

Vekemans himself had defused and removed mines from under the smaller bridge. A Canadian company commander, Major Bob Suckling, set up his headquarters in a tramways office. One of Harry's Resistance workers, who was attached to the company, proved to be a telephone engineer who was able to connect the tramways office phone into a secret main phone line which the Resistance had established. This enabled Suckling to talk direct to his colonel, who had been similarly connected up in an office in a girls' school.

On 5 September Harry's dockers had captured the German port commander, swiftly taken over all strategic points of the docks and were defending them against German counter-attacks. At this point the Belgians could see a magnificent opportunity opening up. An Allied force might well storm along the seaway which connected the docks with the open sea a few miles away. On the other hand, if the Germans were able to occupy that seaway it would mean that, although the docks might be in Allied hands, no ships could move in or out. Harry and other leaders therefore pressed the British commanders to occupy the seaway immediately.

Yet in one of the worst tactical errors of the war, the Allies failed to do so. The major general commanding British troops in Antwerp had no orders to proceed along the seaway, and failed to take the initiative. Within a day or two he was ordered to move his division elsewhere. Three other tiers of British command, up to and including Montgomery himself, also failed to act. In the event it took almost three months more, and massive Canadian casualties, before the first ship could steam into Antwerp docks.

Consequently, for two weeks from the day they liberated the docks, Harry and his tiny army had to defend the territory they occupied until Canadian reinforcements joined them. Colson had posted a group of 21 dockers in a hydro station which supplied power to the harbour. In the bitter fighting, all 21 gave their lives. Many other dockers were killed during this period. To this roll of honour should be added 198 members of the Belgian Resistance who were arrested and killed by the *Gestapo* during German attempts to root out the secret army which was forming in the docks.

Once the Canadians had arrived it was Lieutenant Colonel (later Brigadier) Denis Whitaker, DSO, of the Royal Hamilton Light Infantry – the 'Rileys' – with whom Colson's unit worked most closely. Whitaker gives perhaps the best pen portrait of the often invisible Harry: "This short, stocky fighter with the hook nose and the ready smile … this obviously audacious and well-informed young *maquis* officer who offered his services and those of his men. A feeling of mutual respect and accord was immediately established, especially over a couple of shots of good Canadian rum."

For many years after the war, Colson, an Antwerp resident, organised Remembrance events, in particular facilitating the return of overseas veterans and families to battlefields and cemeteries. In 1994 the Canadian Government awarded him the Meritorious Service Medal, very rarely given to non-Canadians. Shelagh Whitaker, wife of Denis, stated: "He has been a staunch supporter to Canadian veterans as well as to the families of those men who were killed during the liberation of Antwerp."

Piet Van Den Hoek, *Militaire Willems-Order*

Piet was a 'Crosser'. He was one of a daring group of sturdy young men who rowed small boats on clandestine operations through the *Biesbosch*. This was a wilderness of marshes, tanglewood and narrow, tortuous waterways between enemy-occupied, starving northern Holland and joyfully liberated southern Holland from late 1944 into 1945. The two zones were separated by the vast River Maas, into which the *Biesbosch* projected.

The Crossers, on journeys from north to south, conveyed to safety crashed Allied air crews, Jews, survivors from Arnhem or Resistance organisers whose cover had been blown. Eminent among these was wounded Arnhem commander Brigadier (later General) Sir John Hackett. On return journeys the rowers carried medical supplies and other precious cargoes to the north, where a ruthless German transport and travel embargo meant that some people were having to eat tulip bulbs. At that time areas north of the Maas witnessed *De Hongerwinter* (the hunger winter), the worst famine in modern European history, one that was man-induced.

On 13 January 1945, Piet, with friend Thijs as the other skuller, set off towards Werkendam to pick up some escaping men. Normally they would row in close to overhanging trees, brushing through foliage, to avoid detection by German guard posts or patrol boats. That night it was freezing hard and the only navigable route was along a narrow rift in the ice down the centre of a wider waterway. They were fatally exposed in the frosty air. Suddenly gunfire sounded from both banks. The lads lay down in the boat and began throwing overboard their load of sealed packages, which were weighted to ensure that they sank in an emergency. Steering in towards the bank, they saw German soldiers moving amid the rank undergrowth. As the boat jammed into tall reeds, they hoped to be able to leap out and hide. But in front of them stood a German soldier, his machine pistol firmly levelled at them, shouting "*Hande hoch!*".

A corporal hurried up and demanded their *Nachtausweis* (permission to be out during curfew hours). They had no such document. The corporal then grabbed Piet's binoculars. The young Dutchman instantly realised, to his great horror, that the glasses were British issue and should have been thrown overboard with the rest of the incriminating freight. The corporal examined the unusual binoculars curiously and became fascinated with their design, much larger than the compact German *Zeiss*. It seemed that the binoculars were of such consuming interest or value that he merely marched the two lads to a labour camp without any intensive interrogation, retaining the binoculars for himself.

The forced labour camp was crowded and badly supervised, with many comings and goings. It took Piet and Thijs only a short while before an opportunity came to escape. Without further delay they were back at the oars in the wild reaches of the *Biesbosch*.

Another couple of Crossers were less fortunate. Towards the end of the war, one of the Crosser leaders, Arie van Driel, and his colleague Kees van de Sande were transporting three intelligence agents when their boat, old and difficult to maintain,

Piet van den Hoek, no heroic escape route for him
from the horrors. (Courtesy of Floris van den Hoek)

started leaking badly, reducing their speed through the waterways. A German patrol boat overtook them. The two Crossers were taken to Rotterdam prison, interrogated, tortured and given to understand that they were soon to be shot. Some time elapsed. The delay in executing them was due to negotiations between the Resistance and German forces for an orderly handover at the imminent ceasefire ending the war. One condition was that no more prisoners were to be executed. However, a drunken German soldier decided to take matters into his own hands, shooting both Crossers dead for no apparent reason.

In 1941, aged 21, Cornelis Pieter van den Hoek, a house painter by trade, had been conscripted by the Germans into the labour corps. Escaping in November 1942, he hid in the *Biesbosch* and eventually became a Crosser. During *De Hongerwinter* he rowed across 37 times, as well as organising communications. Each crossing involved a venture in a tiny boat against incredible odds though the 15-mile wide wilderness. Perhaps even more audaciously, as Allied troops moved to liberate northern Holland, Piet and his companions began to capture individual fully armed German soldiers or small groups, imprisoning them in empty houseboats in the *Biesbosch* until the liberating forces arrived.

Piet was awarded the *Militaire Willems-Order*, the Dutch equivalent of the Victoria Cross, for "distinguishing himself by performing excellent acts of bravery, planning and loyalty". As the German troops of occupation surrendered or withdrew, members of the Resistance were co-opted into interior security forces. Piet van den Hoek was put in command of an internment camp until it closed in 1946. In civilian life Piet set up his own flourishing house painting company and became very active in the community of Werkendam. He served on the city council and the board of his church, and for 19 years was chairman of the Shopkeepers' Association.

His son, Floris, comments: "My father was a modest quiet man as were most of these heroes." Because his father held the supreme *Willems* award, Floris was able to meet several other heroes who had achieved the same distinction. He observed: "All of them were not in for telling about what they did, but more about why they did it."

However, Piet had always wrestled with memories of the horrors of war. In 1973, aged 52, he became so overwhelmed by Post Traumatic Stress Disorder that he could no longer cope with normal work situations. He found some solace and justification in writing his book, *Biesbosch Crossing, 1944-1945*. He never fully recovered from the hauntings of war. However, he campaigned ceaselessly to ensure that adequate and visible remembrance was set up for those who gave their lives, such as Arie and Kees. It was no coincidence that in 1989 the Line Crosser Monument was unveiled. Piet van den Hoek came to his own 'eternal crossing' in February 2015.

The hidden cost of Resistance

It should be remembered that some heroes of the Resistance were not universally revered, or even supported by their own communities. They did not always receive the near unanimous acclaim accorded to returning warriors in Britain, Canada or the United States. In German-occupied countries there were Nazi sympathisers who happily and openly collaborated with the invaders, as could have happened with Mosley's Fascists if Britain had been invaded.

Furthermore, there was a considerable proportion of the occupied population who lived in fear of reprisals triggered by the successes of the Resistance. It is relevant to mention the 600 and more innocent civilians slaughtered at Oradour in France or the thousands of Dutch people starved during *De Hongerwinter*, as a vicious enemy exacted reprisals out of all proportion to the losses which they had suffered. At the time, every piece of news about a local Resistance triumph evoked justified fears in the hearts of the inhabitants that the Germans, with no moral inhibitions or legal restrictions, would react with acts of diabolical cruelty.

Resisters had to live and work in virtually a parallel world of peril, distrust, betrayal and loneliness, with a torture chamber and a dawn bullet as a final prospect. The very secrecy of their missions could lay them open to suspicion in the turmoil of blame allocation after the war. This surely implies that the Resisters, who risked and frequently gave their lives in the cause of freedom, often without due recognition, should rank high among those honoured at times of remembrance. Their circumstances ensured that they could be the most modest of all.

20

Conclusion

Regimental Duties
A typical tank regiment engaged in
routine battle duties, D Day to VE Day, 1st
Northamptonshire Yeomanry, 33rd Armoured
Brigade

*Mirroring and inspired by those who willingly submitted to the supreme test of ulti-
mate valour, these, each in his own insignificant moment, stood firm where a bullet
or shard of shrapnel could have rendered him a mere fatal statistic, not identified
in the Gazette.*

The superlative term 'the Bravest' needs to be employed with considerable sensitivity.
It might appear to imply that there could be a category of 'Less Brave'. This could
reflect adversely on individuals who might have achieved the peaks of valour but who
were never afforded the unique opportunity to show it.

The supreme acts of battle heroism did not emanate solely and entirely from the
character and actions of an individual. Rather were they generated by a symbiosis of
personal commitment, training, individual opportunity, timing, location, terrain,
enemy dispositions, tactical urgency, outcome and so on. To highlight how these
supreme acts differed from the welter of commendable routine actions, it may be
interesting to survey some of those everyday battle acts which might be classified,
not as 'Less Brave', but perhaps as 'Brave but responding to a lesser opportunity'. The
comparison could highlight the parameters of extreme valour.

Twenty-year-old Trooper Bill Higham's tank, 'Orel', had advanced from a recently
liberated village, along a country lane and into apple orchards. There they were caught
up in the full fury of battle, unable to see much through the boughs laden with ripe
cider apples. One massive explosion rocked the tank. They had been hit. The turret
had been dislodged from its bearings. And this was the 'Tommy Cooker' Sherman,
liable to explode and incinerate the crew within seconds. Everybody bailed out. The
commander had been badly wounded. Two crew members lifted him up and helped

Ron West (right) and author unveil memorial at La Roche, junction of the Battle of the Bulge.
(Photo by Jai Tout)

him stagger back through the trees to wherever the medics were working. Bill and Mickey Tull were left alone to guard the tank.

The Sherman had not exploded. The engine was still working, as was the intercom of the wireless set. There then appeared through the trees a Black Watch sergeant. He had three badly wounded men in the orchard. Obviously this tank could not fire its gun, could not fight, so, "could they load the wounded men on the back deck of the tank and ferry them into the village?" They could! Carefully, and ever aware of mines, Bill talked Mickey back along the marks of their advance. In the village, willing hands received the wounded men. The two troopers were alone again. They had a common thought: "There might be some of our own lads needing to be brought out. Shall we go back and look for them?" So Bill Higham's unique ambulance service returned to the orchards. During the day they ferried out several other wounded comrades and a number of sullen prisoners. They received no award, but a lesson in savage oaths as the corporal armourer later assessed the danger presented by the dislodged turret.

Two hundred metres from the Higham tank position, Trooper Joe Ekins sat in his Sherman Firefly tank, code 4 'Charlie', wedged into a thick belt of trees. He could see a wide stretch of empty open ground with the national road beyond it. Outside, guns were firing from several directions. Then the huge dread shape of a Tiger tank rolled into the orbit of Joe's periscope. His eye switched to the precision of the telescopic sights: it was clearly a Tiger. Orders over the intercom held his foot off the trigger for a moment while other tanks were alerted. A second Tiger had appeared, trailing the first. These were the great beasts of the battlefield. Joe had not yet had the opportunity to match his 17-pdr gun against the massive armour of the Tiger, but he had seen the wreckage of the weaker 75mm Shermans smashed by the 88mm guns of the enemy. Then a third Tiger loomed.

The order came: "Gunner! Take the rear one! Fire!" Joe's first shot at about 800 metres bored into the third Tiger, causing belching smoke, the crew leaping out. Immediately the second Tiger began to traverse towards Joe as he swung his gun towards that tank. Shots came from both. The second Tiger began smoking, but a shot had crashed against a turret flap on Joe's Firefly. Then the lead Tiger was traversing with dangerous speed and intent. Joe's commander slid down behind him, badly wounded. The troop leader came climbing in, ordering the driver to back out, speed left and bore into another thick tangle of branches. Joe again was able to see the third Tiger, its gun narrowly off target. The 17-pdr thundered out and the third Tiger was slain. This was still comparatively rare in Normandy or elsewhere, a Sherman slaying a Tiger, let alone three, but there was no award for routine regimental duty.

Four hundred metres to the left, Trooper Ernie Wellbelove, one of the smallest and youngest men in his squadron, sat gazing through the sights of his Firefly, code 2 'Charlie'. For some hours he had been staring at an empty skyline. Now, as though alerted by the sounds of battle elsewhere, a *Panzer* Mark IV appeared over the skyline. Then another, and another. Almost instinctively, Ernie sighted and fired. One *Panzer* was blazing. He sighted and fired again, destroying a second *Panzer*. The third *Panzer* accelerated past the others and disappeared behind a huge haystack. Carefully calculating distance and movement, Ernie fired through the haystack three times. Smoke swelled up from behind the obstruction. That was three down: a moment to savour, to cheer. But at that same moment another *Panzer*, familiar with a deep gully which was still largely unknown to the British, crept up behind Ernie's troop and set Ernie's tank on fire. The young lad wrestled his way out of the gunner's tight seat and up onto the turret, where a co-axial burst of enemy machine-gun fire tore the life from the young gunner. Again, there was no award for routine regimental duty.

Captain Ken Todd noticed that tank 3 'Baker' had pushed forward into a dangerously exposed position. A battle was raging in the course of which some 80 tanks – British, Canadian, Polish and German – would be knocked out within a mile or so of the village in only about an hour. The wireless was jammed with urgent orders and dying screams. Hesitant to transmit, Todd therefore instructed his driver to break cover and move across the bows of 3 'Baker' while Todd gesticulated to its commander, urging him to retire a way. As the two tanks crossed each other, a German self-propelled gun thrust its way through a hedge, spotted the pair, focussed on Todd's tank and fired. The familiar explosion on Todd's tank sent the crew bailing out, Todd himself wounded. Another of the crew, Eric Marchant, fell out of the turret burning bodily. The remainder threw themselves on Marchant, beating out the flames and saving his life. Never to recover fully, he was discharged as "no longer fulfilling the physical requirements for active service". Meanwhile, 3 'Baker' and other Shermans wreaked vengeance on the German SP. Once more, there were no awards for routine regimental duties.

Trooper Ron West was firing the big gun of his tank, 'Culworth', aiming at the vast factory of Colombelles. West felt exposed because the squadron had lined up along the crest of the hill above the River Orne, under direct fire from the enemy. Suddenly the commander's voice snapped, "Stop firing!" Moments of silence ensued. West spoke into his mike: "What's happening, Sarge?" A quavering voice answered: "I don't believe in all this war business any more. I am declaring a ceasefire." It is very risky for a crew member to challenge a sergeant in battle, but West had to act. He squeezed up past the now silent, staring commander and out of the turret. Fortunately, Captain Bill Fox and RSM George Jelley were nearby, superintending the ammunition truck as it replenished the tanks. RSM Jelley, a First World War veteran, climbed on to the tank and quickly diagnosed the situation: "Shell shock! Get him out!" As the medical half-track rattled up, Captain Fox turned to West and ordered: "Right, West, take command. Just keep on firing at those damned chimneys. Good lad!" West called the co-driver to come up and take the gun, disturbing the brief peace which the shocked sergeant had declared. There was no promotion yet for West: a corporal returning from hospital later took over 'Culworth'.

A Black Watch advance is held up by an enemy machine gun, invisible behind a typical huge impenetrable *bocage* hedgerow. Tank 'Brixworth' is sent to "sort it". The Black Watch platoon leader, a sergeant, joins the tank commander on the Sherman turret, 9ft up from road level. Together, aloft and exposed, at full stretch they peer cautiously over the top of the dense 14ft high hedge, the only way to view the farm and orchards beyond. The machine gun fires again, betraying its position. A brief co-axial tank barrage, cannon and machine gun aimed and fired in tandem, destroys the enemy gun, or drives it away. Job done, the Highland sergeant raises a thumb: "Thanks, Mac!" Another case of routine regimental duties.

Major David Bevan surveyed the aftermath of battle. Half of the regiment, and most of the Black Watch infantry, still stood firm amid the blazing wrecks. Tank crews, determined but battered, huddled down within their armour plate as if for greater security. Infantry dug down nearer to the centre of the Earth. David Bevan decided that it was opportune to take a country stroll, this sunny August Bank Holiday. He descended from his tank carrying the traditional riding whip of the Yeomanry officer. Tank gunners continued to traverse slowly, watching for the next move of the elite SS still out there. As the turrets traversed, Bevan was visible moving from tank to tank.

The crew of 3 'Baker', myself included, watched the squadron leader approach, rapping on the tank hull with his whip. "Everybody OK in there? Keep your eyes open. Take it in turns to do co-driver and relax a bit. Well done!" The tall figure moved nonchalantly on to the next tank in the hedgerows. Within 3 'Baker' the crew straightened up. If Bevan could walk the fields where none other dare appear, then we could at least sit closer to controls and be ready for the enemy's next move. Bevan was handed no award for routine regimental duties.

In their light Honey tanks, Reconnaissance Sergeant Jack and Corporal Knoth explored a street devastated by the mass Allied air attack on Caen. The bigger Shermans up the hill had been unable to drive through the mountainous ruins. Down below, Jack and Knoth too found their way totally blocked. So, undeterred, Kenny Jack decided to get out and walk. Totally exposed, he traced a kind of goat's trail, climbing, scrambling and stumbling towards the city centre. This was an empty zone. French residents lay dead under the ruins of their homes; the wily enemy had retreated. Jack went back to report. Two weeks later the streets were still impassable for tanks. While getting no award for this, Kenny Jack later won the MM in Holland.

After a devastating bombardment, tank 3 'Able' led the advance up the hill to the vast naval barracks. At dawn, 3 'Able' and 4 'Able' fired one shot each at the main doors of the fortified complex. A door opened, a white flag waved and more than 2,000 naval personnel marched out to surrender, in good order and led by an admiral. Ongoing regimental duties brought no awards.

Lance Corporal 'Reb' Reboles was appointed as a Sherman tank commander but with no promotion or extra pay. This was a complaint of some tankies. Simply to fly in an RAF bomber one must be a sergeant, but in a tank, a lance corporal (often called "unpaid, unwanted") may command a crew of five. Their task may be to take the tank face-to-face against the same 88mm guns which fire at the bombers 20,000ft up, but on the ground wait at point-blank range. The two lead tanks, Reb's one of them, had to dash around the blind corner into the Dutch village street and hope that one survived. Others in support watched the two tanks accelerate and disappear around the bend. Two massive explosions, more like volcanic eruptions, sent huge clouds of black smoke back around the corner. Reb is written off as "k.i.a." (killed in action). He has received no awards and was not even paid for the job.

No doubt all those mentioned would have been ready to take up a further challenge to action if it had arisen. Having disposed of three Tigers, Joe Ekins might have been happy to see yet another Tiger appear within his sights across that open ground. However, the disposition of friendly and enemy forces meant that the other 17 *Panzers* knocked out that day were more convenient prey for other gunners, several of whom saw only one enemy tank within the confines of their periscopes.

This illustrates one of the peculiar features and requisites of an award for supreme valour, an unusual concentration of peril and responsibility within the scope of the one destined individual. It was an occurrence beyond the power of that individual to arrange. He could only act in response. Of the 'Bravest' mentioned, John Bridge was perhaps the exception in being predestined to certain extreme incidents and not dependant on an unpredictable coincidence of circumstances.

In cases such as George Eardley's charge, fate conspired to confine and restrict the movement of an army corps, until the focus descended to a mere battalion, and then to a company attack. Finally, the siting of the enemy machine guns meant that, within that company, only Eardley and one or two others were in a position to locate and attack the guns. Effectively it was one man as the focus and spear point of an operation involving perhaps 10,000 men. On the other hand, Joe Ekins' Firefly was part of a three armoured regiment defence plan with perhaps 30 other Firefly tanks available within wireless call, all able and available to replicate or replace Ekins.

Another factor appears in the actions of Higham and Bevan. Both were exposed to heavy enemy fire in the course of a battle of considerable dimensions. However, little or none of that fire was deliberately focussed on them as individuals, being concentrated *en masse*. Chapman, ascending his hill, and Harper, leaping his wall, and Cardy, squeezing between burning vehicles, were the concentrated targets of a number of enemy arms alerted to the danger of the one approaching target. This exposure of the single individual as sole target was a major factor in several of the feats of valour described in the previous pages. Even Bridge, operating in an area cleared of all other humans, was an individual target of his current bomb. Kenny Jack, walking through the Caen ruins, had valiantly taken a perilous route exposed to any hidden enemy gun. In the event, he was not fired on, the area was found to be unoccupied by the enemy, so he was not considered for an award. The commander of 'Brixworth' and the Black Watch sergeant, exposed whilst looking over the hedge, were only momentarily at risk and were not targeted.

In the case of Ekins, there were, as mentioned, other Firefly tanks available which, if less conveniently, could have been directed against the Tigers. In contrast, when Hollis and his commander first noticed the German pillbox, there were no alternative actors available. It was one of the two who must gamble with his life and, in the order of things, the sergeant major, rather than the officer, who must rush the machine guns. From time to time in battle, fate focussed on an individual in such a way that no other person could assume responsibility. Only Harper was available to take the fatal canal walk. With casualties on all sides, Tilston, although a major, was the only person available to go back and forward time and again, under murderous fire, to maintain ammunition supplies. Similarly, Blackburn and Murphy, as they brought their own artillery fire down on their own positions, were the only individuals in place and in communication, and therefore competent to act. Had Major Bevan on his stroll been knocked out, there were subordinate commanders able to take over immediately.

There is also the consideration of outcome and impact on the enemy. 'Reb', sacrificed at a blind bend, and his fellow commander were eliminated without causing any harm to the enemy and without affecting the course of the battle. Joe Ekins did have an impact, but that battle would still have been won if, say, Bill Higham had been firing the gun. Exclusivity was a vital consideration.

Long experience often produced the same effect as formal training. Close, bailing out of yet another burning tank, had developed a self-preservation instinct from sore experience, as had Hollis, a Dunkirk survivor, and Blackburn, the longest surviving Forward Observation Officer. Wittmann at Villers-Bocage may have triumphed more because of instant reaction founded on experience than through tactical acuity and forethought.

More difficult to analyse is the power of charisma or force of personality, ranging from Murphy's *coup d'oeil* to the almost electric field of inspiration which appeared to surround Rose with his jodhpurs and unmarked jeep. Cain's continuing example of self-sacrifice and mastery of the impossible, and the subversive energy of undercover 'Harry' at Antwerp, inspired individuals to fight and suffer far above their normal expectation. In the case of Bridge, his inspirational leadership would be bolstered by an expertise in mechanics beyond most people's comprehension.

Another asset not indigenous to battlefields is the ability to remain calm. Jeanne Lotton survived so long on her underground missions because she exuded calmness to the point of anonymity. Piet van den Hoek, more than most, needed to stay calm in a situation where speed was impossible and only the slowest devious moves were advisable. Bridge was in a similar situation where an impulsive action could have triggered disaster. Cardy, pausing a moment to garner slaughtered chickens, is perhaps a more humorous example of assured indifference to turmoil.

Fundamental for the warrior at the peak moment of peril are the virtues of determination and durability. Both Ekins and Wellbelove were presented with three targets only, which they demolished within minutes. The opportunity then ended, with no call for further durability. In both cases the excellence of gun sights and guns reduced the period of actual action. In contrast, nowhere was the need for determination more pronounced than in the case of Göstl. At the conclusion of a bitter, prolonged battle, the *Panzergrenadier* was in a state which might be described as 'consciously dying' in his ditch. Comparatively safe cellars were within reach and there would have been every excuse for withdrawing to a deeper pit. Figuratively, Göstl's determination was a gritting of the teeth ratcheted up to a grinding away of the molars. In all the instances cited in earlier pages, the individual demonstrated grim determination, even sheer stubbornness, to follow his own objectives. He was not to be a mere pawn sliding meekly across the chessboard of fate.

A more subtle aspect of valour was that of inspiration or motivation. The Yeomanry tank men mentioned, about their regimental duties, were genuinely patriotic and wholly loyal to their family of comrades. Yet in the acts of supreme bravery a further element was often added. The exiles Rossey and Jarzembowski were inspired by something even beyond normal patriotism. Theirs was a cocktail of love of country, thirst for revenge, concern for their loved ones far away beyond aid and a sense of the bitter stigma where their national flag had suffered ignominy. Equal inspiration could spring from a compound of extreme horror and anger, such as Chapman having his company commander shot dead in his arms or Hollis and Rossey wading ashore, colliding with the bodies of comrades killed alongside them.

Such motives were of a different nature from, but of the same value as, Bridge's sympathy for civilian victims of air raids and his calculated desire to intervene in some way. Preconceived personal principles also fired others. Hammerton's immediate post-war concern for war-scarred youths, Bazalgette's and Rose's religious backgrounds and Blackburn's later battle against discrimination suggest dedicated men maintaining a moral high ground. Their dedication led to diminished concern about threats to their own wellbeing or future prospects.

In assessing the outcome of an individual's courageous actions, judgement should not depend too closely on statistical calculations. When 3 'Able' and 4 'Able' fired at the naval barracks and produced thousands of prisoners, the statistic did not reflect extraordinary gunnery by the two tanks' crews. An entire regiment lay behind the two tanks, and all were available to join in a longer fusillade against the barracks. The outcome did not depend solely on the two tanks. Equally, the immediate emergence of the naval force, surrendering in parade order, revealed that capitulation was already in progress before the warning shots.

Similarly, Bill Close would have considered that his netting of an entire battalion of surrendering enemy artillerymen called for less courage than some of his apparently less productive actions in the midst of dire defeat. Those earlier desperate actions at least reduced casualties and gained a modicum of ground where all else had failed. In contrast to the naval barracks episode, the lesser statistics of Harper's modest dozen prisoners taken and Eardley's three machine guns destroyed evidenced an extraordinary willingness to be exposed to extremes of peril.

Rarely was the bravest act a mere automatic performance of duty. No doubt each named warrior had that basic sense of duty, a discipline officially owed to the Crown or State but becoming more compelling when funnelled through various formations down to platoon, troop or similar level. Yet at the supreme moment of self-sacrifice it is likely that considerations of duty would have been swamped by more personal allegiances. Hollis made it clear that for him the prime impulse was that of friends bonding together, rather than regimented formalities. Blackburn's radio operator referred to a bonding "more than family".

The old concept of the path of duty being the way to glory may have been appropriate to Wellington's lined-up, static infantry, firing mechanically. But regimented duty needed to be greatly enhanced by addition of the individuality, adaptability, fluidity and technological skills required across the D Day beaches in 1944.

Lurking in the background of any discussion on bravery is the subject of fear. The enforced British 'stiff upper lip' tradition in the Second World War made it difficult for individuals to speak about fear, even when coping with it before and after battle. Yet the open discussion of fear is the best antidote to the malaise.

Many accounts tend to agree that, at a climactic moment of battle, fear may be subverted by other more pressing emotions, like pain, anger or sheer concentration, as the pace of action accelerates. Sir Philip Sidney touched on this point centuries ago, observing that "a true knight is fuller of bravery in the midst than in the beginning of danger".

So what is 'fear' and what is 'bravery'? There are various technical definitions and descriptions of fear in the academic literature. However, fear, in its battle impact, is fairly simple to dissect. It can function for the mind in the way that pain alerts the body. Pain is an essential warning device, a red light. If pain did not exist, a wound in the back of the body, out of sight of the eye, could bleed to death with the afflicted individual unaware.

Similarly, fear, acting far faster than logic, can produce an effect of restraint in the mind at a moment when judgement might err on the side of imprudence. The soldier might instinctively perceive an opportunity to attack, and leap into action prematurely and fatally, as reflected in Joe Ekins when sighting the Tigers, itching to fire, but ordered to await support. At such a point fear could cause a momentary pause, giving the mind time for swift further reflection, then switching to a wiser option. In the dread, dead moments before the onset of danger, fear can be a useful consultant, advising against precipitate action. The individual who is aware of the essence of fear can use it as a tool, can sit and discuss with it, and then act with redoubled assurance and confidence. Failing that familiarity, fear can paralyse or pervert all action.

Where fear exists, 'bravery' is primarily a reaction to that fear rather than to the actual material motions of a battle. If there were no fear, the options on a battlefield might require little more personal commitment than the decision to move pieces on a chessboard, in this case the warrior being both chess player and pawn. Certainly, the vast majority of warriors will experience some concern about possible wounding, life being cut off suddenly or whatever hellish afterlife or empty void the individual may contemplate. But it is fear that colours, amplifies and adds the sting to such thoughts; and, if not dealt with, can paralyse totally.

Over the centuries, wise and experienced observers have sought to define or illustrate bravery. The Roman Sallust commented: "In battle it is the cowards who run the most risk. Bravery is a rampart of defence." Mark Twain observed: "Courage is resistance to fear, mastery of fear: not absence of fear." An outstanding soldier, American Civil War general William T. Sherman, stated: "Courage is a perfect sensibility of the measure of danger and a mental willingness to endure it." This definition was most apposite for crews of the eponymous tank with its inclination to burn up its residents. Franklin D. Roosevelt is credited with saying: "Courage is not the absence of fear but rather the assessment that something else is more important than fear." When considering courage in battle, there might be added to FDR's words, "and worth the sacrifice of one's own life or well-being".

In action there is no space for fine words or reflections. For most front-line warriors, at the ultimate moment when thought erupts into action, it becomes simply a job to be done with total focus and precision. For many, there is the almost atavistic kick-start propulsion of the nervous system, at the precise moment of moving from contemplation into action, as at the crack of the starter's pistol, the referee's whistle for the kick-off, the striking of the first ball of the first over or the plunge from the highest diving board. Perhaps the imperative reactions of the wild beast may lie only lightly subdued in the human brain under layers of civilised notions.

So, who were they, the 'bravest'? If these pages appear to be biased towards cases of bravery carried out by the quiet, inoffensive man, it might be pertinent to mention at least one other warrior who did not naturally fall into that category. Lieutenant Colonel Paddy Mayne, SAS, winner of four DSOs but denied a VC, has been described as having "a total disregard for danger and a genuine love of fighting for fighting's sake". However, it was also noted that, as the war dragged on, he became more withdrawn, turning to reading more often; and that after the war he spoke little of his heroics. Was this again the case of a physically ferocious man who was, as much as any other, prey to human feelings, but who was denied the open culture in which he might have spoken freely about them?

Long after the perils of the consummate moment, bravery often had an enduring cost. The frank admissions of some of the bravest, and the observations of families and comrades, lead to the subject of Post-Battle Traumatic Stress Disorder or syndrome. Typical cases are the intrepid hero Hollis alone in a locked room with the ghost of an *SS* boy, or the supposedly fearless Murphy with a revolver under his civilian pillow. In addition to the prodigious mental and physical efforts these heroes expended on the day, and the physical pain often suffered later, there must be considered also the price that many paid in the form of long-continuing PBTSD. An intriguing example is seen in the Resistance 'Crosser', Piet van den Hoek; in his late 50s he was still so haunted by wartime experiences that he was unable to concentrate on daily work and had to retire prematurely.

As observed earlier, no professional battle-related consensus existed before the American Psychiatric Association's meeting of 1980, which published what is known as *DSM-III*, defining PTSD. Many who suffered most were therefore never available for detailed study. Anecdotal information from sources such as veterans' reunions strongly suggests that, at the end of the Second World War, a very considerable number of former combatants suffered from the condition; that very few received any form of treatment or recognition; and that significant numbers continue to experience symptoms into retirement age.

To be fair, in 1945, not only was there no consensus among psychiatrists about 'battle fatigue', there were not the skills, clinics, military organisation or financial resources sufficient to cope with the myriad of those who may have needed review or treatment. In any case, many 1945 servicemen, upon discharge, would not have appreciated being labelled as suffering from what they might then have regarded as some kind of mental deficiency. Cowardice or funk were terms familiar to D Day soldiers and accepted by most as an inevitable occurrence in the course of life-and-death combat, but not open to discussion.

The publicity now afforded to the existence and treatment of PTSD in war zones such as Afghanistan and Iraq should have helped to direct attention to its largely unreported incidence in the Second World War. There were two constituents of Post-Battle TSD which Second World War veterans experienced to a greater extent than most non-combatants, such as bombed civilians, may have done. The first is the intense sense of guilt where the combatant feels that the bullet which killed his comrade was destined for him, as with Chapman's company commander killed in the corporal's arms. Or, in the case of tank 3 'Baker', the question "Why did the SP choose to destroy Todd's tank and not ours?" The 'bullet with my name on it' syndrome is well understood and frequently encountered in the front line. When one's destined bullet hits a comrade it sparks off pent-up anger and inescapable guilt.

The second trigger of PBTSD resides in the forcible transformation of the peaceful, possibly even pacifist civilian into a deliberate instinctive killing machine. This transition was especially frequent and violent in an era when many youths were still brought up strictly according to the Ten Commandments and similar ideals, with their "Thou shalt not kill" and "love thine enemy" injunctions; and where Sunday School might have contributed as much to a child's formation as day school.

It was an initial abuse of the mind when the raw recruit was drilled to thrust a bayonet into the stomach of a sandbag, remembering, as had been demonstrated, to twist the disembowelling bayonet during extraction. This was then exacerbated when, on demobilisation, the individual was ejected in an abrupt seismic discharge, without any form of counselling. He was propelled straight back into an uncomprehending civilian society with mores radically different from those of the barrack square. Murphy contrasted such treatment of humans with the humane rehabilitation treatment afforded to army dogs on demobilisation.

In brief, for the majority of the heroes described there might have been added another medal acknowledging the untold agonies suffered in a more secretive, long-term battle: that of wrestling with PBTSD. That battle might have been waged whilst still in a slit trench, later behind a closed door or even later still on returning to a Normandy war cemetery for the first time many years after. For some that latter experience was the unique opportunity for psychological release after years of torment.

As to honours awarded for valour, various considerations were taken into account by the military authorities. The most obvious was the tactical importance and urgency of the individual's act within the larger framework of a battle. This was an aspect over which the recipient rarely had any control or even knowledge. Bridge is again a conspicuous exception, especially in Messina harbour, where he shared full awareness of the implications. At the moment of action someone like Chapman was not to know, and someone like Harper was never to know, the importance and timeliness of his heroism within the complex ramifications of a major conflict.

It is difficult to decide whether those who had to recommend or countersign an award were always totally disinterested, or whether a battalion commander or brigadier might consider that some previous misdemeanour could preclude an individual from consideration; or conversely that a more favourable view of the individual might shade a decision in his favour. Bill Close was well aware of having offended a certain brigadier, but that did not prevent the same brigadier from countersigning an award for the tank commander.

However, certain officers in the hierarchy of countersignatories did appear to act beyond the purest consideration of merit. Notably Bridge, Hollis and Paddy Mayne appeared to have suffered from someone's opinion that "he has enough awards already". Obviously a high award, such as the Victoria Cross, required an inviolable system of proof and approval. Lower down the award scale, instances were reported of what the troops called "medals coming up with the rations", being awarded according to availability. Nevertheless, in spite of the confusion which reigned in major battles such as the Normandy campaign, it does appear that, on the whole, awards were made in a just and rigorous manner.

What, then, of the plot and proposition of 'The Dirty Dozen', its brutalised criminals recruited to carry out a mission considered too terrifying for normal troops? How do they relate to the deeds of those chosen here?

In choosing to study Rose, with his family line of rabbis, and Tilston and Bridge, with their university degrees, and Blackburn, Bazalgette and Hammerton, with their musical sensitivities, and Göstl, with his quest for a doctorate, might not this selection have erred on the side of the highly cultured and well educated?

On the other hand, considering Hollis, driving a lorry, Close, crashing his delivery bicycle, Eardley, in the print shop, Chapman, escaping from the coal mines, Rossey, harvesting olives, Harper, cutting peat, and Murphy and Wittmann, hunting of necessity to fill the cooking pot, could not these be said to contribute to a sensible balance of class and culture?

In more than one case there is some evidence of bad or even violent conduct after the war. A better understanding of and response to PBTSD at that time might have prevented some such behaviour. That would be true not only on the part of those persons mentioned but as also affecting incalculable numbers of veterans who suffered, and may still be suffering, from what is now a fully comprehended and treatable condition.

To sum up: the most extraordinary heroic deeds required a blend of circumstance over which the pivotal hero had no or little initial control. Opportunity was often the operative factor which went hand-in-hand with the valour of the individual concerned. That person then needed to exert an outstanding combination of battle skills, with full awareness that a horrific personal fate could attend any momentary misjudgement or hesitation. In battle so much was happening, in a state of uncontrollable confusion, that sustained logical thought was an unlikely luxury.

What is perhaps most striking is the unanimity of modest and sometimes derogatory comment on their own extraordinary feats by these individuals from such varying backgrounds of nationality, culture, rank and social standing. They deserve the last word.

Their responses include Bridge's attribution of survival to sheer luck, Blackburn's "Any reader looking for adventure must look elsewhere", Tilston's quip that bravery was due to "inexperience" and his later rebuke that "I was not in the Hochwald Forest on my own", Cain's "I was shouting like a hooligan … I blubbered and yelled", Merle's "I just stood there, dazed and drained", Hammerton's "Fear stalks at the soldier's side", Hollis's "If I hadn't done them, somebody else would have", Göstl's "I could not do anything else at the time", Eardley's "If I had known that there were three of the b*****s in there, I wouldn't have gone", Murphy's "I just fought to stay alive, like anyone else I suppose" and Rossey's "But not to crow about it, no! no!"

And, away in the incomprehensible distances of eternity, Baz might be indulging in a wry grin and, disdaining all ostentation, might conclude :"I have just had a couple of beers, and hence the rather high-sounding verbiage."

Eardley bombing statue in Congleton street. (Photograph by Simon Cooper; thanks also to Congleton Photographic Society and *Chronicle*)